Reframing the History of Family and Kinship:
From the Alps towards Europe

Reframing the History of Family and Kinship: From the Alps towards Europe

Volume 25

Edited by / Edité par
Michel Oris

PETER LANG
Bern • Berlin • Bruxelles • Frankfurt am Main • New York • Oxford • Wien

Dionigi Albera, Luigi Lorenzetti, Jon Mathieu (eds.)

Reframing the History of Family and Kinship: From the Alps towards Europe

PETER LANG

Bern • Berlin • Bruxelles • Frankfurt am Main • New York • Oxford • Wien

Bibliographic information published by Die Deutsche Nationalbibliothek

Die Deutsche Nationalbibliothek lists this publication in the Deutsche Nationalbibliografie; detailed bibliographic data is available on the Internet at ‹http://dnb.d-nb.de›.

British Library and Library of Congress Cataloguing-in-Publication Data:
A catalogue record for this book is available from The British Library, Great Britain.

Library of Congress Control Number: 201694920

Cover illustration: © MAK/Georg Mayer. MAK – Österreichisches Museum für angewandte Kunst / Gegenwartskunst

ISSN 1660-6043 pb.
ISBN 978-3-0343-2127-3 pb.
ISBN 978-3-0343-2390-1 MOBI

ISSN 2235-6878 eBook
ISBN 978-3-0343-2388-8 eBook
ISBN 978-3-0343-2389-5 EPUB

This publication has been peer reviewed.

© Peter Lang AG, International Academic Publishers, Bern 2016
Hochfeldstrasse 32, CH-3012 Bern, Switzerland
info@peterlang.com, www.peterlang.com, www.peterlang.net

Contents

Part 3: Towards Europe

DIONIGI ALBERA, LUIGI LORENZETTI, JON MATHIEU

Introduction

In recent years the interdisciplinary field of family and kinship history in Europe has seen the emergence of a number of studies aimed at developing comparative viewpoints that encompass a wide range of geographical and temporal contexts. Some of these general studies have covered the whole of Western Europe and focused on common evolutionary traits in different historical processes across the region since the Middle Ages. After a period in which localised studies and monographic approaches were dominant in the academic field, these works now appear, in some respects, to echo certain comparative elements that were already present in the field of family history during the 1960s and 70s. From this point of view it could be said that this field of studies is characterised by alternate recurring cycles of underlying trends which could leave one with the impression that we are witnessing the "corsi e ricorsi" ("occurrences and recurrences") of which Giambattista Vico wrote. Yet, as Vico himself pointed out in his philosophy of history, a cyclical sequence should not be understood as a series of identical replicas of preceding phases. Recent studies accordingly display substantial differences compared to their precursors, with families and households no longer being seen as separate from kinship, and with a widespread focus on historical changes in kinship conception and practice. It should also be noted that it is not possible to speak of a unified field with regard to these more recent trends. Hypotheses and interpretative models differ somewhat concerning which factors scholars choose to take into account, and the underlying logic that they apply to these processes. These differences can be seen clearly among some of the most prominent recently proposed theories on kinship evolution in European history.

In a number of his writings the French historian Gérard Delille has presented a model which owes a great deal to the alliance theory developed by anthropologists like Claude Lévi-Strauss and Françoise Héritier[1]. According to Delille it is possible to identify what he defines as a "European" (or "Christian" or "Western Christian") system of marriage in large parts of the continent during the medieval and early modern periods. At the heart of this system were the regulations imposed by the Church after the Fourth Lateran Council in 1215, which prohibited marriages within the fourth degree of consanguinity and affinity. European populations absorbed these guidelines and even complemented them with other tacit prohibitions, like that against marriage between two people sharing the same surname (or with a partner whose surname could be found among the women of the other partner's parental line). Delille, then, believes that Europe was characterized by an alliance system in which marriages systematically linked distant relatives at degrees outside the canonical prohibitions. The exchange of women between alternate lines (mostly patrilineal, sometimes in combination with matrilineal ones) would constitute a core element of this system at the Western European scale.

According to Delille, this system of marriage circulation underwent a radical transformation in the eighteenth and nineteenth centuries and was replaced by a different system under which an increase in marriages between close blood relatives or affines was accompanied by a parallel growth in the number of marriages between unrelated people. In this way there were both a contraction and a divergence with respect to the earlier comprehensive endogamy organised through long term cycles, spanning over several generations. In the twentieth century this new phase gave way, in turn, to the effective disappearance of consanguineous marriages.

Delille's theories have raised a number of questions. Some authors have noted that it is difficult to prove that historical actors had a very extended memory of kinship, going back five or six generations. They observed that few families in the past, aside from the elite, possessed written documents, and most of the people were unlikely to have been able

---

1   Gérard Delille, "Échanges matrimoniaux entre lignées alternées et système européen de l'alliance: une première approche", in Jean-Luc Jamard, Emmanuel Terray, Margarita Xanthakou (eds.), *En substances. Textes pour Françoise Héritier,* Paris, Fayard, 2000, pp. 219–252; *Id.,* "Réflexions sur le système européen de la parenté et de l'alliance", *Annales. H.S.S.,* 2, 2001, pp. 369–380; *Id.,* "Représentation, généralisation, comparaison. Sur le système de parenté européen", in *Annales. H.S.S.,* 11, 2007, pp. 137–157; *Id.,* "Parenté et alliance en Europe occidentale. Un essai d'interprétation générale", in *L'Homme,* 1, 2010, pp. 75–135; *Id.,* "La France profonde. Relations de parenté et alliances matrimoniales (XVIᵉ–XVIIIᵉ siècle)", in *Annales. H.S.S.,* 4, 2015, pp. 881–930.

to produce the genealogical records that would be necessary to adequately identify exchanges between alternate lines[2]. Some critics emphasise the fact that Delille's study is weighted in favour of families who remained in one place for several generations and is almost always based on incomplete genealogies with data for some marriages completely missing, especially those on the matrilineal side[3]. This patrilineal bias would have a general weakening effect on the general model, causing the cognatic character of kinship in medieval and modern Western Europe to be underestimated[4].

The theory proposed by Delille raises questions about how short-term dynamics might relate to mechanisms of exchange between alternate lines that can play out over centuries. Another issue is that of the connection between the underlying principles of kinship and more concrete factors like the influence of economics and politics. Delille puts forward a fascinating analysis of the latter, but (following the structuralist tradition developed in the field of anthropology) he remains, nonetheless, convinced that the symbolic (cultural) aspect is in a position of primacy. For instance, he proposes a reversal of the thesis whereby the acceleration of economic exchange was responsible for the disarticulation of kinship and alliance. He believes that it was, on the contrary, the system of matrimonial exchanges which by encouraging exogamy, was at the origin of an increase of economic exchanges in early modern European history[5]. This culturalist approach recalls ideas that were proposed several decades ago by Peter Laslett, John Hajnal and Alan Macfarlane, who suggested that the European economic take-off had its origins in a kind of cultural matrix that materialised itself in the predominance of the nuclear family and of late marriage. On the other hand, Delille's vision of a contraction in kinship from the eighteenth century has some points in common with that of a

---

2   Jon Mathieu, "Kin marriages: Trends and Interpretations form the Swiss Example" in David Warren Sabean, Simon Teuscher, Jon Mathieu (eds.), *Kinship in Europe: approaches to long-term development (1300–1900)*, New York, Berghahn Books, 2007, pp. 211–230 (see pp. 220–221); François-Joseph Ruggiu "Histoire de la parenté ou anthropologie historique de la parenté? Autour de Kinship in Europe", in *Annales de démographie historique*, 1, 2010, pp. 223–256 (see p. 228).

3   François-Joseph Ruggiu "Histoire de la parenté", art. cit.

4   Élie Haddad, "Deux modèles récents de la parenté à l'épreuve de la noblesse française d'Ancien Régime", in *L'Atelier du Centre de recherches historiques. Revue électronique du CRH*, 9, 2012 (on-line: URL: http://acrh.revues.org/5086.)

5   See for instance his recent book, *L'économie de Dieu. Famille et marché entre christianisme, hébraïsme et islam*, Paris, Les Belles Lettres, [2013] 2015.

number of historians, including Lawrence Stone, who in the 1970s wrote extensively on the decline of kinship in the English upper classes, situating this decline earlier, between the sixteenth and the eighteenth centuries[6]. On a more general scale, Delille's ideas are akin to the master narrative of the decline of kinship in connection with modernisation.

This central narrative has been criticised by the historian D. W. Sabean, another author who has undoubtedly had a crucial influence on the development of new approaches to kinship history. In proposing a rather different vision from Delille's, Sabean has formulated several important hypotheses concerning changes in the practice and representation of kinship in Europe[7] and has encouraged collaborative studies which led to a book co-edited by Sabean himself[8]. This volume (covering the development of kinship over an extended period, from 1300 to 1900) presents a coherent research programme, the aims of which are clearly outlined in the introduction[9] and in the introductory notes to each section. The definition of kinship is broad, and includes inheritance and succession models, alliance systems, the circulation of goods amongst relatives, terminology and cultural representations. According to Sabean and Teuscher we should move on from the idea that kinship is always different for each specific context, and is associated with other types of relationships in an unsystematic way. They also believe that we should reject the theory embedded in the subconscious of social sciences according to which kinship has witnessed a decline in Europe due to the growing importance of other institutions such as the market or the State[10]. In order to stimulate comparative research and encourage debate among different research traditions, the book suggests two major historical transitions in kinship dynamics that took place across the whole continent.

---

6   See Lawrence Stone, *The Family, Sex and Marriage in England, 1500–1800*, New York, Harper, 1979 (especially the chapter 4).

7   David Warren Sabean, *Property, Production, and Family in Neckarhausen: 1700–1870*, Cambridge, Cambridge University Press, 1990; *Id.*, *Kinship in Neckarhausen, 1700–1870*, Cambridge, Cambridge University Press, 1998.

8   David Warren Sabean, Simon Teuscher, Jon Mathieu (eds.), *Kinship in Europe: op. cit.*

9   David W. Sabean, Simon Teuscher, "Kinship in Europe: A New Approach to Long-Term Development", in David W. Sabean, Simon Teuscher, Jon Mathieu, (eds.), *Kinship in Europe: op. cit.* pp. 1–32.

10   *Ibid.*, pp. 1–3.

The first of these transitions dates to between the late Medieval period and the beginning of the early modern period, approximately from 1400 to 1700[11]. This transition was marked by a strengthening of the patrilineal penchant of kin organization, through the development of agnatic or single-heir models of inheritance, the interlocking of client relationships and marriage alliances, and the growth of vertically structured kinship networks. Social structures accentuated the role of descent, agnatic kinship, paternal authority, domestic discipline and exogamy. According to Sabean and Teuscher, spouses in European societies before the second half of the eighteenth century were generally not related to each other (here they are in sharp disagreement with Delille). This transition was interwoven in the process of modern state formation, and connected to a more precise definition of property rights as well as the establishment of less permeable social hierarchies. The differences that can be observed in the rhythm of this transition are thought to be due to local variations in the timing of each States' consolidation and reconfiguration of property rights.

The second transition began in the eighteenth century, around 1750, and continued into the following century. While the previous period had glorified agnatic kinship, we see here the development of new models based on alliance, bilateral kinship networks and social and familial endogamy. Sabean and Teuscher argue that, from the second half of the eighteenth century, marriages increasingly tended to take place between couples closely related by consanguinity or by affinity, thanks to the gradual disappearance in Europe of laws prohibiting these unions. Moreover, this transition was embedded in those social dynamics which were characterised by the rise of capitalism, the development of a class structure and the modernisation of the political machine.

While Delille's model was inspired by the alliance theory of French structuralist anthropology, the interpretative framework proposed by Sabean and Teuscher seems to have more in common with the "descent" theory formulated by British social anthropologists. Sabean and Teuscher had emphasised the occurrence of a process of "verticalisation" during the first transition, which enhanced linearity and especially patrilinearity in kinship relations, along with the development of dynastic configurations. It is only with the second transition, during the late eighteenth century and the nineteenth, that alliance and kin marriages took a central position within the context of a process of "horizontalisation". Thus the situation as

---

11   *Ibid.*, p. 10.

envisioned by Sabean and Teuscher is diametrically opposed to that suggested by Delille who, as we have seen, believes that there was a contraction in kinship from the eighteenth century and that preexisting exchange networks were disrupted. For Sabean and Teuscher, on the other hand, this period saw an intensification of kinship relationships, resulting in what they define as a "kinship hot society".

Sabean and Teuscher's model has become an important reference for those working in the field of kinship and family in European history and stimulated comparative discussions. Some authors have suggested that the empirical basis on which *Kinship in Europe* relies is mainly focused on the elite and have called for a wider analytical scope in order to test the model with other social groups[12]. In an influential essay, François-Joseph Ruggiu remarked that the behavioural patterns highlighted in *Kinship in Europe* may not be so much the result of a temporal evolution as they are of social selection. In other words, they might be mainly concerned with the elite, with the addition during the nineteenth century of the middle class. Citing results published in the studies of French authors, Ruggiu suggests that, when considering other social groups it is possible even for the sixteenth and seventeenth centuries to identify 'kinship-hot' sub-societies, meaning groups of families who routinely practiced close-kin marriage[13]. On the other hand he states that even in the eighteenth and nineteenth centuries the percentage of consanguineous marriages remained low, and this casts some doubts on the relevance of a phenomenon which has been described as structuring for European populations[14]. Putting forward a more radical opinion, another historian has argued that this numerical increase of cousin marriages did not reflect a change in attitudes, and was simply a side effect of demographic transformations that generated a higher probability of kin marriages[15].

We can now turn our attention to a different approach toward kinship and family history in Europe, which Dionigi Albera has proposed in several works, principally in a book published in 2011 that aims to combine

---

12   François-Joseph Ruggiu "Histoire de la parenté", art. cit., pp. 244–245; Fabrice Boudjaaba, Marie-Pierre Arrizabalaga, "Les systèmes familiaux. De la cartographie des modes d'héritage aux dynamiques de la reproduction familiale et sociale", in *Annales de démographie historique* 1, 2015, pp. 165–199 (see p. 190).

13   François-Joseph Ruggiu, "Histoire de la parenté", art. cit., pp. 240–241.

14   *Ibid.*, p. 235.

15   Christine Fertig, *Familie, verwandtschaftliche Netzwerke und Klassenbildung im ländlichen Westfalen (1750–1874)*, Stuttgart, Lucius & Lucius, 2012.

history and anthropology with a long-term approach stretching from the fourteenth to the twentieth centuries[16]. In comparison with the aforementioned works, Albera's book has a narrower scope since it focuses on just one portion of Europe, namely the Alpine region which hosts a great variety of political and ethno-linguistic configurations. This reduction in scale makes it possible to delve deeper into an empirical study of local evidence in order to corroborate more generalised conclusions. Albera is also interested in an intermediate sphere, between the large vision of kinship promoted by Delille, Sabean and Teuscher and the household and family structures that have been central to the research tradition founded by the Cambridge Group in the 1960s. In order to delineate this intermediate thematic area, Albera formulates the concept of *domestic organisation* to indicate a series of relationships formed through activities related to common residence, production, distribution, transmission and reproduction. These elements are not isolated from their social framework, since the author also takes into consideration the legal context, access to collective resources, settlement structures, social relationships within villages and rural communities, and the nature of local political institutions.

Albera's comparative analysis takes form through successive stages. His theoretical foundation rests, initially, on a micro-analytical approach which makes it possible to define a first typology, with the formalisation of three ideal-types ("Bauer", "bourgeois" and "Alpine agnatic"). This typology is then supported through an analysis of a large body of monographic studies on the Austrian, Italian and Swiss Alps. This enables the author to define three rather compact regional sets whose main characteristics correspond to the ideal-types, with a regional polarisation of domestic practices that reveals substantial continuity over time, and is sometimes still recognisable in the nineteenth and twentieth centuries. These long-standing divisions within Alpine Europe do not seem to be connected to environmental or ethno-linguistic factors, but mainly to divergent historical processes rooted above all in the political and juridical domains.

Using the knowledge obtained from his Alpine observatory, Albera discusses the model of historical transformation put forward by Sabean and Teuscher. He argues that the chronology of the first transition, from the Middle Ages to the early modern period, should be more flexible, and observes that the growth of agnatic tendencies does not necessarily imply

16   Dionigi Albera, *Au fil des générations. Terre, pouvoir et parenté dans l'Europe alpine (XIVᵉ–XXᵉ siècles)*, Grenoble, PUG, 2011.

an increase in dynastic inclinations and the succession of a single heir. This process seems to apply to the nobility and to leading urban groups, but it is scarcely present in Alpine rural societies, among the peasants upon which Albera's study is, essentially, focused. On the whole, by situating itself at a meso-level, *Au fil des générations* builds a set of theoretical instruments that may help renew, at a more general level, the history of the family and kinship in Europe, by putting the issue of the difference between regional blocs and among social groups at the centre of the discussion, along with the issue of scale and of the relationship between micro, meso and macro methodologies. This approach requires cross-fertilisation between micro-history, Albera's meso-analytical approach, and wider visions that emphasise the existence of common transformations, at a continental level, in kinship conceptions and practices. The articles contained in this volume represent an attempt to move in this direction. They are closely connected to Albera's work, although the theories of Delille and, above all, those of Sabean and Teuscher, will often be evoked in the following chapters and have inspired the research presented here.

The first section of this volume presents a broad discussion of recent developments in kinship history, with contributions from two of the editors of *Kinship in Europe* and from the author of *Au fil des générations*. In his chapter, Jon Mathieu first considers certain features of the genesis of the latter book, going on to examine different processes of historical transformation described or suggested by Albera within the framework of his spatialised typology. He then formulates several arguments suggesting that Albera's "contextual typology" of Alpine domestic organisation is compatible with the model of historical transformation proposed by the editors of *Kinship in Europe*.

For his part Simon Teuscher discusses the opinions outlined in *Au fil des generations* and responds to Albera's criticism of the chronology of transitions described in *Kinship in Europe*. In his dialogue with *Au fil des generations,* he also notes the existence of a number of parallels between certain Alpine patterns and the general interpretative framework that he and David Sabean delineated at a European level. Teuscher's discussion of Albera's book leads him to address the issue of scale in historical research and the problem of mediation. This latter problem has to do with the multiple articulations of kinship, which manifest themselves as signs and symbols as well as material entities like property and practices, and Teuscher convincingly argues for a better appreciation of this issues.

Dionigi Albera's article proposes a discussion of recent reactions to *Au fil des generations*. After attempting to better define what he means by the expression "third phase" in the history of family and kinship in Europe, he summarises the main elements of his comparative approach. He then provides an overview of the connection of his regional typology with other scales of analysis, both smaller and larger. In particular he is interested in how his approach relates to microhistory. He suggests that microhistory is fundamental, but that it should be integrated within a wider historical narrative. He also argues that the models of Alpine historical processes which he developed in *Au fil des générations* may be compatible with, and complementary to, the broad hypotheses presented in *Kinship in Europe*.

The Alpine region is the common thread that unites the chapters in the second part of this volume, which deal more or less directly with the theoretical framework proposed by Dionigi Albera. In the first chapter Luigi Lorenzetti reflects on the regional typology put forward by *Au fil des générations*. He is interested in the degree of uniformity, flexibility and variability present in the different components of Albera's Alpine domestic organization types. He picks out a few examples of transversality which overlap these three ideal-types. By focusing on the agnatic region, he also highlights the internal diversity to be found in this area.

In Margareth Lanzinger's dialogue with Albera's book she refers to the Bauer type of the Eastern Alps. Her study compares two areas, Lower Austria and Tyrol, which shared the same prevailing principle of impartible succession while at the same time having different marital property regimes. In Lower Austria marriage created a joint and indivisible estate, while separation of marital property predominated in Tyrol's rural areas. Lanzinger suggests that, along with inheritance practices, marital property regimes helped to shape power structures, distribution of property, relationships across different generations and gender, giving more strength to marriage in Lower Austria, and to the line of descent in Tyrol. Relatives seem to enjoy a more important position in Tyrol, especially in the case of childless couples. On the basis of an analysis of marriage dispensation applications in the nineteenth century Tyrol, Lanzinger examines the importance of relatives in the context of male widowhood. On the whole, Lanzinger brings attention to other, more horizontal, relationship axes which intersect with the vertical rationale of succession to property control and patrilineality.

Sandro Guzzi-Heeb proposes an alternative view to the analysis of kinship structures and inheritance patterns, demonstrating the importance of kin networks in Valais during the eighteenth and nineteenth centuries. Guzzi-Heeb recognises that a structural orientation, as exemplified by Dionigi Albera's work, is a useful instrument with which to scrutinize basic elements of the social construct and to analyse the different paths along which societies evolved. Nonetheless, he believes that both this approach and that advocated by Sabean are unable to explain how kinship networks function, since the latter cannot be described as simply a result of formal kinship structures. From this point of view Guzzi-Heeb makes a distinction between what he defines as *primary kinship*, or "the tightly interconnected group of kin on which one relies for primary necessities", and *strategic kinship* which designates a more fluid pattern of social relations between kin, in the sense of "related persons able to provide political or strategic support in order to achieve a goal". While it is possible to examine primary kinship through the lens of kinship structures and inheritance patterns, he maintains that strategic kinship should be situated within the broader range of local networks.

The articles that make up the third part of the book broaden the field of studies further. They leave behind the Alps to concentrate on an exploration of various European contexts, and are generally influenced by Albera's analysis of Alpine Europe. Following in the footsteps of the methodological approach of *Au fil des générations*, Elie Haddad's article proposes a transposition of Albera's interpretation of spatial variations in Alpine domestic organisation to the study of social variations within a single state. He does this by studying the specific history of domestic organisation in a social group belonging to the Kingdom of France, namely early-modern nobility. He argues that the aristocracy underwent discernible transformations, and analyses to what extent these were different from the transformations experienced by other social groups. Haddad's analysis of mid to high level aristocratic families links the specific evolution of French noble domestic organisation to the political and social history of the Kingdom as a whole.

The link between general and regional patterns that caracterises Albera's work on the Alps is at the center of the following chapter in which Fabrice Boudjaaba develops a regional approach designed to test the validity of what are seen as the main trends in the history of family organisation in Western Europe. Boudjaaba is particularly interested in the second transition in the kinship system as proposed by Sabean and Teuscher, pointing to the growth of new models based on alliance and bilateral kinship. In order to test one particular element of this transformation, the author has looked at Normandy between the eighteenth and nineteenth centuries. Here the prevailing domestic arrangement was the nuclear family, but customary family law during the early modern period had a strong patrilineal bias, with daughters generally being excluded from succession and married under the dowry system. And yet, in line with the hypotheses put forward by *Kinship in Europe*, the Norman family system seemed, from the eighteenth century, to move away from its patrilineal bias and towards a preference for bilateral arrangements. This change is key in explaining the widespread acceptance in Normandy of the new family law imposed by the Civil Code at the beginning of the nineteenth century.

Jérôme Luther Viret's article uses a regional approach which is intended to test wide-ranging historical theories concerning Western Europe. He is chiefly concerned with John Hajnal's well-known Western demographic model which, predominantly, is characterised by late marriage. Viret calls into question a purely economic interpretation of this phenomenon, explaning comparatively late marriage with the fact that young people needed wait until they had the means to set up a new household. Aside from this, he stresses the need to take into account questions of power, particularly that exerted by the spouses' parents. By analysing marriage contracts and the body of common law, Viret makes a comparison between patterns of family life in the Paris area and in Normandy. The age of newlyweds at their first marriage is fairly similar for both areas, as is the presence of the nuclear family, despite radically diverging ideas regarding the couple and inheritance transfer.

In the following chapter, Michaël Gasperoni responds to Albera's invitation to investigate local and regional processes in a *longue durée* perspective, in order to understand how they interact with broader dynamics. His focus, then, is on a long-term analysis (from the sixteenth to the nineteenth century) of the kinship system in an area of Central Italy which includes the Republic of San Marino and Rimini. By working on this intermediate scale (midway between the local and the regional), and through an exhaustive study of the available demographic documentation along with the reconstruction of an entire population and the creation of a genealogical dataset designed for computer analysis, the author is able to test the viability of general theories of kinship transitions at a European level like those advanced by Delille and Sabean and Teuscher.

Lastly, Vincent Gourdon presents a broad summary of recent advances in the history of godparenthood in Western Europe, a growing field of study to which this author has made a decisive contribution. Gourdon points out the existence of converging dynamics on a Europe-wide scale, which coincide with the development of a familialisation process in godparent-hood throughout Western Europe and beginning in the eighteenth century (a shift which seems to match the second transition identified by Sabean and Teuscher). He also emphasises the fact that important differences and nuances exist between national and regional patterns, with regard both to the results they produce and to their respective time-scales.

This book began with a workshop, held in Ticino (Switzerland) at the Laboratorio di Storia delle Alpi of the Università della Svizzera italiana in May 2013. The workshop was entitled *A third phase in historical and anthropological family research? Towards a regional and dynamic typology*. Some contributions to the workshop did not make their way into the book, while some authors were recruited after the gathering. Our thanks go to the Laboratorio di Storia delle Alpi for its splendid organisation and its patient engagement, to the Swiss National Science Foundation for its financial support, and to all the participants in the workshop and the authors of the present book for their great efforts. As stated above, our main aim was to rethink recent empirical and theoretical contributions to the history of the family and of kinship in Europe in the light of a new approach proposed by Dionigi Albera in his monograph about *alpine Europe*. The approach raises important general questions: How can we conceptualise regional trajectories within widespread or continental processes of transformation? How useful are notions on a meso-analytical level like Albera's ideal types compared to micro- and macro-historical studies? Can the notion of domestic organization cover the most important elements necessary to discuss major spatial and temporal differences in family and kinship history? And last but not least, which are the relationships of this approach to other general approaches proposed in recent research?

Part 1:
Alpine Europe? Reconsidering
Recent Research

Jon Mathieu

Transitions in the Domestic Organisation of the Alpine Area, from the Late Middle Ages to Modernity

This chapter offers a historical reading of Dionigi Albera's recent book *Au fil des générations*[1], with special attention to two points: the transitions from one ideal type of domestic organisation to the other, and the relationship of the text to the model of kinship history as proposed by David Sabean and Simon Teuscher[2]. At the beginning, however, I would like to hint at the long and interesting making of *Au fil des générations*. Since I have followed the process over the years, albeit from some distance, I permit myself to adopt a personal tone.

A book with a history

The book *Au fil des générations* originated from a dissertation entitled *L'organisation domestique dans l'espace alpin. Equilibres écologiques, effets de frontières, transformations historiques*. It was a "thèse d'ethnologie", accepted by the Université de Provence in 1995 – not very short, two volumes, a few kilos. I have an idea of that intellectual and physical weight because Dionigi Albera was so kind to give me a copy at the train station of Torino Porta Nuova in June 1996. The two volumes could barely fit in a plastic bag, and I carried the bag during my journey

---

1   Dionigi Albera, *Au fil des générations. Terre, pouvoir et parenté dans l'Europe alpine (XIVᵉ–XXᵉ siècles)*, Grenoble, PUG, 2011.

2   David W. Sabean, Simon Teuscher, "Kinship in Europe: A New Approach to Long-Term Development", in David W. Sabean, Simon Teuscher, Jon Mathieu (eds.), *Kinship in Europe: Approaches to the Long-Term Development (1300–1900)*, New York, Berghahn Books, 2007, pp. 1–32.

around the alpine area. The effort was paid off by the content. Albera and I had had some kind of parallel intuition about the way one could deal with family and household in alpine history, but he was first to put it down, and I could use it very well in my current research. Two weeks later I wrote him a letter:

> "I thank you very much for your help in Torino and for your most interesting book. I learned a lot from this text and I fully agree with the main conclusions, especially the attention you pay to the socio-historical context of domestic organisation. I am very glad you gave me the chance to join you in this exciting journey through the alpine valleys, past and present. We should have the opportunity to talk for a long time, in this letter I can select only a few points and I will select first of all the minor points where I cannot share your views. I think this is more useful." (personal letter 18.06.1996).

In his dissertation, Albera proposed an outline of three ideal types of domestic organisation that should cover the main features of the variegated forms of household, family, and kinship in the alpine area, from Nice to Vienna. They could be called the *Bauer* type, the *bourgeois* type and the *agnatic* type, and were defined by particular configurations of inheritance, co-residence, authority, relationships beyond the domestic sphere, settlement patterns, and other criteria. Thus the socio-historical context played a great role[3]. In my critical comments, I pointed above all to the uneven treatment of the bourgeois and the agnatic types, and proposed to pay more attention to the political dimension and to the public role of notaries (for the agnatic type).

At that time I was working on a book about economic and socio-political issues of alpine history from the sixteenth to the nineteenth century, and I planned to use Albera's approach to frame the chapter on family history. I was therefore interested in a quotable publication, and wrote him again in 1997 saying that I hoped that he already finished his *opus magnum* for publication. I also asked him if he could possibly send me a copy of the proofs so that I could give the correct pages in my own book (personal letter 27.10.1997). This turned out to be a

---

3   Dionigi Albera, *L'organisation domestique dans l'espace alpin. Equilibres écologiques, effets de frontières, transformations historiques*, unpublished Thèse d'ethnologie, Université de Provence, 1995. In chapter 18 there was also a subvariant of the agnatic type.

total misjudgement of the situation! My book appeared in 1998[4], listing Albera's manuscript as "demnächst als Buch" (soon in book format). But time passed by, one year after the other, and no publication was in sight, until, to my big surprise, I received a postal package from Albera in spring 2010. It was a new version of the manuscript, rather different from the original one. Not only was the title new, but also several parts and ideas were completely new. Some principal concepts, however, survived the whole period. It was a good text in the first version, but it was even a better one in the second version.

Again, I wrote a lengthy letter to Albera (meanwhile the internet had become common and speeded up communication) telling him that I very much admired his work and the intellectual energy that he had invested over all these years. I proposed to change the first sentence of the manuscript, since it started with an excuse, an unnecessary sign of modesty in my view. And I added a few comments on the typology, for instance the following one:

> "At the end of your well-made summary you come to the "situations intermédiares" and "transformations qui oscillent entre plusieurs processus". I wonder if it would be interesting to give some more thinking and weight to these "inconsistencies". To my mind they are extremely interesting and possibly capable of showing your model from another side, and prove effectively that the typology is a real tool, which can produce interesting and important questions. Perhaps you could make a list of all the transitional regions and processes that you have in your work (there are quite a lot of them) and then you could see to what degree the different forms are compatible and which transitions are more likely to occur than the others." (personal letter 16.05.2010[5]).

We discussed these propositions when we held a private celebration of the published book, in Torino on 29 October 2011, more than fifteen years after he had given me the first version at the same place. They turned out to be over-ambitious for the time being. Nonetheless I take the opportunity of the present publication to test one of these ideas in a very restricted way in the following section.

---

4   Jon Mathieu, *Geschichte der Alpen 1500–1900. Umwelt, Entwicklung, Gesellschaft*, Böhlau Verlag, Wien, 1998 (english version: *History of the Alps 1500–1900. Environment, Development, and Society*, Morgantown, West Virginia University Press, 2009).

5   See now Dionigi Albera, *Au fil des generations*, *op. cit.*, p. 331.

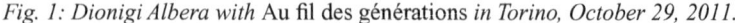
Fig. 1: Dionigi Albera with Au fil des générations *in Torino, October 29, 2011.*

Domestic organisation on the move

Similar to the 1995 version, the published version of 2011 proposes a threefold "contextual typology" of the domestic organisation in the alpine area. It distinguishes a *Bauer* type (in the Eastern Alps) from a *bourgeois* type (in some regions of the Central Alps) and an *agnatique alpine* type (in the Southern and Western Alps). Among the three, the latter has evolved most between 1995 and 2011[6]. Each type has a starting point in an important earlier microstudy of household and family. From there Albera moves to a regional level of generalisation. He is careful in delineating the spatial contours of the distinct forms of domestic

---

6   The agnatic type was not presented with a fixed nomenclature in 1995, and the spe-
     cification "alpine" was completely new in 2011.

organisation in most parts of the Alps. The alpine area measures at least 180,000 square kilometres and more than 5,000 communities. Tracing, reading, and treating the available literature were therefore a major task. The book offers also a detailed definition of the three types centring on the household and its intergenerational transmission, but including a series of other characteristics like the form of habitat, the patterns of coresidence, the economic and social stratification, the relationships beyond the domestic sphere, and special corollaries. The types are seen as "ideal types", that is, as heuristic tools for research, a kind of *ensembles*, with a certain flexibility.

A well-explained, evidence based, and spatialised typology can be used in different ways. First of all, it gives an idea of the overall social structure of the area. In the case of the Alps, this is especially interesting, since they appear as a contact zone of different household cultures and thus a privileged place for comparative research. The *Bauer* type, for instance, seems to stretch from Austria up to Denmark, while the *agnatique alpine* type is linked to similar forms in Northern Italy. So the unusual expression "Europe alpine", given in the subtitle of the book, is not farfetched. In my view, typologies are also useful when they generate new questions. What about the regions "in between" not really fitting into a principal type of domestic organisation? And what about the transitions from one type to the other during the long period under investigation from the fourteenth to the twentieth centuries? Being a historian I am principally interested into questions of change and continuity, the time dimension of social phenomena. I have therefore tried to single out the different transformation processes described, or hinted at, in *Au fil des générations*. Since intergenerational transmission is at the centre of the three ideal types, I focus on that specific indicator, and this leads me to the following tentative chart.

Fig. 2: Transitions of domestic types in the alpine area as addressed by Albera 2011.

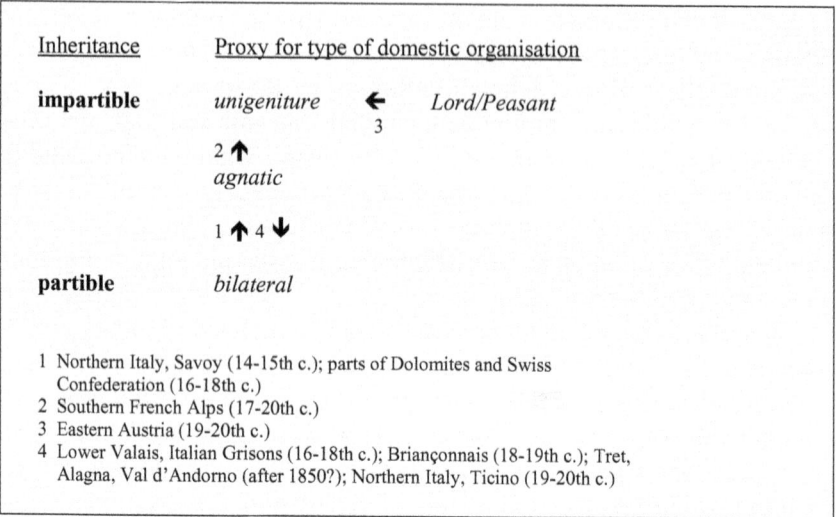

Figure 2 places the types of domestic organisation in a spectrum from impartible to partible inheritance: unigeniture (one heir only) for the *Bauer* type, agnatic (male heirs, with daughters being paid off with a dowry) for the *alpine agnatique* type, and bilateral (ungendered inheritance for sons and daughters) for the *bourgeois* type. I have added a *Lord/Peasant*-category for the feudal context of the *Bauer* type. Up to the nineteenth century, in many regions of the Eastern Alps the property rights of the peasant were generally weak, the transmission of the farm being a kind of transmission of a public office controlled by the lords. The figure shows that Albera's book describes or suggests at least four kinds of transitions. At the bottom of the figure I have listed the regions and the approximate periods thereof, mentioned in the text.

Before looking at the transitions separately, we can go over them in a cursory way and see that some regions are large and some regions are small. Category 4 includes even three communities: Tret, Alagna, and Val d'Andorno where intergenerational transmission moved from the agnatic to the bilateral type probably during the late nineteenth century. These are localities well known in alpine anthropology and history through the research of John Cole and Eric Wolf[7], Pier Paolo Viazzo[8], and Patrizia Audenino[9]. Albera points to them in order to suggest that the bilateral structures, described in their monographs, were a rather recent phenomenon evolving out of former agnatic type. In doing so he also illustrates another usage of the typology, namely its heuristic power in detecting "anomalies". As long as we have no idea of regional patterns, we have no measure for usual as well as unusual configurations. But let us now briefly follow the single transitions from 1 to 4:

(1) Northern Italy and Savoy in the late Middle Ages and parts of the Ladin Dolomites and Swiss Confederation during the early modern period saw the establishment of agnatic types of domestic organisation. In some cases we do not really know the former type, so that the given bilateral starting point is somewhat dubious. The cases of the Ladin Dolomites and the Swiss Confederation are in need of further research as well. But the main movement towards agnatic structures, originating in the important cities of Northern Italy and Southern France during the later Middle Ages and reaching out to most of the alpine valleys through the notarial system, is plausible and well substantiated. It seems to have been driven by politico-cultural factors.

(2) In the case of the Southern French Alps, the restriction to heirship continued with a move towards unigeniture from the seventeenth century onwards. It is one of the very important findings of the final version of the research, and Albera links it to a similar movement of the French *Midi* in the early modern period. In this case, too, the Alps were open to the changes of the surrounding areas. We could perhaps point to the fact that this new form of unigeniture transmission is not really included in the basic threefold typology. The *Bauer*-type of the Eastern Alps manifested rather different features.

(3) As already mentioned, the *Bauer* type, in the early modern period, was shaped by the lords' authority regarding farm management and transmission, which turned it into a kind of public office. There were

---

7   John Cole W., Eric R. Wolf, *The Hidden Frontier. Ecology and Ethnicity in an Alpine Valley*, New York, Academic Press, 1974.

8   Pier Paolo Viazzo, *Upland communities. Environment, population and social structure in the Alps since the sixteenth century*, Cambridge, Cambridge University Press, 1989.

9   Patrizia Audenino, *Un mestiere per partire. Tradizione migratoria, lavoro e comunità in una vallata alpina*, Milano, Franco Angeli, 1990.

different degrees of interference by the lords, but generally the interference grew stronger at first and then weaker from the eighteenth century onwards, parallel to the restructuring of statehood and feudal domination. Through the so-called *Grundentlastung* after the 1848 revolution it ended up in most cases in a unigeniture system. Now the dominant discourse concerned the economic viability of the farmsteads in modern market competition.

(4) The other option of the nineteenth and twentieth centuries was a move towards ungendered, bilateral inheritance, motivated by the social discourse of equality. In our study area, Northern Italy and Ticino were the foremost examples thereof. Other sites of the forth category were border regions between two types of domestic organisation shifting with the political belonging. The Lower Valais, for example, was savoyard in the Middle Ages, and became a subject territory of the Swiss allied *Landschaft Wallis* (Valais) in the late fifteenth century. Briançonnais bordered on Piedmont/Italy, and seemed to have been a forerunner of its modern development for several reasons. This was in sharp contrast to the development in the southern parts of the French Alps tending to unigeniture during the same period.

The state of the historical knowledge about the single transitions is very diverse. *Au fil des générations* describes some of them broadly and with convincing clues and sources. Some, on the other hand, remain rather obscure and uncertain. On the whole, the clearest and most extensive change discussed in the book concerns the agnatic type of domestic organisation. It was established in large areas during the late Middle Ages, reached its apogee during the early modern period, and declined in the nineteenth and twentieth centuries, giving place to bilateral or unigeniture inheritance according to regional circumstances.

Types of domestic organisation and a model of kinship history

The basic idea of the book under study is a "contextual typology" of domestic organisation. Spatial variations, not historical transitions, are the author's principal concern. Another starting point was chosen by David

Sabean and Simon Teuscher in their model of kinship history[10]. The book is organised around a two-phased model: The first transition leads from medieval to early modern kinship patterns, through a process of "verticalisation" which stresses linearity and especially patrilinearity, that is dynastic structures. The second transition, during the late eighteenth and nineteenth centuries, can be described as a process of "horizontalisation", where alliance and kin marriages became central to the system. Both transitions were part and parcel of wider political and economic changes such as state formation, intensified administration, commercial and industrial take-off, and so forth.

Dionigi Albera takes up and discusses the Sabean-Teuscher approach in a rather detailed fashion, approving of some parts and criticising other parts. He is especially critical about the first transition, pointing out that its periodisation is rather vague and the evidence scarce. Furthermore, according to Albera, there are cases where the gradual restriction of authority and inheritance in the early modern period cannot be documented, especially in the *bourgeois* type regions[11].

In my view the two approaches are compatible in many ways. The prominent historical trajectory of the agnatic type, for example, can also be read as an illustration of the first transition in the Sabean-Teuscher model (establishment of exclusive vertical relationships with the advent of male-centred inheritance and patrilinearity), and its transformation from the eighteenth century onwards seems to be compatible with the second transition in that model (the increasing important of alliance and kin marriages). Albera is, of course, right in pointing to the regions where bilateral inheritance was institutionalised in the early modern period like in Valais or in the Grisons. Yet in both regions, during that period, there was also a trend towards the restriction of inheritance, in the Grisons above all with the instrument of the so called "Mannsvorteil" (male advantage). This trend involved only elite families that amounted to few percent of the population. But there are indications that linearity and intergenerational authority were strengthened in peasant families, too[12].

---

10   David W. Sabean, Simon Teuscher, "Kinship in Europe", art. cit.

11   Dionigi Albera, *Au fil des générations, op. cit.*, pp. 44–45, 486.

12   Jon Mathieu, "Die ländliche Gesellschaft", in Verein für Bündner Kulturforschung (ed.), *Handbuch der Bündner Geschichte*, vol. 2, Chur, Verlag Bündner Monatsblatt, 2000, pp. 11–54.

Thus it ultimately depends on the definition one gives to "vertical-isation" and "horizonalisation": Do we take a broad or a narrow view? What can be regarded as an exception, and how many exception are tolerable? These are very legitimate questions. Yet the same questions can be raised for the regional typology in *Au fil des générations*: How do we treat the elite instrument of the "Mannsvorteil" within the bourgeois type of domestic organisation? Is it a tolerable exception or not? What about a male preference for the inheritance of the house, a custom documentable in some Grison valleys where strict bilateral inheritance was observed regarding the financial assessment of material goods?

An interesting contribution to the discussion comes from Margareth Lanzinger with her recent habilitation thesis on marriage prohibition and the politics and practices of dispensation in the diocesis of Brixen in Tyrol and the adjacent dioceses of Salzburg, Trento, and Chur from 1780 to 1890[13]. The region under study enables her to compare two types of domestic organisation with regard of alliance politics: the *Bauer* region east of Innsbruck and the *bourgeois* region west of Innsbruck. This comparison was one of the working hypotheses at the onset of her investigation. She thought that the bourgeois, bilateral type would generate more kin marriages. But the detailed work on thousands of cases of dispensation made her aware that there was a dynamics of its own in this kind of kin administration on both the demand side and the supply side. The dispensations were, for example, influenced by the competition between state and church for authority in the field of marriage, and if some close kin marriages were allowed in one region this could set an example for others and produce a snow ball effect.

At this place I want only to stress that Lanzinger's work lies exactly at the interface between Albera and Sabean-Teuscher. She has much to say about the domestic organisation and focuses on the alliance patterns of the second transition, challenging its general label ("horizontalisation") and bringing in a new factor (the dynamics of dispensation politics and practices). Thus her investigation increases the complexity of the question. Generally speaking, the mentioned authors and studies force us to rethink the interplay of different dimensions and variables in the field: How many of them do we need on the micro and macro level of family history? How do we combine regional and chronological variations? How much weight

---

13   Margareth Lanzinger, *Verwaltete Verwandtschaft. Eheverbote, kirchliche und staatliche Dispenspraxis im 18. und 19. Jahrhundert*, Vienna, Böhlau Verlag, 2015.

should we assign to path dependence in a given territory and to context pressure of the overall society at a given moment?

Conclusion

Looking back at the historical and anthropological family research in the alpine area, one becomes aware of its advances. Fifty years ago, the anthropologist Robert Burns outlined a "Circum Alpine Area" with one family type – the so-called "stem family" –characterising the entire area and contributing to its unity[14]. He relied on his field experience in one particular village of the French Alps and on a few rather general studies. In 1974, when John W. Cole and Eric R. Wolf published their monograph on two villages at the border of South Tyrol and Trentino, the standards for research had already improved considerably. The authors procured much more information, historical and contemporary, about their subject than Burns, and besides the ecological similarities between the two villages they emphasised the differences and tried to insert them into a larger framework. Pier Paolo Viazzo (who worked for some time with Dionigi Albera) published his pioneering *Upland Communities* in 1989. He brought in modern methods of historical demography and quantitative household research and problematised the *idées reçues* about alpine societies in several ways.

Dionigi Albera's book of 2011 enlarges the empirical basis again, and quite massively. His work is more systematic than the precursors, and the focus is now clearly on the diversity of domestic practices. He sees the alpine area as a *lieu de croisement*, a contact or transitional space, of a wider European history[15]. The mountain environment is no longer generating unity, but contributing to differences in the cultural and political field that shaped the domestic dimension. Albera focuses on a typology that is explicitly contextual and dynamic. In the present chapter I have singled out the transition processes described, or hinted at, in his book in order to obtain an overview. The forms of intergenerational transmission

---

14   Robert K. Burns, "The Circum-Alpine area: a preliminary view", in *Anthropological Quarterly*, 36, 1963, pp. 130–155.

15   Dionigi Albera, *Au fil des générations, op. cit.*, p. 494.

have been used as a proxy for the types of domestic organisation. Perhaps this attempt at systematisation can be helpful for future studies that would inform us more precisely, for instance, on the speed and modalities of the transitions. With respect to the two-phased model of kinship history proposed by Sabean and Teuscher I have argued that it is compatible, by and large, with Albera's typology. Much depends on the rigidity or flexibility that we give to the definitions of the regional and chronological types.

Simon Teuscher

Problems of Scale and Mediation in Studies of Kinship in the Past

What is the future of studies of kinship in the past? It probably looks as if I wanted to make a big question even bigger by raising all kinds of problems about scale and mediation. But what follows is little more than a few thoughts departing from Dionigi Albera's important book *Au fil des générations*[1]. I will also try to reply to some of Albera's critiques of the volume on *Kinship in Europe* that Jon Mathieu, David Sabean and I have edited[2]. I will begin by highlighting a few of the many merits of Albera's book, in particular with regard to how it positions itself vis-à-vis an extended historiography on kinship in Europe. I will then continue with questions of scale, that is, about whether and where we should apply micro or large-scale perspectives – or perhaps something in between. Kinship in Europe seems to have provoked such questions and they are at the heart of the future prospects of kinship history. I will next address the issue of mediations, of how kinship depends on its articulations in language, signs, and symbols or in property and practices. I will argue that more attention to these problems may help to overcome certain controversies and help relate changes in kinship to broader historical developments.

Dionigi Albera's book is a comparative study of the structures of household organization, settlement, and kinship in the Alps. He invites his readers on a journey not only the length of the Alpine arch but across time. He revisits the last three decades of anthropological and historical research on Alpine societies, including classic examinations such as that of John Cole and Eric Wolf on Tyrol, of Robert Netting on Vallais, of

---

1   Dionigi Albera, *Au fil des générations. Terre, pouvoir et parenté dans l'Europe alpine (XIVᵉ–XXᵉ siècles)*, Grenoble, PUG, 2011. The chapter repeats and further develops some of the observations I made in my article "A proposito di Quattro libri sulla storia della famiglia", in Quaderni Storici. *Nuova Serie*, 143, 2, 2013, pp. 611–616.

2   David W. Sabean, Jon Mathieu, Simon Teuscher (eds.), *Kinship in Europe: Approaches to the Long-Term Development (1300–1900)*, New York – Oxford, Berghahn Books, 2007.

Giovanni Levi on Northern Italy, of Laurence Fontaine or Alain Collomp on the western Alps, and Jon Mathieu's comparative studies of the social history of Alpine regions. At the end of this trajectory, Albera presents a number of original theoretical and methodological reflections that merit notice beyond the community of Alpine research.

A great deal of Albera's methodological innovations can be described as a search for middle grounds and intersections. He tries to find intersections between history and anthropology, between research into household organization in the tradition of the Cambridge group and new approaches to the history of kinship, between micro and macro-history, between detailed descriptions of historical states and models of long-term development. An important instrument in establishing these middle grounds are the three ideal types with which Albera operates – of the "Bauer," the "Bourgeois," and the "Alpine Agnates." These types serve as shorthands for structures that affect household, settlement, and kinship organization. One the one hand, each has a foundation in micro-studies – the "Bauer" type in Cole and Wolf's study of the village of St. Felix in Tyrol, the "Bourgeois" in Netting's examination of the village of Törbel in the Swiss Valais, and, the "Alpine Agnate" in Albera's own examinations located in the Piedmontese Alps[3]. On the other hand, these three ideal types are an effective means for distinguishing major Alpine regions – and possibly even entire sectors of the European continent – that possess quite different social structures.

Sometimes Albera radically distances himself from those poles between which he is searching for the middle ground. Thus he is fairly critical of the Cambridge group's tradition of examining household structures without looking into kinship organization. Probably more controversial is his rejection of both micro-studies and general statements about European developments in household and kinship.

The latter can serve as an entry point into our discussion of questions of scale. The editors of this volume suggest that the future of kinship research belongs to yet another middle ground, namely to examinations at the regional level, while both micro-studies and generalizations regarding

---

3   John W. Cole, Eric R. Wolf, *The Hidden Frontier: Ecology and Ethnicity in an Alpine Valley*, New York, Academic Press, 1974; Robert Mc C. Netting, *Balancing on an Alp: Ecological Change and Continuity in a Swiss Mountain Community*, Cambridge, Cambridge University Press, 1981; Dionigi Albera, *L'organisation domestique dans l'espace alpin. Equilibres écologiques, effets de frontières, transformations historiques*, Thèse, Aix-en-Provence 1995.

all of Europe belong to earlier periods of research and are now outdated. Dionigi Albera blames micro-history for hiding the important regional developments in an anthill of local findings[4]. And he finds that the sketch of long-term developments in the volume *Kinship in Europe* operates with time-frames that are too vague and that he underestimates regional path-dependencies.

This criticism is fair enough to the extent that one decides to read both micro-historical examinations and *Kinship in Europe* as contributions to a greater understanding of those regional developments that form the main interest of *Au fil des générations*. Yet both ask entirely different questions. Micro-historical work, on the one hand, uses its perspective to challenge modernization's narratives, to solve theoretical problems and to reveal interconnections that can only be seen on the local or individual level. On the other hand, the intention behind our *Kinship in Europe* was not to replace micro-history but rather to promote its findings. Our concern was that the results of micro-historical work on kinship had not been taken seriously enough in broader historical debates. We are the last ones to deny that kinship was significantly different among the peasants of Neckarhausen, the small town patricians in Manduria, or the peddlers from the Alpine valleys of Savoy. But our main intention was concerned with a point about which there is considerable consensus: Almost all micro-studies raise serious doubts about the master narrative of a constant decline of kinship since the Middle Ages, as has been suggested by most theories of modernization. Despite this unanimous criticism the old tale of decline remains largely unaffected in more general historical debates, where it keeps being repeated and used in all kinds of arguments. Because we grew impatient with micro-history's failed attempts at getting the message across, we tried to conceptualize a narrative that was as abstract as the old one but more congruent with recent findings on the local and regional levels. Our intention was not to teach lessons to specialists working on kinship locally and regionally, but to draw the attention of a broader scholarly community to the importance of kinship as a factor of historical change.

Our suggestion was to organize future research around two transitions. The first one would lead from the thirteenth century well into the early modern period, the second one from the mid-eighteenth into the beginning of the twentieth century. The first transition was characterized

---

4   Dionigi Albera, *Au fil des générations, op. cit.*, p. 8.

by a new stress on familial coherence and hierarchy. This was accompanied by a growing concern with descent, heritage, and linearity in property devolution, often but not always in the form of patrilinearity. All of this helped to keep particular goods undivided and to make their devolution from one generation to the next more predictable. Prominent examples of such goods were heritable offices, monopolies, castles, and estates as well as entire states, i.e. things that had not only material value but gave access to social positions and political power. In many cases property that was less loaded with political and social significance was not – or at least not fully – affected by these patterns of devolution and, for instance, still passed on in equal amount to both daughters and sons. During the second transition families organized less around immutable "things" than around attempts at pooling and hedging capital. Now alliance, affinity, sibling and cousin-relations became more dominant. And marriages became more endogamous in terms of class, milieu, and consanguinity, all of which helped to provide the financial investments needed in industrial enterprises, a more capital-intensive agriculture, and for careers in the *professions libérales*.

That the two transitions are simplifications and that local developments can diverge significantly is something we both explicitly stated and underscored by including conflicting chapters in our volume. Perhaps we have not sufficiently explained that we did not primarily aim at describing representative forms of kinship organization and therefore did not discuss in depth just how representative they were within specific regions, social settings, and timeframes. In many respects these are very important questions, and during the last years there have been made interesting attempts at answering them[5]. But our main concern was to overcome the old story according to which kinship in the course of history merely declined and was replaced by newly emerging phenomena such as the commune of the thirteenth century, the state of the sixteenth, the associations of the eighteenth, or the welfare system of the twentieth. Instead we wanted to explore how changes in kinship played a productive role in bringing about new phenomena. That kinship was involved in processes of historical change is something which had first been explored in studies at the micro-level.

---

5   François-Joseph Ruggiu, "Histoire de la parenté ou anthropologie historique de la parenté? Autour de Kinship in Europe", in *Annales de démographie historique*, 1, 2010, pp. 223–256; and Jon Mathieu, "Verwandtschaft als historischer Faktor. Schweizer Fallstudien und Trends, 1500–1900", in *Historische Anthropologie*, 10, 2002, pp. 225–244. See also Fabrice Boudjaaba in this volume.

We tried to transpose this to those major processes such as state-building and class formation which are so much on the agenda of "big histories of different kinds."

To recall this may help to explain the status we gave to our own model. Our first transition is to a large extent about the interrelationship between processes of state formation and the organization of kinship. It is uncontested that state formation was one of the major processes in Western history. But it is also uncontested that this process did not happen everywhere, neither everywhere at the same time nor at the same pace[6]. The same is true of our first transition. Dionigi Albera is right to state that the temporal delimitation of this transition is vague. It is as vague as the temporal delimitation of state building. The latter can be seen at work in city communes of the thirteenth century as well as in territorial administration of the sixteenth. The first transition took place in a world where we should probably not even look for the kind of fast, coherent and continental transformations we know from modernity.

Class formation is different in this respect, since it is more precisely datable and more generally spread out over the entire European continent. But there are still considerable differences. Class formation made a stronger and earlier impact on heavily industrialized cities of England and the Ruhr than, say, on Mediterranean islands or northern Norway. The same is true for our second transition. It did not happen everywhere, nor everywhere at the same time and to the same extent. Our attempt in *Kinship in Europe* was to discuss how kinship was involved in larger historical processes, and it did not aim to replace examinations that focused on other scales.

Dionigi Albera's book successfully demonstrates the benefits of examinations on a third scale, neither micro nor macro but meso, and at the regional level. The great merit of Dionigi Albera's approach to regions as the main units of examination is, I think, that it allows for reconceptualizion of the political system. He helps us to understand that constitutional history with its stress on political bodies and offices tells at best half the story concerning the way power was organized in pre-modern societies. The other half that remains to be told, for most regions, deals with how constitutions interact with kinship, household, and settlement patterns.

---

6   For an approach that stresses variation, see Willem Blockmans, André Holenstein, Jon Mathieu (eds.), *Empowering Interactions: Political Cultures and the Emergence of the State in Europe, 14ᵗʰ to 19ᵗʰ Centuries*, Aldershot, Ashgate, 2009.

It will be hard to return to classic institutional-history approaches to early modern states after having read *Au fil des générations*. The book explains how for instance the feudal structures of Tyrol were supplemented and reinforced by hierarchically structured households and unigeniture in the devolution of dispersed farms. None of this resulted from adaptation to the environment, as Dionigi Albera convincingly demonstrates, but was part of political culture and political organization in the wider sense.

Once kinship organization is no longer relegated to the effects of the natural environment – what we tend to think of as stable – but is instead understood as an aspect of political organization, which historians have always perceived as dynamic, change becomes the key topic of kinship research. Dionigi Albera marvelously shows such changes, while emphasizing regional path- dependencies and particularities. A good example of this is the succession of changes in the French Alps. Here patterns of patrilineal inheritance, with compensations for daughters in the form of dowries, were already widespread during the late Middle Ages. In the early modern period these systems of equal inheritance among male descendants tended toward unigeniture and often but not always assumed the form of primogeniture.

If we depart from the general assumption that kinship organization is dynamic and undergoes changes over time then we can take a more critical look at older literature which assumed its stability between the Middle Ages and industrialization. If Dionigi Albera finds less change in feudal Tyrol and communal Valais than in the western Alps, this may be owing to the fact that he relies on the work of other scholars who did not have as keen an eye for the dynamics of kin organization as he himself did. Moreover, the description of the system of primogeniture in Tyrol is based on evidence from the nineteenth century. We ought to be open to the possibility that patrilinearity in Tyrol could have developed only after the Middle Ages. And the description of partible inheritance in Valais stems from older legal historians who mainly built their case on normative sources from the late Middle Ages. But despite rumors to the contrary, things can change even in Switzerland. Meanwhile we know from more micro-studies (!) that even where the law kept prescribing equal inheritance, the leading families found strategies to circumvent the law. They founded *fidei commis*, they downgraded the values of the estates left to the firstborn, so that they had to pay little compensation to their younger siblings, or found ways of passing on communal – in the main not hereditary offices – to their firstborn[7]. There are reasons to believe that communal Switzerland became increasingly patrilinear, while Tyrol had not been so since time immemorial but did become so after the Middle Ages. Both regions would then have had developments that were perhaps slower but not so different from those south of the Alps and the ones sketched in *Kinship in Europe*.

As much as I admire Dionigi Albera's distinctions on the level of major regions, I do not subscribe to his idea that this is the only thing the history of kinship should be doing in the future. Yet today there are many reasons to look at developments on many levels, on the micro as well as the meso and the macro and, maybe most important, to go back and forth between them. This is necessary, for instance, to answer a question Dionigi Albera does not address: Did his regionally diverse kinship systems only belong to the traditional world or did some of them find their way into modernity?

While it makes sense that structures differed from one more or less coherent region to the other in a pre-modern world where the political system was largely about controlling agricultural production and its returns, we should be prepared to find a wide range in the spatial distributions of differences in recent centuries. Thus industrialization spread less from one region to the next than it did more generally across Europe and more specifically between individual urban and urbanized centers within the various regions. And even before that, the difference in the prevalence of literacy and of notaries was less between regions than within regions, where they successively spread from major urban centers to the most important villages. This matters because notaries brought new ideas about the organization of inheritance and matrimonial property that probably helped bring about changes in kinship. There are good reasons to maintain that in the future the choice of one's scale of examination will also depend on the questions one asks. And kinship research today raises many questions.

---

7   Hans Conrad Peyer, "Die Anfänge der schweizerischen Aristokratien", in Kurt Messmer, Peter Hoppe, *Luzerner Patriziat. Sozial- und wirtschaftsgeschichtliche Studien zur Entstehung und Entwicklung im 16. und 17. Jahrhundert*, Luzern, Rex-Verlag, 1976, pp. 1–28, here p. 19; Anton Philipp von Segesser, *Rechtsgeschichte der Stadt und Republik Luzern*, Luzern, Gebrüder Räber, 1850–1855, vol. 2, p. 528. See the observations for Zurich in Johann Caspar Bluntschli, *Staats- und Rechtsgeschichte des Kantons Zürich*, Zürich, Orell-Füssli, 1838–39, vol. 2, pp. 196–198.

Quite a number of these questions are related to my second topic, namely how kinship emerged in different media or forms of mediation. It is no trivial matter that kinship never per se becomes visible. Kinship organization emerges from coats of arms, genealogical paintings and diagrams, theological theories about incest prohibitions, medical treatises, but also in less explicit terms from patterns of inheritance, the circulation of property or settlement patterns, from naming patterns, expectations of getting help, and much more. Such mediations not only make relationships accessible to experience or visible but they also serve in shaping them. David Sabean has stressed that relationships are usually not merely *between* persons but also *about* something. With regard to rural societies, he asked for a richer conceptualization of landed property as a mediation that gives shape to relationships. When two farmers quarrel about a piece of land they are not each enacting their relationship to the land but are expressing a relationship with each other that is about the land[8]. It makes a difference for the relationship whether it is about a piece of land or a house or about a farm, each of these coming with its own built-in risk of conflict, needs for cooperation, temporal rhythms of throwing people together as well as pitting them against each other.

How relationships are affected by the materiality of the things they are about is a problem that has been preoccupying the social sciences since their early days. Georg Simmel in particular explored such mediations in *The Philosophy of Money*[9]. His discussion of societies before monetization contains vivid descriptions of how the materiality of things that people exchanged or owned affected their relationships. Simmel understood the structuring effect of things mainly in terms of limitations. He made the controversial argument that money and monetary value, once they replaced concrete things (land, farms, castles, workshops etc.) as being the main expression of property, had a liberating effect and allowed new and less constraining forms of relationships.

Even if one disagrees with Simmel's evolutionary model, it is hard not to be compelled by his examples of how relationships depend on the

8   David W. Sabean, "Young Bees in an Empty Hive: Relations between Brothers-in-Law in a South German Village around 1800", in David W. Sabean, Hans Medick (eds.), *Interest and Emotion: Essays on the Study of Family and Kinship*, Cambridge, Cambridge University Press, 1984, pp. 171–186; here p. 171f.

9   Georg Simmel, *The Philosophy of Money*, ed. David Frisby, trans. Tom Bottomore and David Frisby, 3rd enlarged edition, London, Routledge, 1990, pp. 283–356.

concrete objects of exchange and pieces of property that they are ultimately about. Along Simmel's line of thought one could even ask whether
what we tried to apprehend as the second transition in *Kinship in Europe*
could in part be explained by a change in the nature of that property which
kin primarily organized around and which kinship was mediated through.
Thus when kinship organization between the late Middle Ages and the
middle of the eighteenth century tended toward linearity and patrilinearity,
this was also due to the importance of passing property that was hard to
divide from one generation to the next, for instance castles, farms, monopolies, or patrimonialized offices. It was starting in the mid-eighteenth century that attempts at accumulating and pooling capital rather than the control of particular "things" became key to social positions, which came with
a kinship organization that laid more stress on horizontal organization and
endogamous kin and class marriages.

One could probably extend the analysis of how things mediate relationships even further. From the perspective of the history of science and
with regard to measuring instruments, Norton Wise developed the argument that things can also mediate between ideas and tangible realities[10].
Maybe this thought could be translated to kinships studies, so that we
might understand a castle or a farm that is passed on from one generation
to the next as mediating between a material building and the idea of a
dynasty. The mediation would then, in Wise's words, both reify the idea of
a family order and idealize a building as the expression of such an order[11].
Albera's book is filled with wonderful examples of such mediations, but
he does not explicitly address mediation in his discussion of why kinship
systems differ.

We should begin to examine more closely how concepts of kinship
are affected, filtered, and modified by the media that convey them. In
rural societies people were probably most familiar with thinking kinship
through the mediation of names or property and its devolution. We probably ought to understand attempts at representing kinship in more abstract,
systematic, and explicit forms in coats of arms, kinship diagrams, and
pedigrees in their relation and in competition with the mediations people
were more familiar with – and not, as modern scholars often do, as a kind

10   Norton Wise, "Mediations: Enlightenment Balancing Acts, or the Technologies of
      Rationalism", in Paul Horwich (ed.), *World Changes: Thomas Kuhn and the Nature
      of Science*, Pittsburgh, University of Pittsburgh Press, 2010, pp. 207–256.
11   *Ibid.*, p. 214.

of media or as transparent sources through which some kind of uniform medieval or early modern kinship system becomes visible.

As we approach change in kin organization we should be interested in how different mediations speak to each other and at what points in time, in what social setting and for what reasons new mediations emerged, threatened or supplemented the existing ones. A highly significant moment for the nobility was certainly the emergence of coats of arms, of arms rolls, and of heralds as specialists of knowledge about kin relations and the conventions of their representation[12]. Another important change in the political significance of kinship is probably indicated by the emergence of parish books that from the middle of the fifteenth century began to be kept in ever more regions in Europe. These books represented a first attempt at systematically recording childbirths along with the names of parents and godparents and marriages and thus providing written evidence for kin relations. We should probably also examine the spread of notaries and the marriage contracts and testaments issued by them as indicative of an upheaval in the meditation of kinship. According to Dionigi Albera, it was the gradual spread of the notary from the big cities in northern Italy to the Alpine villages that enhanced his "agnatic" type.

To look at how kinship is mediated may also help solve some old controversies. Let me take the example of the controversy about patrilinearity. Scholars such as Anita Guerreau and Joseph Morsel contest that kinship ever became patrilinear in Europe[13]. When patrilinear successions appear, be it in the examples of George Duby from the period around 1200 or in those of the German nobility's obsession with *Geschlechter* that began in the fifteenth century, they ascribe this to the system of lordship rather than to that of kinship. Regardless of such developments, Guerreau and Morsel maintain that kinship as such – as it was discussed in theological prohibitions of incest – remained bilateral. This is true. But why should the theological writing about kinship be more true or closer to real kinship

---

12   Georg Scheibelreiter, *Heraldik*, Wien, Oldenburg Verlag, 2006, p. 131; Michel Pastoureau, *Une histoire symbolique du Moyen Âge occidental*, Paris, Seuil, 2004, pp. 213–243.

13   Anita Guerreau-Jalabert, "Sur les structures de parenté dans l'Europe médiévale (Note critique)", in *Annales E.S.C.*, 36, 1981, 6, pp. 1028–1049; Jospeh Morsel, "Die Erfindung des Adels. Die Soziogenese des Adels am Ende des Mittelalters – das Beispiel Frankens", in Otto G. Oexle, Werner Paravicini (eds.), *Nobilitas. Funktion und Repräsentation des Adels in Alteuropa*, Göttingen, Vandenhoeck & Ruprecht, 1996, pp. 312–375.

than patterns of succession to political offices? It is probably more productive to look at *both* as mediations within their specific contexts of communication and interaction and conveying kinship in different and at times conflicting manners.

Dionigi Albera examines kinship structures mainly as they emerge from rules of inheritance law and inheritance arrangements. This too is a particular set of mediations, one that – as Albera's book convincingly demonstrates – has an exceptionally strong structuring effect on peoples' lives. Yet there were other mediations of kinship that one could look into: the choice of god-parents, credit relations, marriage patterns and more[14].

Not all mediations were specific to places and regions. Some were, even before modernity, outright cosmopolitan. Good examples are the kinship diagrams that medieval theologians and lawyers at universities throughout Europe developed as tools for the calculation of degrees of kinship[15]. In order to sharpen incest rules, they devised notions of kinship that were explicitly meant to bypass any notion of relatedness that could possibly be articulated through property devolution. Incest should be forbidden beyond the circle of kin that had the slimmest chance of inheriting from each other, beyond any kind of relatedness that could be imagined with regard to inheritance of goods[16]. Thus the diagrams gave kinship an unusual extension, beyond what could be memorized on a regular basis, including the descendants of the great-great-great-great-grandparents. Moreover, these new conceptualizations of kinship were unusually systematic and operated with quantifications of kin-relations in a complex system of graduation. Commentaries on the diagrams were constantly discussing how kinship as it was defined with respect to incest prohibitions ran counter to common sense[17].

---

14   Some of these are explored in David W. Sabean, *Kinship in Neckarhausen, 1700–1870*, Cambridge, Cambridge University Press, 1998.

15   Christiane Klapisch-Zuber, *L'ombre des ancêtres. Essai sur l'imaginaire médiéval de la parenté*, Paris, Fayard, 2000; and Hermann Schadt, *Die Darstellungen der Arbores Consanguinitatis und der Arbores Affinitati. Bildschemata in juristischen Handschriften*, Tübingen, Wasmuth, 1982.

16   Kurt Reindl (ed.), *Die Briefe des Petrus Damiani*, part 1, *Monumenta Germaniae Historica. Die Briefe der deutschen Kaiserzeit IV*, Munich, Monumenta Germaniae Historica, 1983, p. 181 (no. 19).

17   Anton Schütz, "Les données immédiates de la parenté. L'Eglise, la filiation, le mariage, le droit canonique", in Pierre Legendre (ed.), *Le dossier occidental de la*

Mediations made of drawings on paper came with fewer practical restrictions than did heavier ones like castles and farms. Over time the diagrams were modified for use in ever more contexts to which systematic conceptions of kinship could be applied, for instance in order to represent dynasties of royal, noble and patrician families[18]. The old canon-law kinship diagrams since the twelfth century were often wrought in the form of a human body with the ancestors on top and the descendants below. And it was from the fifteenth century onward that the diagram was sometimes flipped around to become a family tree in the modern sense, with younger generations growing out of the roots and trunks of the older ones[19]. Thus a linear temporality and linearity in the structure of kinship, often in the form of patrilinearity, moved to the foreground of visual representations of kinship among the elites in all of Europe.

Other advancements of the old diagrams were used to establish notions of the purity of noble descent in *Ahnenproben*; or pure Christian descent as in notions of *limpieza de sangre*[20]. Systematic ideas about descent and kinship became main ingredients in the establishment of the great abstract and all-encompassing social divisions of the modern period: the divisions of race, estate, citizenship and nationality. None of this, I believe, would have been possible had kinship continued to be primarily mediated through property of different kinds. It took the more abstract paper mediations to make it emerge with such a high degree of system and such prescriptive power.

Even ideas about the bodily substances kin share can operate as mediations of kinship – and they too undergo radical changes[21]. In specialized treatises about kinship and its calculation, lawyers and theologians of the Middle Ages led intensive debates not only as to how one might visualize

---

    parenté, Paris, Fayard, 1988, pp. 189–220. See also Thomas Aquinas, *Summa Theo-logica*. Supplementum L 54 art. 1–4.

18   Christiane Klapisch-Zuber, *L'ombre des ancêtres, op. cit.*, pp. 159–206.

19   *Ibid.*, pp. 236–250.

20   Simon Teuscher, "Verwandtschaft in der Vormoderne. Zur politischen Karriere eines Beziehungskonzepts", in Elisabeth Harding and Michael Hecht (eds.), *Die Ahnen-probe in der Vormoderne. Selektion – Initiation – Repräsentation*, Münster, Rhema Verlag, 2011, pp. 85–106.

21   Anita Guerreau-Jalabert, "Flesh and Blood in Medieval Language about Kinship", in Christopher H. Johnson, Bernhard Jussen, David W. Sabean, Simon Teuscher (eds.), *Blood and Kinship: Matter for Metaphor from Ancient Rome to the Present*, New York, Berghahn, 2012, pp. 61–82.

kinship – how to represent it in images and diagrams – but also as to its nature and physiology. While kinship in the literature up until about 1400 was mainly spoken of in terms of flesh and unions of the flesh, the late Middle Ages brought about a new language of blood and admixtures of blood[22]. The language of flesh was firmly rooted in the idea that sex and marriage constituted *una caro* – one flesh. Both relationships of marriage and of descent were thought of in terms of being one flesh. When the language of blood took over, this changed. Blood is not united but mixed. Children get an admixture of the bloods of their parents. Only relations of descent are characterized by shared blood. Affines were not thought of as sharing blood. Thus the change in ideas about the physiology of kinship gave increasing weight as well to lines of descent. In the passage to the modern period, ideas about shared and mixed blood became operative in ideas about race and hereditary noble qualities.

I think that we have to give up the idea that each society or social group in any given time period simply has its one and only kinship structure. Kinship is referred to in many ways, conveyed in many media and mediations, in learned treatises as well as in the distribution of land plots in a village, and people use different and at times conflicting patterns. This does not mean that there are no general trends in its development. But introducing change into the world of kinship also means leaving the idea of unambiguous structures in the sense of Lévi-Strauss behind. There may have been several different kinship structures around during the same period and within the same social group, and moreover we have no immediate access to such structures but approach them across the very mediations that also structured people's interactions within relationships.

To conclude: The history of kinship is no longer solely about the development of kin organization. Kinship is about to become one of the core topics of a new social history. This is because in several respects kinship operates as an episteme and as such has taken over roles previously assumed by class. It has proven to be a productive approach to a great number of problems – to problems of demographics, as we have long known; to state formation in the wider sense, as Dionigi Albera's

---

22   Simon Teuscher, "Flesh and Blood in the Treatises on the Arbor Consanguinitatis (thirteenth to sixteenth centuries)", in Christopher H. Johnson, Bernhard Jussen, David W. Sabean, Simon Teuscher (eds.), *Blood and Kinship, op. cit.*, pp. 83–104.

book so impressively demonstrates; to the emergence of a class society, as David Sabean has shown; to thoughts about heredity, race, and ethnicity. In order for kinship to work as a springboard into broader questions, we need all scales of research and we need to talk about the different mediations of kinship. And this will confront us with contested and conflicting structures.

Dionigi Albera

From the Alps to Europe: Combining Long-Term Approaches to Family and Kinship History

"It must be admitted from the beginning: I am a poacher". This was the first sentence of the original preface to the manuscript of *Au fil des generations*, in which I acknowledged that the historical orientation of this work did not originate from a certified training which could make me a legitimate member of the circle of Clio's disciples. Therefore, I added several lines to signify I was partly aware that I was taking a gamble. As he reminds in his chapter in this book, Jon Mathieu suggested to me that this kind of *captatio benevolentiae* was inadequate and pointless. "You are an historian", he wrote, and he recommended that I delete this prologue from the final version. After some reluctance, I accepted this battlefield promotion and followed his counsel.

As a matter of fact, I was somewhat anxious about the possible attitude of professional historians towards my adventurous forays into their hunting grounds. I am part of a generation of anthropologists who were formed when the conversation with history was still very active. In common with other "apprentices", I was influenced by a cultural climate that allowed not only the "consumption" but also the "production" of history by anthropologists. The example of prestigious figures such as Eric Wolf or Jack Goody clearly indicated the way. So it seemed quite natural to build our enquiries upon historical ground. From this point of view, the development of the field of family history has been a powerful factor encouraging a crossing of disciplinary boundaries, offering a stimulating setting for anthropologists interested in the study of kinship in the European field. My dialogue with history began by exploring local archives during my ethnographic research in a valley of the western Alps; I then familiarised myself with the techniques of historical demography and became acquainted with micro-history's methods and theoretical arguments. This journey finally led me to attempt a broad synthesis of alpine domestic organisation over several centuries.

Now, five years after these hesitant beginnings, it clearly appears that my worries were groundless. In fact I have been extremely pleased with the serious reception that historians have accorded my book. Several prestigious journals devoted reviews and discussions to it, and numerous leading historians in the field have involved themselves constructively in the debate. I am very grateful to all of them for the interest they have shown in my work and for their warm reaction to it. I would like to offer here some discussion of the remarks generated by *Au fil des generations*, including those that are presented in several chapters of this book, concentrating on what I consider to be the main issues.

A third phase?

Let us start by dismissing what I see as a misunderstanding. Some authors have assigned to me the role of initiating a third phase in the history of family and kinship, in which the approach outlined in *Au fil des generations* constituted a kind of manifesto. According to Simon Teuscher, I saw my own research as the beginning of a third phase in the study of kinship. After a first phase composed of micro-historical approaches and a second phase characterised by new long-term models, this third phase would require one now to adopt comparisons and generalisations situated within a medium-term perspective, both temporally and geographically[1]. Luigi Lorenzetti suggested that I was aiming to delineate a third phase, but he sees this as intermediate between the macro perspectives proposed by family history in the 1960s and 1970s and the micro-historical focus of subsequent research[2]. For Margareth Lanzinger (in this volume), I conceptualised a third phase of the history of the family by treading an intermediate path located midway between "the old history of the family and the new historical anthropology of kinship".

I am ready to acknowledge that *Au fil des generations* was quite ambitious, but certainly not to this extent. Since several scholars have shared

1   Simon Teuscher, "A proposito di quattro libri recenti sulla storia della famiglia", in *Quaderni Storici*, a. XLVIII, 2013, n. 2, pp. 611–616 (612).
2   Luigi Lorenzetti, "A proposito di quattro libri recenti sulla storia della famiglia", in *Quaderni Storici*, a. XLVIII, 2013, n. 2, pp. 600–610 (601).

the above interpretation, which was certainly far from my intentions when I wrote the book, it is likely that the misunderstanding derives from a lack of clarity on my part. It therefore feels important to clarify my point of view on this question. I will start by referring briefly to the analysis I presented in the first part of the book, where I tried to place my approach within the broader context of the development of the study of family and kinship history in Europe[3]. Therefore I highlighted two main periods. The former period spanned the 1960s to the 1980s. In this phase some "strong" comparative perspectives occupied the centre stage, helping to delineate an area of studies that was experiencing a vigorous expansion. Expanding the seminal taxonomy proposed by Michael Anderson[4], I mentioned four main perspectives, which gave shape to the field in this period.

First, several studies generated what Michael Anderson has described as "the sentiments approach", including the work of authors like Philippe Aries, Lawrence Stone, Jean-Louis Flandrin, Randolph Trumbach and Edward Shorter. The focus was on constellations of symbols and feelings, on sexual and emotional relationships within the family space. A wide range of topics was discussed: from the choice of the spouse to the emergence of a private sphere, from attitudes about sex to parenthood and childhood. In general, in spite of the different chronologies and processes evoked by these authors, they agreed that there was a weakening of kinship ties and a growing independence of the nuclear family.

Second, in the same period, the historians and demographers of the Cambridge Group inaugurated the approach that Michael Anderson defines as "demographic". They developed a method for analysing sources hitherto relatively neglected – the lists of inhabitants – and subsequently made bold assumptions on the basis of their findings. These historians tried to overthrow the myth of a patriarchal order, which had dominated for a long time in European history, suggesting that the nuclear family had a chronological priority in European history. A family "system" based on the nuclear family, combined with a demographic regime of "low pressure"

---

3   A remarkable overview of this development has been recently provided by Fabrice Boudjaaba and Marie-Pierre Arrizabalaga, «Les systèmes familiaux. De la cartographie des modes d'héritage aux dynamiques de la reproduction familiale et sociale», *Annales de démographie historique*, 1, 2015, pp. 165–199.

4   *Approaches to the History of the Western Family, 1500–1914.* London, Macmillan, 1980. (New expanded edition: Cambridge, CUP, 1995).

based on late marriage, would have been the breeding ground for the rise of capitalism and modern industry.

A third contribution to the history of the family and of kinship came from research conducted in France, within the framework of an historical anthropology where the structuralist school of Lévi-Strauss merged with that of the *Annales*. This produced a fruitful context for numerous detailed case studies. In the work of synthesis, the empirical data was organised within a conceptual framework which lay at the crossroads of structuralism, the history of mentalities and the revitalised tradition of Le Play. The central phenomena analysed were the residence and the transmission of property. In this case too, scholars tried to isolate the main European "family systems".

A fourth approach to family and kinship corresponds to what Michael Anderson defines as the "household economics approach". Influenced by the social sciences, this approach made economic relations within the co-resident group the centre of attention. Work done within this framework sought to understand how a set of resources became available to family members, how it was used and how it interfered with power relations. Norms, meanings and symbols associated with behaviour in the household sphere were therefore not considered as independent variables, but as results of the constraints of the environment, the economy or the social structure. The currents that make up this approach have often been peripheral and less coherent and influential than those emerging from the mainstream research centres, principally located in the United Kingdom and France. For instance, greater weight was given to ecological and economic variables by research conducted in Scandinavia, Italy and Austria.

In this first period, through bold hypotheses about the spatial distribution of family forms and their historical transformation in Europe, the work of the Cambridge Group – and to a lesser extent that of "the sentiments approach" and of French historical anthropology – dominated a large part of empirical research in Europe. They had considerable influence on scholars who were less inclined to generalisation and who were more cautious about awarding an autonomous status to the field of family studies. A quite eclectic, and often quite empirical, practice developed in response to stimuli from "supreme theories", and ineluctably absorbed a series of conceptual and methodological principles that arose from these theories, even when it manifested a critical attitude vis-à-vis the latter by accumulating empirical material that seemed to undermine them.

Thus the growth in this research field, and the attendant emergence of criticism, led to what I saw as a second phase, which became discernible in the 1990s. An increasing body of localised knowledge on gender relations, on rituals and emotions showed that the linear perspectives proposed by "the sentiments approach" in the 1970s had to be be reformulated. More generally, the research focus shifted: from collective attitudes, mentalities and structures towards the concrete behaviour of historical actors. The search for correlations between variables such as age at marriage, the composition of domestic groups and the rules for the transmission of inheritance, partially gave way to approaches focused on practice and on transactions between groups and individuals. In general, a vision in strategic terms of family dynamics acquired increasing importance.

The criticism of structures and systems identified by the approaches that had dominated during the first phase was mainly supported by a micro-analytical approach. The latter was able to show the gap that existed between the density of relationships at the local level on the one hand, and the abstract models on the other. Focusing on people and actions also allowed the research to be emancipated from arbitrary conceptualizations and ideological representations formed from particular sources, such as censuses. Attention also focused on the social uses of kinship, often beyond the sphere of co-residence. In particular, the emergence of the Italian *microstoria* profoundly affected the field through a series of methodological and theoretical proposals that have exerted a wide influence and represented the most advanced and sophisticated formulation of an orientation centred on the study of action and context.

In this second phase, the history of the family as a recognisable interdisciplinary study lost some clarity, spread across many different areas of investigations. The production of historical studies remained considerable, but it lacked a unitary character. Efforts to generalise and offer an overview (by formulating more or less reformed versions of theories developed in the previous period) were still present, but they remained in a secondary position, within an epistemological context characterised by a fascination for detailed sectorial surveys. Increasingly sophisticated tools were sometimes mobilised in low value-added analyses (in terms of developing cumulative knowledge). Alternative explanatory models to the grand theories of the past were mainly trying to account for the complexity of local configurations. Some work experimented with sophisticated types of quantification, inspired by the formal network analysis, with its statistical procedures and technical vocabulary derived from graph theory. The complexity of this approach made it difficult to design a standardisation that could allow systematic comparisons.

After having identified these two periods, I noted that a number of recent works felt the need to broaden again the temporal and spatial perspectives: these presented large-scale perspectives radically different from those of the first period. In other words, I saw the possibility of the emergence of a third phase. In relation to the development of these new comparative trends, the work of Bernard Derouet, Gérard Delille and David Warren Sabean appeared particularly significant to me. Their theoretical propositions laid the foundations of what I defined as a new historical anthropology of kinship in Europe. In particular, the collective work that resulted in *Kinship in Europe* was for me the most ambitious attempt to promote this new perspective[5].

This broad historiographical outline was aimed at delineating the purpose of my work, which was to contribute to the renewal of the study of the history of the family and kinship in Europe, by adopting a rather different and somewhat complementary comparative perspective. In other words, I was trying to help (along with many others) with the emergence of a third phase.

It may be helpful to clarify what I mean by "phase". It does not refer to an all-embracing model or episteme that would provide a clear and strong direction to the research. However, neither should we conceive this periodisation in terms of "turns". This kind of rhetoric is typical of the US academic environment and tends to multiply the statements concerning research orientation's changes, with a frequency that betrays a certain professional need to display continuous novelty in a highly competitive knowledge market. The language of "turns" implicitly suggests that there is a single path taken by research, albeit with a series of twists, and this obscures the variety of approaches and intellectual trends that coexist at any one moment.

The phases I identified in the field of family history have broader echoes. Some aspects of the first phase are linked to macro-historical trends that originated in the 1950s, promoting a "scientific" approach in response to traditional narrative history. The second phase corresponds

---

5   See David W. Sabean, Simon Teuscher, Jon Mathieu (eds.), *Kinship in Europe. Approaches to long term development (1300–1900),* New York – Oxford, Berghahn Books, 2007.

to some general trends across several intellectual fields, which provoked the evanescence of major theories and the overall fragmentation of research (and this approach was openly advocated by the supporters of post-modernism). The foreshadowing of what I have called a third phase corresponds to an increasing concern with the long term in recent historical research[6]. However, we must be careful to avoid too clear-cut a characterisation of processes that are highly composite.

Within the field of the history of the family and kinship in Europe, it is unrealistic to consider rebuilding the entire field around a small number of new methodological slogans. Disparate trends coexisted in the previous phases, and everything leads us to believe that this will also be so in the future. In my view, what identifies a phase is the presence of an orientation that exercises hegemony over a share of the scientific field and, more or less directly, manages to steer it. This orientation gives a pervading tone to the epistemological landscape, but without erasing the diversity and the contradictions. During the first phase of the history of the family, a number of broad approaches (in the paths of Lawrence Stone, Peter Laslett or Emmanuel Le Roy Ladurie) produced general theories that provided the guidelines for a wide research front that has corroborated or, more often, rebutted them. The demographic approach of the Cambridge Group has probably made the most consistent efforts to achieve a theoretical and methodological uniformity, giving shape to a fairly coherent research program. But even in this case, formalisation remained restricted to some segments of the research. Conversely, even when the epistemological bases of these exercises have been undermined by the appearance of specific criticisms, the fascination with these simplified explanatory models has not ended, and it is likely that this path will continue its journey for a long time in some academic circles.

The return of the long-term in the study of family and kinship in European history does not mean that we can expect an automatic expansion of the chronological span considered by individual researchers or a standardisation of research techniques. What we can reasonably hope for is the development of a number of general interpretative lines, over a broad expanse of time and space, which may be able to interact with a substantial part of the research. These lines may propose issues and stimulate

---

6   See for example Jo Guldi and David Armitage, *The History Manifesto,* Cambridge, Cambridge University Press, 2014 ; "La longue durée en débat", in *Annales. H.S.S.,* 2, 2015, pp. 285–287.

discussion, while adjusting to a plurality of scales and of methodological approaches. The interpretative lines proposed by Sabean and Teuscher
seem to me an important step in this direction[7].

I completely agree with Teuscher when he questions the idea that
there should be a single scale adopted in historical research[8]. A plurality
of scales is not only inescapable but also fruitful. In this framework macro
and meso hypotheses may be highly productive. This is what *Kinship in
Europe* attempted, when it proposed to replace a master-narrative about
the constant decline of kinship in European history by a more articulated
counter-narrative based on two major shifts in the configurations of kin
across Europe between the Middle Ages and the modern era.

The comparative questioning that I have pursued over the last few
years seems to offer a complementary perspective. Both *Kinship in Europe*
and *Au fil des generations* were inspired by the hope of using the results of
the numerous case studies that had discarded the grand narratives of the
first phase of family history, in order to build new comparative perspectives. The former was mainly concerned with the arguments of historians
such as Lawrence Stone concerning the inescapable antagonism between
state organisation and kinship, while the latter wished to construct an
alternative to the generalisations of the demographic approach, or to the
geography of the family forms outlined by French historical anthropology.
Moreover, the scope of my analysis was more modest from both a geographic and a thematic point of view. Instead of ranging across the European continent, my comparative endeavour remained focused on the Alps.
Besides, I concentrated on an intermediate dimension, between the large
vision of kinship promoted by Sabean and Teuscher and the "family structures" that have been extensively investigated in comparative studies since
the 1960s. The central concept in this intermediate thematic area was that
of *domestic organisation*. By that I meant a set of relations mobilised in
activities related to common residence, production, distribution, transmission and reproduction. I was concerned in particular with the node of the
transmission of goods and positions, which is an essential element of social

---

7   David W. Sabean, Simon Teuscher, "Kinship in Europe: A New Approach to Long-
     Term Development", in David W. Sabean, Simon Teuscher, Jon Mathieu, (eds.), *Kin-
     ship in Europe, op. cit.*, pp. 1–32.
8   Simon Teuscher, "A proposito", *art. cit.* p. 612.

reproduction, acting on the structuring of interpersonal relationships[9]. I paid much attention to the context that forms a direct interface with the domestic dimension, namely the management and the transfer of rights to collective resources, the forms of settling, the social relationships within the villages and rural communities, the local political structures.

Types and processes

The construction of my comparative analysis was quite complex and I would like to recall here some aspects of its internal architecture. The theorisation was, so to speak, "bottom up", proceeding in successive stages: it started from a micro-analytic base and then, through an accumulation of data, broadened out, allowing the analysis to pass from one level to another. Attention focused at first on the research done by Eric Wolf and John Cole in the southern Tyrol, Robert McNetting in the Valais and myself in a valley of the Piedmontese Alps. These case studies were not only used to deny some general assumptions (for instance about the constraints of the Alpine environment that would produce a uniformity in property transmission practices), but also to provide the foundation of an analytical construction. Thus, an initial typology was extracted from these monographic explorations, with the formalisation of three types ("Bauer", "bourgeois" and "Alpine agnatic"), set up as contextualised contrasts from these three micro-analytical situations. I will summarise here the salient features of these types.

The Bauer type is characterised as a system of relationships focused on the estate, which is transmitted undivided from one generation to the next. The public role of the holder of a farm is the basis of the social articulation of the community. The lands that make up the estate are often compactly gathered around the house; or, if the properties are not in one piece, they are composed of a limited number of plots. The dispersion of farms generates a fragmented habitat structure. The area of private property may also include the pastoral areas. Otherwise, the access rights to common land are attached to the farm. Siblings, who are excluded from

---

9   Jack Goody, "Introduction", in Jack Goody, Joan Thirsk, Edward P. Thompson (eds.), *Family and inheritance. Rural society in Western Europe 1200–1800,* Cambridge, Cambridge University Press, 1978, pp. 1–9.

the succession to the farm, occupy secondary positions at the village level. When they remain within the family of the brother who controls the estate, they hold a subordinate position and can be considered as servants. The local community displays a polarisation between the holders of property and those who are excluded. Relationships outside the domestic group are sporadic and tend to be formal. The network of relationships linked to kinship and neighbourhood remains weak

In the "bourgeois type" the transmission of property is characterised by bilateral equality. The public roles are set from birth. All children inherit the paternal and maternal goods on an equal basis; all the sons become automatically "bourgeois", that is to say full citizens, when they reach their majority. The population is grouped in compact villages. The estates consist of a number of parcels of land very scattered around the territory. Access to common land is reserved for the bourgeois citizen or assigned to members of residents' associations. In this last case, the rights over pasture land fall into the egalitarian division of inherited property. The nuclear family is predominant. When the inherited unit exceeds the co-residence, it gives rise to cognatic coalitions. Economic diversification across the village is not very pronounced and does not result in a rigid social stratification. The equal division of assets in each generation and widespread access to collective resources and to the decision-making process in the local community contribute to maintaining this balance. Kinship relations between cognates and affines are intense. The agnatic ties are important in village politics. Neighbourly relations are close and effective.

The Alpine agnatic type is marked by a devolution of property that benefits male descendants (and sometimes male collateral) over female descendants, who receive a dowry. Public roles in the local community are related to the position of household head. Each estate is configured as a collection of dispersed plots in the local territory. Habitat structure is characterised by compact nuclei: small villages and hamlets (sometimes quite tiny), which frequently have a patronymic character. Access to common land is related to residence and the possession of property in the municipality, or to the fact of belonging to a neighbourhood. The residence after marriage is usually patrilocal. The assets are managed in joint ownership for a certain period of time by agnatic sets (father and sons, brothers, uncles and nephews, patrilateral cousins). The agnatic management may also involve periods of co-residence for two or more married brothers, with their families. Groups that combine landed property with successful emigration and the exercise of notarial activities compose the local elite, which dominates the local credit system, controls the land market and holds political office, while ensuring coordination with wider political entities. Apart from the common property management, which is reserved to agnatic kin, there is a dense network of bilateral kinship relations. Neighbourly relations are intense and blend with those of kinship, especially in small hamlets.

I subsequently did a comparative evaluation of this typology through the analysis of a larger number of anthropological and historical case studies in the Austrian, Italian and Swiss Alps. The comparison was oriented towards a polythetic classification. I examined a large body of monographic examples, ensuring that many of the important characteristics of these three clusters were present. This procedure resulted from the dispersion of the documentation and its heterogeneous and partially random nature. Although all the elements were not corroborated to the same extent, the documentation has consistently confirmed the plausibility of this taxonomy.

It was thus possible to define three quite compact sets, which reproduce the polarisation previously illustrated at the microanalytical level. The relationships described by the Bauer type are significant in the Alps of Austria and Slovenia. The traits of the bourgeois type appear in several Swiss regions, particularly in the Valais and Grisons cantons; the attributes of the Alpine agnatic type appear to be significant in all the Italian Alps and in substantial parts of the French Alps.

As a whole, this typology permits us to inventory and systematise the results of the comparison. It captures a regional polarisation of domestic practices that was still visible in the nineteenth and twentieth centuries. However, this typology provides a fixed frame without chronological determinations. A significant part of my work has tried to understand how these differences were implemented. A journey into a disparate literature, covering various periods, suggested substantial continuity over time of the main elements that make up the three types. This allowed me to advance a general hypothesis and led to more synthetic results: as a consequence, the discussion shifted from static types to more dynamic models that took account of historical processes, the geographical base of which largely corresponds to the previously identified regional blocs.

The first historical process describes most Austrian alpine areas, where the medieval spatialisation of society and the establishment of the territorial State during the modern period have involved the formation of interdependent relationships between the lords and the wealthy peasantry. By controlling the intergenerational transmission of estates, land lordship built its economic foundation and its political influence mainly on the base of peasant taxes. Between the sixteenth and seventeenth centuries, the peasant families experienced a "bureaucratisation" of the state, which transformed the farmer into a sort of "official" at the lowest level of the hierarchy. This led to a polarisation, not only within the peasant community (the powers of which were generally quite weak) but also within each family, between those who had access to control of the farm and those who were excluded. Similar dynamics also affected the Swiss plateau regions (including Emmental) and the Black Forest. Political and legal reforms of the nineteenth century did soften this system, but they did not cut down its main structures.

A second process is seen in the Valais and Grisons cantons (and probably the Länderorte, although here the documentation is incomplete). In these regions, land lordship was collapsing early in the Middle Ages. Successfully opposing feudal rule, the communities of inhabitants underpinned the spatialisation of local society in the late Middle Ages, and the constitution of the territorial state thereafter. To access civil rights and to enjoy the communal resources individuals had to be "bourgeois." The focus of municipal authority was the assembly attended by all the adult citizens, including those who were not at the head of a domestic group. A low level of internal integration characterised the structure of the territorial state, the cohesion of which came rather from a common foreign policy. The prerogatives of the central government were very limited, and taxation was low or non-existent. This composite structure enabled the maintenance of a myriad of local customs and practices. The practice of law and jurisdiction was slightly specialised and essentially embedded in the community. Even notarial practice was little developed, and written law was long in competition with oral custom. Local legislation stipulated equal treatment of children in terms of inheritance rights, regardless of gender. The transformations in the political, legal and economic spheres that occurred in the nineteenth and twentieth centuries do not seem to have seriously modified the main characteristics of the system in most of these regions.

A third historical process, starting in the final centuries of the Middle Ages, involved the Italian Alps, but also Ticino, Savoy and the French

Alps. The medieval spatialisation of the area and the development of the territorial state relied on the mediation of a written legal culture, managed by a body of specialists (notaries, lawyers) whose presence extended to all levels of the territory. The constitution of the state was accompanied by an early definition of jurisdictional rights. The assertion, negotiation and transfer of property rights were conditioned by an agnatic orientation encouraged by the adoption of written law which spread from Northern Italy urban centres to the countryside and the Alpine foothills. In this written law jus commune (mainly Roman law) and jus proprium (statutory laws drawn up by communities) overlapped. Similarly, the character of the territory, through the legitimisation of rights and obligations (especially with regards to taxation) concerning different types of residential units (villages, neighbourhoods, towns, municipalities, federations of municipalities), was based on an agnatic matrix. The formation of the territorial state was superimposed on these microscopic and widely spread arrangements. From the nineteenth century, the agnatic order was weakening in several areas, giving way to a bilateral orientation, encouraged by the new legislative provisions and in the context of the collapse of local economies and of strong definitive migration.

Overall, through a process of generalisation that, from a micro-analytical level, reached a meso-level (which was nevertheless quite extensive, encompassing much of the Alps), this work proposed a set of theoretical tools to investigate the history of the family and kinship in Europe. The issue of differentiation was placed at the centre of the discussion. From this point of view, at least three levels can be isolated.

First, the discovery of huge differences in the Alps contradicts the view that suggested a standardisation of domestic practices arising from the constraints of the mountain environment, whether in terms of the transmission of the inheritance or of labour organisation. Second, the significant differences between regional blocs and the establishment of divergent historical processes can help define meaningful contexts within which the practices of historical actors are positioned. Local contexts are certainly marked by incertitude, to borrow a definition of Giovanni Levi, but certainly not from the same kind of incertitude. They are not equivalent and cannot be conceived as indistinguishable environments that allow a free play of individual and group strategies. Third, the differences between these regional blocs, and the continuity of their partitions from the point of view of domestic organisation, put into question the vision that emphasises the existence of general, common transformations, at the continental level, in conceptions and practices related to kinship.

I am very pleased that all comments directed at my work acknowledge the general plausibility of its architecture and of the types and models that I was proposing. Several remarks have helped to enrich these interpretive frameworks, to qualify, clarify and refine them, and to discuss their articulation with other scales of analysis, smaller or larger[10]. I will turn now to an examination of these issues.

Frontiers, internal variations, and intersecting processes

Even if this topic has not been specifically addressed, some comments leave the impression, when they are considered globally, that in *Au fil des generations* there was some unbalance between the agnatic side and the rest, from the point of view of the solidity of the theoretical construct. Jon Mathieu (in this volume) rightly observes that the most far-reaching discussion of long-term historical processes in the book concerns the agnatic sector of domestic organisation. Even if I am conscious of the boldness of some generalisations I made concerning the latter, the problems arising from the limitations of my competence and the insufficiencies in the available documentation, were more serious for the bourgeois and the Bauer sectors. I hope that future research may help to refine my models through a deeper understanding of the processes in these areas.

Luigi Lorenzetti has pointed to a rural bias in the delineation of my typology. For him, some important aspects of Alpine economic history, like temporary migration or industry, are given insufficient attention in my typology, as well as in my models of historical transformation[11]. Admittedly, even if the diversification of the Alpine economy is not completely

---

10   I cannot examine here the interplay between my typology and some well-established comparative concepts like Claude Lévi-Strauss' "house" or Frédéric Le Play's "stem family". For a discussion of this issue see Élie Haddad, "Qu'est-ce qu'une "maison? De Lévi-Strauss aux recherches anthropologiques et historiques récentes", in *L'Homme*, n° 212, 2014, 4, pp. 109–138, as well as the review by the same author of *Au fil des générations*, *Annales. H.S.S.*, 70, 2015, 4, pp. 1001–1004.
11   Luigi Lorenzetti, "A proposito", *art. cit.*, p. 602.

absent from the variables I have considered, it remains quite peripheral. One may add that the urban dimension is also rather neglected. The comparative framework that I have delineated is the result of a number of compromises. In order to be viable, my typological effort was based upon a conscious attempt to simplify. Thus I was compelled to make choices to avoid constructing overcomplicated tools, which would inevitably be exceedingly difficult to handle. For instance I had to resign myself to giving up a more formalised treatment of the migration parameter, in the absence of sufficiently solid data that could be articulated with the other elements of the typology (and this was a somewhat painful choice, given my longstanding interest in Alpine mobility…). Certainly, with regard to this and other parameters, it would be possible to improve my analytical instruments.

In my book I argued that the regional level is crucial to an understanding of the dynamics of kinship in Europe. My argument for this mesoscale was perhaps too resolute and this has led some commentators (for example Guzzi[12], Lanzinger and Teuscher, in this volume) to interpret my position as a desire to promote only this dimension for future research. Therefore I should reaffirm that this unilateral perspective is very far from my vision. Regional types and models are not, in my view, a point of arrival but simply a step along the way, which enable one to ask new questions. They form provisional results, which need to be clarified, confirmed or modified through articulation with other scales of analysis.

From this point of view, various commentators have raised some important issues. For instance, Luigi Lorenzetti (in this book) states that some elements of the three ideal types of alpine domestic organisation do overlap, in particular the agnatic and the bourgeois ones. He remarks, for example, that in both situations private property is fragmented into small plots, the management of the estate may be undivided and there is a profusion of common land. This is certainly true, and it is clear that the differences between these types cannot be seen as absolute, but are instead a matter of degree. As Sandro Guzzi[13] has observed, the agnatic type is somewhat intermediate between the other two. As a consequence, some

---

12   Sandro Guzzi-Heeb, "Rezension zu : Dionigi Albera, *Au fil des générations. Terre, pouvoir et parenté dans l'Europe alpine (XIVᵉ–XXᵉ siècles)*, Grenoble, Presses universitaires de Grenoble, 2011", in *Schweizerische Zeitschrift für Geschichte,* Vol. 63, 2013, Nr. 1, pp. 165–169.

13   *Ibid.,* p. 167.

resonances with the latter are quite predictable. I would add that the contrast is stronger between the agnatic and the Bauer types, while the agnatic is closer to the bourgeois type. Some historical processes linked to the control of local resources are similar in both the agnatic and the bourgeois types. For instance, to quote another example mentioned by Lorenzetti, the restriction in the access to common land on the basis of effective residence in the community for the whole year (or at least for a large part of the year) is present in both the "agnatic" and the "bourgeois" zones, showing a shared (and often growing) concern to relieve the pressure on the common land. However, overall these elements of transversality between different areas, which historical and ethnographic data show, do not obliterate, in my view, the essential differences between the three regional types.

Lorenzetti also observes that in the Valais, in spite of the equality between heirs of both sexes, as well as the joint ownership of the family assets by husband and wife, the latter has a subordinate role. Moreover, he notices that in the Alpine sectors of the agnatic bloc, responsibility for care of the elderly was assigned to both sons and daughters. These observations draw attention to a more general question. The distinctions that can be made between agnatic and cognatic propensities in European history are never absolute. We should rather think in terms of a bias towards one, within a register that involves some cohabitation of the two trends. Even the strongest bilateral system has some traces of male supremacy; even a robust agnatic pattern does not entirely eliminate the other propensity.

Several authors have addressed the crucial question of the internal uniformity of the types. Some very interesting remarks (for example by Mathieu, Lorenzetti and Teuscher) have focused the attention on what we may define as a vertical variation within local societies. The principal difference is apparently linked to divergent behaviours that, in several cases, a small elite adopted, with respect to the rest of the society. Jon Mathieu asks if this is a tolerable exception within the framework of my regional typology. My answer tends to be "yes". I do not consider that the diverging attitude of the elite discards the general logic of the types. Yet vertical variation is an important point, of which I was only partially aware when writing the book, and it has significant consequences for the interpretation of historical transitions. I will come again to this in the next section.

Another form of internal diversity may be defined as horizontal: it concerns differences between localities within a particular region. Luigi Lorenzetti has argued that several components of the agnatic type do vary somewhat from place to place even within restricted zones in the Italian Alps. These differences concern, for example, the forms of settlement and of dwelling, or the land market's intensity. As Lorenzetti himself suggests, these dissimilarities may be seen as "variations on a theme", within the agnatic domestic organisation. In my view they do not undermine the solidity of the overall construction. Clearly the perception of such nuances depends upon the scale of observation and on the theoretical and method-ological choices of the observer. A closer scrutiny will undoubtedly permit one to grasp better the meaning of these partial discrepancies (and perhaps to construct sub-regional types, depending on specific research interests). I think that a similar conclusion may be made concerning the examples of internal differences observed elsewhere in this volume by Lanzinger, regarding the Austrian Alps (Bauer type), and by Mathieu, regarding the Grisons (bourgeois type).

Jon Mathieu has remarked that my typology may be a useful tool to detect 'inconsistencies' and transitional regions and processes that depart from the main tendencies. In *Au fil des generations* I dealt with some of these. Without being able to pursue a thorough analysis, I focused the attention on the cases of the Western Tyrol and Vorarlberg, the domestic organisation of which presents an eccentric nature compared to other Aus-trian territories and appears characterised by traits that are largely incom-patible with the Bauer type. Moreover, I mentioned some transformations that fluctuate between several paths. For example, after sharing the agnatic orientation of the Italian Alps in the Middle Ages, the southern valleys of the Grisons and those of the Lower Valais shifted towards a pattern of domestic practices that pertains to the bourgeois type. As a first general hypothesis, I suggested that this transition was induced by a narrow incor-poration into a new political structure, which affected the foundations of the local society, so stimulating a transformation in the domestic sphere. On the contrary, in other instances the domestic practices seem to persist even if the wider political context changes. In these cases the new domi-nant system does not seem to impact the political structure, the juridical idiom and the principles of domestic organisation at the local level (in this respect I discussed some Alpine examples from Lombardy, Ticino, and Veneto). In other words, the stability of the political microstructure contributes to local inertia that can be described in terms of path depend-ency. Nevertheless, Luigi Lorenzetti (in this volume) rightly emphasises that loyalty to past structures may also be seen as a badge of resistance to pressures implemented by the dominant powers in order to change the rules related to the domestic sphere.

A broad typology may also permit one to identify areas of interaction and phenomena of opposition or cultural osmosis between contiguous spaces. In *Au fil des generations* I examined some osmotic processes of dissemination between adjacent territories of practices and conceptions related to the domestic sphere. In particular, I scrutinised the spread of a new lexicon based on unigeniture in Upper Embrunais and Queyras (Southern French Alps) from the end of the seventeenth century. Much work is still to be done in this respect in relation to other contact zones through localised surveys (see Lorenzetti and Mathieu, in this volume).

Micro, meso and macro

The issue of the interplay of my typology with other scales is particularly relevant in relation to the extremes of scale variation, in both a micro and a macro direction. As I noted above, the micro-analytical dimension is fundamental in the comparative approach I have developed. Starting from a core of anthropological case studies, it tries to utilise ethnographies in a comparative undertaking, through the construction of a typology derived from the micro-level analysis, further tested through the examination of a body of qualitative and quantitative data. This permitted a gradual process of generalisation by isolating a number of significant variables.

While the micro dimension of ethnography does not seem to pose serious problems to commentators, the question of the relationship with micro-history is apparently more intricate. It should be taken into account that the latter is not simply a methodological position adopted by some historians through a particular opening of the focal length, but it is also a specific research school with its own physiognomy. Several commentators have pointed to my critical attitude towards this orientation. So I would like to emphasise that I have learned a lot from micro-history, with which I had the chance to familiarise myself in its formative period in Turin, particularly through the teaching of Giovanni Levi. Moreover, my book draws on some results from micro-history, although its main debt on the micro level is to ethnography. I should add that I do not have the slightest intention to argue for the obsolescence of micro-history or to propose replacing it with another approach. I am quite convinced, like Guzzi, Lanzinger and Teuscher, that to grasp the concrete action of kinship (in its manifold configurations) in European history, the approach of micro-history is unavoidable. That said, it is true that I made a series of criticisms concerning the ability of micro-history to integrate its results within a cumulative programme of research, by embracing comparative techniques. Doubtless, the monographic approach advocated by several micro-historians is supported by a strong theoretical framework. Yet while such historians are at ease contesting the relevance of general theories, their own theoretical generalisations display a reluctance to engage in comparative reasoning. In spite of the evident merits of micro-history, I am not ready to change my mind on this specific issue.

According to Guzzi, I did improperly assimilate local history approaches into "a true micro-historical approach", because "in the philosophy of micro-history, the purpose of the local investigation is not to examine a village or valley in itself, but precisely to grasp on a smaller scale general phenomena that escape to a more distanced observation". In order to substantiate this point, Guzzi provides, among others, the example of the work of Giovanni Levi on the "kinship fronts" in seventeenth century rural Piedmont, advancing that "his goal was not the formalisation of certain kinship structures, but to stress the social importance of kinship solidarity, against a tradition that for decades had emphasised the primacy of the nuclear family. The main – and perfectly generalisable – result was not some kinship structure, but a certain social and economic use of kinship".[14] Even in Guzzi's opinion, the critical dimension of micro-history (that it is to say contesting on a small field the relevance of grand theories) is emphasised. As for the constructive dimension, it should be added that the general conclusion of Levi was not without ambiguities. The social and economic use of kinship that he discovered in the European past (inspired by anthropologists who had been working on this topic in different settings) was undoubtedly a very stimulating result, but it remained slightly formalised. Levi's analysis places the action of kinship fronts in a decidedly agnatic frame, but he offers also some statements that lend themselves to equivocation, by expanding the range of the relations considered when describing the "kinship of fronts." This vagueness has perhaps been the origin of some misinterpretations. For example, Jacques

---

14   *Ibid.*, p. 168.

Revel and Francis Zimmerman completely changed the scope of this concept. For them, Levi's kinship fronts are located in a fully cognatic dimension[15], which is far removed from the context of the seventeenth century Piedmontese sharecroppers. A similar interpretation is given by Martine Segalen, who equates the concept of "kinship front" with that of kindred (*parentèle*), conceived as an undifferentiated whole, including affines and bilateral kin[16]. It is difficult to escape the impression of a lack of clarity in the circulation of this concept.

More generally, I am not sure that it would be possible to identify "a true micro-historical approach" or a single " philosophy of micro-history", like Guzzi suggests. As a matter of fact, the field of micro-history appears quite dispersed. There is the Italian microstoria, along with French and German versions and Anglo-Saxon variations, without counting more recent developments in several countries. Each tradition shows some shift in methodological principles, and it would be hard to look for unanimity among micro-historians on the issue of the micro-macro link. Zoltan Boldizsàr Simon has recently observed that while most micro-historians "are convinced that arriving at generalities is one of the most important defining characteristics of micro-history, the extent of agreement is significantly lessened when it comes to identifying that way. Such identification is usually regarded as the most puzzling and mysterious question one might ask about micro-history".[17] Significantly, the authors of a recent book that gives an overall account of micro-history present two radically different, and irreconcilable, views on this issue[18].

Doubtless, in its multiple manifestations, micro-historical work may be crucial in confronting grand theories, as well as in discovering new connections and contexts that become more visible at a reduced scale. Yet the approach of micro-history leads to a kind of rhetoric that is not very compatible with a historical approach that aims to develop broad perspectives in time and space and is written from an all-embracing point of view. Micro-history is important, but it should be placed alongside more

---

15   Jacques Revel, "L'histoire au ras du sol", in Giovanni Levi, *Le pouvoir au village. Histoire d'un exorciste dans le Piémont du XVIIe siècle*, Paris, Gallimard, 1989, pp. I–XXXIII; Francis Zimmermann, *Enquête sur la parenté*, Paris, PUF 1993.
16   *Sociologie de la famille*, 4e éd., Paris, A. Colin, 1996, p. 74.
17   "Microhistory: In General", in *Journal of Social History*, vol. 49, 2015, n. 1, pp. 237–248 (237).
18   Sigurður Gylfi Magnússon and István M. Szijártó, *What is Microhistory? Theory and Practice*, London and New York, Routledge, 2013.

prosaic serialization work based on comparison. This is what I tried to do in my book, which may be seen as an attempt to overcome what I see as a crucial problem in the micro-historians' process of generalisation, namely an uncontrolled shift between the micro-dimension and very general theoretical statements, without establishing proper forms of mediation. From this point of view, my journey in comparative history could also be seen, admittedly in a quite paradoxical way, as an exercise in micro-history.

In other words, small-scale investigation is absolutely relevant to answer "great historical questions", but a microanalytic method can rarely do it alone. An important parallel step is to build a historical narrative, articulating the facts in a coherent way. The main features of a historical narrative are causal coherence, a definite beginning and ending, a plot and a central subject[19]. The narrative proposed by *Kinship in Europe* presented these features. Being unsatisfied with the traditional narratives incorporated in the grand theories concerning the declining importance of kinship across Europe, the authors endeavoured to build an alternative narrative aimed at promoting the findings of micro-history which, in Simon Teuscher's words, had failed at getting the message across. My attempt was rather similar in its logic, even if I was mainly interested in promoting the findings of Alpine anthropology and in contrasting other grand theories. Our respective central subjects were somewhat different (domestic organisation versus kinship) and the scope was smaller in my book (Alps versus Europe). There are, nevertheless, significant overlaps in the chronological span, in the plot and in the causation processes explored in both historical narratives.

I agree with Jon Mathieu that, despite some discrepancies, the broad perspectives presented in *Kinship in Europe* are compatible, by and large, with the typology and the models concerning alpine historical processes that I developed in *Au fil des générations*. The differentialist perspective I advocated concerning the history of domestic organisation in Alpine Europe does not mean that we should exclude the transverse action of a common "breathing". The trends isolated by Sabean and Teuscher regarding the long-term developments in European kinship may then be read in terms of their refractions in distinct regional processes at the domestic level. Thus, for the Alps, it would be possible to study the interaction between the patterns of transformation that I have identified in relation

---

19   Anton Froeyman, "Concepts of Causation in Historiography", in *Historical Methods*, Vol. 42, 2009, n. 3, pp. 116–128.

to the restricted dimension of the domestic organisation, alongside those indicated, in a broader (both geographic and thematic) perspective, for European kinship[20].

Concerning the first transitions, even in the Alps the consolidation of the modern state seems to have led overall to an accentuation of patrilineality. This transition, however, is not consistent across different alpine areas, due partly to differences in the speed and form of the construction of the modern state. In the Austrian Alps, the influence of patrilineal ideology leads in certain cases to a preference for male successors in the management of the farm and, more generally, gives a dynastic tone to the mechanisms for the transmission of the homestead. As I have already mentioned, some reviewers focused their attention on the emergence of patrilineal principles, evolving then in a dynastic direction, among elite groups in several sectors of the Swiss and Italian Alps. This seems now to have been a much more generalised phenomenon than I supposed in *Au fil des générations*, where I confined it only to limited sectors, and undoubtedly it may be seen as a manifestation of a general pattern described by Sabean and Teuscher.

A fuller attention to diverging dynamics of domestic organisation, and to their inscription in local juridical and political configurations, could perhaps add complexity to the historical narrative proposed by Sabean and Teuscher. Looking from an Alpine perspective, it appears that the growth of a patrilineal orientation shows a wide array of outcomes. The latter may be superficial, confined to some groups; or, on the contrary, they may deeply touch all society over a long duration, as happens in the Southern Alpine areas. The same can be said for the transformation towards a dynastic orientation: this is quite marginal in several areas, while affecting all levels of society in several parts of the Southern French Alps. Here, from the late Middle Ages until near the end of the seventeenth century, the pattern of domestic organisation largely corresponded to the Alpine agnatic type. Then there was a transition towards the devolution of property to only one heir. This raises some interesting questions about how these tendencies spread. How were internal frontiers between groups maintained? Why are some osmotic processes interrupted at a certain threshold, being limited to the superior segments of the society? Elsewhere in this volume Teuscher presents some interesting considerations on mediation, which may help explain these phenomena.

---

20   David W. Sabean, Simon Teuscher, Jon Mathieu (eds.), *Kinship in Europe, op. cit.*

Even for the second transition, it is possible to identify several correspondences. The decline of the agnatic orientation in certain areas of the Italian Alps, from the nineteenth century, rhymes for example with the contemporary accentuation of bilaterality in Europe, underlined by Sabean and Teuscher. But, again, it would be important to locate the character and extent of this change in kinship behaviour, putting it in the context of regional processes that, from the point of view of the domestic organisation, maintained distinctive logics until the twentieth century.

The conversation between the Alpine and European dimensions could also take other paths. I see at least two directions that would permit a dialogue between the analytical framework delineated in *Au fil des générations* and wider scales of enquiry focusing on domestic organisation. First, the tripartite typology, and the historical narrative that accompanies it, may be used to take into account regional developments that are somewhat contiguous to the Alps (even if the use of an Alpine typology in other contexts should be considered with some caution). A second direction could be a broader comparison with other regional processes which are geographically and historically "apart", but which present homologies that make them "comparable". This would further extract the Alps from the peripheral position to which they have often been relegated in historiographical imagination, instead placing them at the centre of continental processes.

Part 2:
From the Alps

Luigi Lorenzetti

Regional Spaces and Domestic Organisation. Homogeneity, Transversality and Trans-Cultural Diffusion in the Agnatic Alpine World (Sixteenth-Nineteenth Centuries)

The emergence in recent years of a vast amount of research on the history of the family reflects a dramatic revision on the part of historians in their interpretation of how their subject changed over the last few hundred years. One of the most significant contributions to this critical understanding of the question was made by David Sabean in the 1990's, and led to the publication in 2007 of a seminal work in which some authors distanced themselves from the paradigm of a gradual weakening of the sense of kinship in the life of the individual. The same authors do, nonetheless, focus on how kinship continued to play a part in the building of social relationships[1], and how this factor assumed different shapes and forms at different times in history. From the Middle Ages to the end of the eighteenth century horizontal lines of consanguinity were abandoned in favor of vertical ones, which brought with them the principle of filiation and patrilineal inheritance systems. Conversely, the period between the end of the eighteenth century and the twentieth century has seen a strengthening of horizontal lines of kinship that emphasised alliance and affinity rather than filiation.

The fact that historical paths and lengthy phases are inherent in the history of the family and common throughout Europe should not, however, lead us to ignore the numerous territorial (or regional) differences that exist across the continent. Dionigi Albera, in particular, has recently shown the presence of long-standing divisions in Europe which, in the

---

1   See David W. Sabean, Simon Teuscher, Jon Mathieu (eds.), *Kinship in Europe. Approaches to long term development (1300–1900),* New York – Oxford, Berghahn Books, 2007; François-Joseph Ruggiu gives an ample, in-depth commentary of the book in "Histoire de la parenté ou anthropologie historique de la parenté? Autour de Kinship in Europe" in *Annales de démographie historique*, 1, 2010, pp. 223–256.

alpine context, are evident in a series of regional family organization patterns that appear to show no sign of environmental or ethno-linguistic conditioning[2]. In other words, Albera highlights the presence in certain regions of deep-rooted "family cultures" which are anchored to political and judicial models – usually from outside of the alpine area – that change over time, yet still retain their distinctive features[3].

With these studies in mind, this paper aims to present a number of reflections on comparative approaches to the history of the family within a regional context. Focusing the analysis on certain areas of contact (political and cultural) of the agnatic nature of the alpine world, the article shall attempt to highlight some of the features that can contribute to our understanding of this regional space.

Family models and regional spaces: uniformity and variability

The studies carried out in the 1990s by D. Albera focused on the presence of several different forms of domestic organization in the alpine region which fall into three categories, or ideal types: *agnatic*, *bourgeois*, and what is known as the *Bauer* type[4]. These ideal types, based on different models of succession, are further defined by "context variables", which refer to the location and structure of the settlement, the residential forms, social and economic profiles, and types of family and social networks. Each type coincides with a "macro-regional" space, characterised by considerable degrees of internal homogeneity and historical continuity. The *agnatic* model is largely equivalent to the region of the Italian Alps and the present-day canton of Ticino, the *Bourgeois* type has much in common with the traditions of some Swiss alpine cantons, including Valais, Grisons

---

2   Dionigi Albera, *Au fil des générations. Terre, pouvoir et parenté dans l'Europe alpine (XIVᵉ–XXᵉ siècles)*, Grenoble, PUG, 2011.

3   For a critical analysis of D. Albera's work, see the commentary published by Luigi Lorenzetti and Simon Teuscher in *Quaderni Storici*, a. XLVIII, n. 2, 2013, pp. 600–616.

4   See Dionigi Albera, *L'organisation domestique dans l'espace alpin: équilibres écologiques, effets de frontier, transformations historiques*, Thèse, Université de Provence, 1995; *Id.,* "Oltre la norma e la strategia: per una comparazione ragionata dell'organizzazione domestica alpina", in *Histoire des Alpes – Storia delle Alpi – Geschichte der Alpen* 6, 2001, pp. 117–132.

and Central Switzerland. The *Bauer* type corresponds in many respects to patterns of domestic organization found in various parts of the Austrian Alps, particularly in Styria, Carinthia and the Salzburg region.

It should be noted that both induction and deduction are contemporaneously used in order to describe these regional spaces. In the case of the former, Albera's study is based on a wide monographic documentation that makes it possible to trace the main features of familial systems in the alpine region, while the demarcation of these areas can be seen as the result of a deductive process, by referring to a model in order to verify whether a given reality does indeed belong to a specific *ideal-type*. This means that, unlike a "typical" research method, which would establish *ex ante* the regional spaces in question and then go on to identify and analyse the relative forms of domestic organisation (along with their specific features and variants), Albera's ideal-types provide for an alternative route whereby the regional areas of domestic organisation can be identified on the basis of their specific attributes. This is a significant change in perspective inasmuch as it transforms the analytical approach from regional delimitation to spatial transversality, and is in turn connected to multidimensional dynamics (ecological, environmental, economic, social, political, cultural).

With this in mind, and borrowing certain elements from the field of regional analysis[5], we can attempt to develop this approach further by working with two possible hypotheses:

a) The spatial delimitation of different models of domestic organisation is dependent upon the degree of uniformity that characterises its various components.
b) The historical variations in the regional spaces of domestic organisation are the result of the flexibility and variability of their different components.

As for the first of these hypotheses, one cannot help but notice a degree of variation in the different components which Albera identifies as characteristic of the various patterns of domestic organisation. With regard to agnation, for example, there are numerous variations in the practice of hereditary transmission and family rights, from the fairly widespread

---

5   See Ulrich Pfister, "Subregioni, regioni e macroregioni nell'area alpina (XV–XIX secolo)", in Andrea Leonardi (ed.), *Aree forti e deboli nello sviluppo della montagna alpina,* Trento, Università egli Studi di Trento, 2001, pp. 219–221.

custom of writing a will, to cases of *ab intestat* inheritance; from situations involving a dowry to those which are inherently indivisible[6]. Nonetheless, even those variables which are a corollary of the agnate model – settlements, precepts of residency, social-economic stratification and systems of family relationship – display notable differences, even within limited areas. There are differing precepts of residency, for instance, and although it is the case for a great many domestic units that the cycle of life continues in the same place generation after generation, in other areas there seems to be more of a tendency to move to a new location. This was the case in the Dolomites, where newly married couples usually set up a new home since sons were acknowledged by their fathers to be individual and independent adults, with the right therefore, as *vicini,* to use the communal resources[7]. Whereas in other areas historical data seem to indicate more complex principles of residency. Particularly in the Aosta Valley and in the alpine valleys of Piedmont, where the presence of *joint families* seems to be linked to the fact that emancipation was foreseen only on the father's death (or by means of a legal document)[8]. An independent household whose head was not emancipated would not receive access to the common goods, since this privilege was enjoyed only by *capofamiglie* who were – by definition – emancipated.

Settlement patterns also varied considerably, even within geographical areas that shared common political and cultural characteristics. Family life in the valley of Poschiavo and the upper Bregaglia Valley (two Italian language areas in the canton of the Grisons) resembled that that of alpine Lombardy, whereas in the low-lying parts of Bregaglia, farmers tended to summer their cattle collectively rather than individually, and the

---

6   There are several examples in Luigi Lorenzetti, Raul Merzario, *Il fuoco acceso. Famiglie e emigrazioni alpine nell'Italia d'età moderna,* Roma, Donzelli, 2005, pp. 40–54.

7   See Cesare Poppi, "Kinship and social organization among the Ladins of the Val di Fassa (Northern Italy)", in *Cambridge Anthropology,* 6, 1980, pp. 60–88 (68).

8   See Lucia Carle, "Identità trasmessa e identità reale", in Stuart J. Woolf (ed.), *La Valle d'Aosta. Storia d'Italia. Le regioni dall'Unità a oggi,* Torino, Einaudi, 1995, pp. 235–236; Floriana Montani, *Famiglia, matrimonio e condizione della donna in una comunità alpina (Usseglio – Valli di Lanzo),* Lanzo Torinese, Società Storica delle Valli di Lanzo, 2004, pp. 40–46.

abundance of cultivation and pasture lands together with the presence of workable land at many different altitudes led to a high degree of mobility[9].

Significant differences can also be seen in the way in which land changed hands. While the peasant small-holding can be seen as representing the fulcrum of the domestic economy in an agnatic society, there is a great deal of variation in the quantity and frequency with which land was bought and sold or transferred, and this can only partly be explained by regional economic differences and the modest interest shown by the merchant classes for land ownership. During the eighteenth century, for example, the land market in Carnia, where trading by pedlars (*Cramars*) was widespread, was essentially static[10], while in some Waldensian communities in Piedmont, where families were also traditionally bound to small-scale trading, land frequently changed hands and the market was intense[11]. The same is also true of other communities in the alpine valleys of Lombardy, where a lively exchange of land also seemed to go hand in hand with the proliferation of the notary class who played an intermediary role in the local market.

From a structural point of view, these differences have been seen largely as "variations on a theme" which have no bearing on the essential nature of agnatic domestic organisation, or as a statistical effect where the reduction in the scale of observation accentuates the dispersion of the phenomena observed[12]. Although they are not without some foundation, these objections prevent us from appreciating how much we can discover from such differences, in that they are directly associated with the degree of internal "coherence" in such a system. In other words, local variations

---

9   Diego Giovanoli, "Edificazione delle fasce gestionali nelle Alpi grigioni (1500–1950)", in Dario Benetti, Santino Langé (eds.), *La dimora alpina. Atti del convegno di Varenna*, Sondrio, Cooperativa editoriale Quaderni Valtellinesi, 1996, pp. 199–230 (213).

10 Alessio Fornasin, *Ambulanti, artigiani e mercanti. L'emigrazione della Carnia in età moderna*, Verona, Cierre ed., 1998, p. 76; Luigi De Corte, *La proprietà fondiaria in un villaggio del canal di Gorto tra '700 e '800. Continuità e permanenze*, in Manlio Michelutti (ed.), *In Guart. Anime e contrade della Pieve di Gorto*, Udine, Società filologica friulana, 1994, pp. 173–178.

11 Marco Battistoni, *Comportamenti di confine. Cattolici e valdesi nell'età della Confessionalizzazione*, Vercelli, 2012, p. 78–97 (http://past.unipmn.it/pubbl/past_m001. pdf).

12 See Jon Mathieu, "Diversity of family practices in mountain societies. Why?", in Bernard Derouet, Luigi Lorenzetti, Jon Mathieu (éds.), *Les pratiques familiales et sociétés de montagne, XVIᵉ–XXᵉ siècles*, Basel, Schwabe, 2010 pp. 173–187 (173).

are valuable indicators of how flexible the ideal-type can be. Moreover, they can help to understand the extent to which the variety of solutions in different contexts is compatible with the transmission processes of the agnatic model.

This can be examined by means of the second hypothesis, which proposes that historical variations in the regional spaces of domestic organisation are the result of the flexibility of their different components. If we allow that the law is fundamentally a social arrangement, changes in the legal norms which govern domestic organisation should, in principle, react to changes necessitated by the passage of time, and meet the needs of the social groups which use them[13]. In the Italian Alps, one of the most significant changes that took place in the Modern Era was probably that of a stricter application of the principle of residency, when dealing either with hereditary rights within the family or of the rights of *vicini* within the local community. At a family level, particularly in places where there was a strong tendency to migrate, there are many indications that hereditary transmission was linked more and more to heirs who were physically present and contributed to the livelihood of the family[14].

Similarly, over the course of the Modern Era rulings concerning *vicini* show a progressive overlapping of transmission by filiation (*Jus sanguinis*) with the principle of residency, so as to temporarily withhold the right to the status of *vicini* from those who had been absent from the community for a long period, those who had failed to pay local taxes and those who did not own land within the confines of the community[15]. The Charters of Leventina (Ticino) prescribed that *vicini* who owned property in the valley did not lose their rights even if they were absent. But those who left the community (*vicinanza)* and did not own property there or pay the local taxes, forfeited their status as *vicini* and were considered *forastieri* (foreigners)[16]. In Valtellina, too, permission to use communal woodland resources was granted less on the basis of an individual's connection to the "founding families", i.e. their descent in the patrilineal line from

---

13   Pio Caroni, "Statutum et silentium. Viaggio nell'entourage silenzioso del diritto statuario", in *Archivio Storico Ticinese*, 118, 1995, pp. 129–160 (147).
14   Luigi Lorenzetti, Raul Merzario, *Il fuoco acceso, op. cit.,* pp. 38–42.
15   *Ibidem.*
16   Emilio Clemente, *Gli statuti della Leventina,* in "Bollettino Storico della Svizzera Italiana", 2, 1944, pp. 49–63; Romano Broggini, *L'acquisto e la perdita del vicinato prima della Rivoluzione francese,* in "Rivista patriziale ticinese", 161, 1981, pp. 8–15 (10).

indigenous inhabitants, than on whether they were recognised as residing or working within the community[17]. The same applied to numerous communities in the central Italian Alps; for example in Villa Rendena (Trentino), *vicini* who were not resident in the community were denied access to communal resources[18] and anyone who transferred their residency outside the *vicinanza* of Val Camonica, or was absent from it for an extended period, lost their community rights[19].

This double evolution concerning the family circle and the community, is generally seen as a strengthening of the patriarchal element in family groups and a response to the growing pressure on local resources. However it remains to be seen whether (and how) this tendency affects succession practices in the following generation of families. The available evidence seems to show that inheritance practices in the agnatic context, including those at a family level, became more rigid. Although these practices were not extended to the reinforcement of primogeniture[20], as was the case in South Tyrol, they laid greater stress on the duty of intergenerational solidarity (that of sons towards their fathers). Nonetheless, the dynamics of these two juridical spheres, the private (or family sphere) and the collective (or *vicinanza* sphere) do not always run parallel to each other. One example of this discrepancy is represented by the valley of Fiemme, a territory which straddles the areas of Trentino and Tyrol which were influenced respectively by the agnatic model and that of undivided inheritance. At the beginning of the Modern Era, despite being under the jurisdiction of the bishopric of Trent (where the agnatic principle prevailed), succession *ab intestato* in Val di Fiemme granted equal treatment to sons and daughters, as it did to brothers and sisters in the event of the death of a sibling[21].

---

17 Dario Benetti, Massimo Guidetti, *Storia di Valtellina e Valchiavenna. Una introduzione,* Milano, Jaca book, 1998, pp. 163–164.

18 See Fabio. Giacomoni (ed.), *Carte di Regola e Statuti delle Comunità Rurali Trentine,* Milano, Jaca book, 1991, p. 297 (n. 56). The ruling is from 1739.

19 Gino Raffaglio, *Le vicinie della Val Camonica e della Val di Sclave,* in Massimo Giudetti, Paul H. Stahl (eds.), *Comunità di villaggio e comunità familiari nell'Italia dell'800,* vol. II. *Un Italia sconosciuta,* Milano, Jaca book, 1977, p. 84.

20 See Margareth Lanzinger, *Towards Predominating Primogeniture: Changes in Inheritance Practices, Innichen/ San Candido 1730–1930,* in Hannes Grandits, Patrick Heady, (Hg.), *Distinct Inheritances. Property, Family and Community in a Changing Europe,* Munster, Lit Verlag, 2003, pp. 125–144.

21 Tullio Sartori Montecroce, *La comunità di Fiemme e il suo diritto statuario,* ed. by Italo Giordani, s.l. Magnifica comunità di Fiemme, 2002 (ed. or. 1892).

Furthermore, the status of *vicino* was granted to males and females on reaching the age of 25, with the only other requirements being that they should either own a property (a house) or reside in the valley. This meant that even *forastieri* (foreigners) who took up residence there with their households were accepted by the community as *vicini*. However, this system was modified in 1584, when women were excluded from the succession to common rights[22]. The new regulation established that "Having a father who is a *vicino* of the Val di Fiemme, and legitimate and natural sons and daughters, of one or more than one mother, be they *vicine* or not, only sons shall inherit the rights and *vicinanza* of the community and daughters who marry a *forastiero* shall not inherit the common rights, but be totally excluded." Exceptions were made only if there were no male descendants, and even then only one female descendent could succeed to the *vicinato*. This decision was based on the fear that a *forastiero* could marry a woman from Fiemme, enabling him to become a *vicino* and enjoy the benefits of communal resources. In terms of family and community organisation, the change in the law created an "asymmetrical" situation. In fact as regards hereditary succession, the agnatic form of testamentary disposition is contiguous with the bilateral form of disposition, although this changed somewhat a few decades later, when hereditary equality between males and females in Val di Fiemme was also subjected to restrictions. The principle of the rightful share[23] (*legittima*) was introduced, which was fixed at two-thirds of the inheritance, while the remaining third was reserved for male heirs only. This principle reaffirms a tendency towards the inequality of the sexes and the agnatic orientation of the inheritance practices. Basically, the example of Val di Fiemme suggests that changes to the defining components of the agnatic alpine model sometimes mean a loss of "congruity" which not only brings into question the logic and principles that govern relations between family and community (expressed in the management of communal resources), but also challenges the very confines of the agnatic space (juridical and, in some ways, geographical).

The final aspect involved in the connection between the agnatic family model and the regional space which delimits it regards changes in the

---

22   See Nadia Delugan, Claudia Visani, *Corpi e territorio. Le trasformazioni della Val di Fiemme nel XVI secolo*, in Cesare Mozzarelli (ed.), *L'ordine di una società alpina. Tre studi e un documento sull'antico regime nel principato vescovile di Trento*, Milano, Franco Angeli, 1988, p. 55.

23   The portion of the estate which a testator cannot dispose of freely.

structure of domestic organisation, that took place during the nineteenth century and in the early twentieth century, along with the adoption of new juridical principles which led to much less agnatic norms of succession. In 1865, for example, Italy's Civil Code abolished the obligatory payment of dowries, established equality between males and females in cases of succession *ab intestat,* and also accorded full hereditary rights to surviving spouses. The standardisation of family rights and the abolition of some local and regional norms, however, did not put an end to practices and strategies aimed at perpetuating the family model in its "traditional" form. The agnatic family model was kept alive for a certain amount of time thanks to its usefulness in marriage strategies (the status of spinsterhood, family alliances) and the forging of the destiny of individuals.

Family models and transversality

A survey of the various characteristics that distinguish the three ideal-types of alpine domestic organization reveals a number of aspects which are shared by two or all types. A comparison, for example, between the agnatic ideal-type and the *bourgeois,* shows several common areas with regard to types of settlement (for example in the organisation of decentralised agricultural activity[24]). Similarly, a great deal of land in both areas was divided into small plots and often, management of the estate was undivided. Such practices originated from a number of factors, including hereditary transmission and the lifestyle of rural mountain communities. Both areas had an abundance of common resources, to which only those who belonged to the "original families" had access. Also similar are the ways in which they are used. In both types of area, with no clear division with respect to the juridical system of the respective models of familial organisation, documentation shows private use of land by families or collectively (through specialised agents).

These examples of transversality seem to corroborate the "weak determinism" hypothesis put forward by J. Cole and E. Wolf. Nevertheless

---

24 See e.g. Paolo Sibilla, *Il gruppo corporato di "vicinanza" e la proprietà collettiva in una comunità alemannica alpina. Ri-considerazioni su un argomento storico-culturale,* in "Cheiron", a. IV, 1987, n. 7–8, pp. 137–171 (154–168).

this transversality has not failed to raise other questions concerning the static nature of such an interpretation. In recent years, therefore, scholars have chosen to focus their attention on the way different regions developed, which in turn is associated with the political processes that can bring about changes in family practice[25]. Such scholarly approaches may have demonstrated their ability to go beyond the impasse of environmental determinism, but one is left with the impression that they are content to avoid the issue, by failing to explore the transversality which characterises the various ideal-types.

One example of this transversality is the presence of the principle of residence (generally associated with the agnatic context) in various *borghese* communities. The *Burgrecht* of Leuk drafted in 1563 decreed that anyone who resided there for at least two thirds of the year should be granted all the privileges of a *communier* (member of the community), although these privileges are reduced by half if residence is for less than six months[26]. Similarly, the regulations stipulated in 1600 for the Binn Valley (in the canton of Valais) declare that "whoever does not stay or live in the valley with a hearth and light for the whole year, cannot benefit from the communal resources, nor have the use of them, nor take his cattle into the mountains other than for the sake of wintering and at the rate of one cow to four *toises* of hay". Those who live there permanently, on the other hand, "can enjoy the use of the mountain pastures, the *allmends*, the woodlands and all common resources"[27].

These regulations, to which we can add others obstructing any *forestiero's* attempt to obtain residence in the valley[28], are quite similar to those adopted by a number of alpine communities in the agnatic area, seemingly adding weight to an ecological interpretation which cites an attempt by local communities to relieve the pressure on their resources. In the case of Valais, however, such regulations can also be interpreted within the framework of regional politics and the growing strength of local communities compared to that of the upper classes. This process led, in some cases, to the common

---

25   Besides Dionigi Albera, *Au fil des générations, op. cit.* See also Jon Mathieu, "Storia delle Alpi tra teoria etnica e teoria ecologica", in *Archivio Storico Ticinese*, 110, 1991, pp. 179–192; *Id., Diversity of family practices,* art. cit.

26   Werner Kampfen, "Les Bourgeoisies du Valais", in *Annales Valaisannes*, t. 13, a. 40, 1965, pp.129–176 (150).

27   *Ibid.*, p. 146.

28   See Louis Carlen, "Zum Fremdenrecht im Wallis vom 15. bis ins 18. Jahrhundert", in *Vallesia*, 8, 1953, pp. 131–144.

resources of the valley being shared out among the various communities. The introduction of the principle that four households could constitute a "rural corporation" led to an increase in the number of *consortages* and, consequently, to restrictions in usage rights on common resources[29].

We also find a certain transversality of family practices within the marital sphere. In Grisons and Valais, for example, inheritance laws treated children of both sexes equally, and the system governing marriages was prevalently one of joint ownership (in the form of joint acquisitions and joint losses), but the administration of these joint resources was entrusted solely to the husband, as it was in agnatic areas. In other words, the over-whelming opinion in the two Swiss cantons characterised by the *bour-geois* ideal-type was that women were incapable of managing their own affairs, and that wives should be entrusted to the care of their husbands. In Valais, the *Landrecht* that came into force in 1514 barred women of all ages (whether they be single, married or widowed) from appearing in court unless accompanied by a guardian. According to Poudret, this rule was a consequence of the principle of *tutelle du sexe* (protection of the [faired] sex) that had become a part of Upper Valais legislation[30], reflect-ing a family model in which the status of women was subordinated by law to that of men, despite the fact that the law recognised equality between the two sexes with regard to hereditary rights.

Signs of transversality are also present in the norms that regulated family solidarity. Some years ago, several studies suggested a distinction between Northern Europe, characterised by weak family ties and South-ern Europe, where family ties are strong[31]. The distinction lay in attitudes toward the care of the elderly, with families tending to look after their aged relatives in Southern Europe, while in the North there is greater depen-dency on public care facilities. In the Alps, however, which straddle the boundary between Northern and Southern Europe, it seems that "cultural boundaries" are very easily crossed. In both agnatic and *bourgeois* areas, the norms of family solidarity meant that the whole family was responsible

---

29   Werner Kämpfen, "Les Bourgeoisies du Valais", art. cit., p. 143.

30   Jean-François Poudret, *Coutumes et coutumiers. Histoire comparative des droits des pays romands du XIIIe à la fin du XVIe siècle.* Partie II. *Les personnes,* Berne, Staempfli Editions, 1998, pp. 279–280, 289, 317–321.

31   See Peter Laslett, "Family, kinship and collectivity as system of support in preindus-trial Europe: a consideration of the 'nuclear-hardship' hypothesis", in *Continuity and Change,* 3, 1988, 2, pp. 153–175; David S. Reher, "Family ties in Western Europe: per-sistent contrasts", in *Population and Development Review,* 24, 1998, 2, pp. 203–234.

for contributing to the welfare of its members, even if they were entrusted to the care of an institution. According to Roman Law it is the responsibility of sons to take care of their elderly parents, based on the rule that only males can hold and administer the family resources[32]. However, alpine traditions (in both agnatic and *bourgeois* areas) assign the responsibility of care to both sons and daughters alike, placing the greater onus on the latter, often by means of a "programmed" spinsterhood aimed at ensuring day to day material support for ageing parents, or prescribe that widows should have access to family and communal resources (providing that they remained a widow), even though the transmission of *vicinato* status was by patrilineal descent, from father to son[33]. In short, these practices show that the norms governing the division of individual roles and status within domestic groups were flexible.

Despite their specific, circumscribed nature, these facts suggest that legal norms (and in some ways their equivalent hereditary customs) may contain patterns that are, to a certain extent, at odds with the consequent defining elements of the model of family organisation regulated by such norms. In other words, the considerations we have made up to this point allow us to presume that the circulation of legislative models does not necessarily imply a parallel and concomitant transmission of the equivalent political and social models. Moreover, their evolution seems to answer to rhythms and logic of a different kind. This would explain why a multiplicity of family structures could coexist even within one overall model of domestic organisation (in this case the agnatic model).

In order to examine this approach more closely, it may be useful to look at what different regional spaces of familial organisation have in

---

32   See Angela Groppi, "Assistenza alla vecchiaia e solidarietà tra generazioni in età moderna", in Ida Fazio, Daniela Lombardi (eds.), *Generazioni. Legami e parentela tra passato e presente,* Roma, Viella, 2006, pp. 51–68 (61).

33   The charters of Croviana (Trentino) of 1727 establish that "after the death of a *vicino* who leaves behind a wife in the house, the said wife – if living alone – may enjoy the communal resources: and on incurring debts will be subject to the same increases as the other *vicini* ". See Fabio Giacomoni (ed.), *Carte di Regola e Statuti, op. cit.,* p. 206 (no. 36). The Leventine charters, for their part, contemplate the existence of a *vicinato femminile* for widows who, even though they had married a member of another *vicinanza,* could come back to enjoy their *vicinato,* but this right was not extended to the children of the *forastiero* husband who, while their mother was alive, were totally deprived of the *vicinato.* See Romano Broggini, "L'acquisto e la perdita del vicinato prima della Rivoluzione francese", in *Rivista Patriziale Ticinese,* 161, 1981, p. 12.

common. If such areas show a high degree of transversality it would be possible to postulate the existence of "trans-cultural diffusion" phenomena, and, vice versa, high levels of dispersion could indicate that the role of contextual variables is more significant.

Family models, areas of contact and trans-cultural diffusion phenomena

Besides the internal uniformity of specific parameters (which define its "structural" relevance), a regional space is defined in terms of its relationship to the outside world, showing the extent to which one space is able to establish a dialogue with another, to share and assimilate reciprocal influences.

This aspect, which brings into play the phenomena of cultural osmosis between contiguous spaces, brings to mind the hypothesis of trans-cultural diffusion which was put forward at the end of the nineteenth century. In the field of alpine studies, the hypothesis of trans-cultural diffusion has been repeatedly questioned and refuted by means of ecological approaches and in studies carried out in the 1980s and '90s, which addressed the expansion of Walser "colonization" in the Alps. These studies showed that, far from imposing their own social and cultural model, the Walser settlements assimilated the customs and practices of the areas that they settled in[34].

In Val Formazza, for example, the arrival of Walsers in the eighteenth century did not lead to any legislative changes. The community was subject to a feudal lord, with a *vicinale* system based on Roman law, until the end of the sixteenth century, when it acquired a new set of regulations of which the civil component was based on that of a neighbouring jurisdiction, whose laws had been promulgated in 1513 by the then dominant Swiss cantons, although they bore the legislative imprint of the Visconti government[35]. As well as enforcing the supremacy of the male line over the female ("Quod agnati excludant cognatos"), these laws stripped women of

---

34   Pier Paolo Viazzo, *Comunità alpine. Ambiente, popolazione, struttura sociale nelle Alpi dal XVI secolo a oggi*, Bologna, il Mulino, 1990, pp. 83–95.

35   Giovanni De Maurizi, "Gli statuti antichi della colonia tedesco-vallesana di Salecchio (1588)", in *Archivio Storico della Svizzera Italiana*, vol. V, 1930, pp. 68–69.

their right to inherit land and their *vicinato* status if they married a *"forast-iero"*, thereby assuming the legislative characteristics of the agnatic area.

In light of these facts, the trans-cultural diffusion hypothesis seems to be without foundation when the focus is on the origins and transmission of certain cultural features, although it could still be useful when trying to understand whether cultural norms and practices correspond to the requirements of the time, and whether they satisfied the needs of the social groups who adopt them[36]. It becomes pertinent, from this point of view, to assume the presence of cultural loans and of interdependent relationships between adjacent areas, and, in the light of the transversality described above, to consider certain analytical approaches.

A number of studies have shown that lifestyles and behavior in alpine communities developed through imitation of city life[37]. Architectural forms, material aspects (like clothing and food), marriage and inheritance patterns and even sexual and reproductive practices[38], documented in the agnatic area originated in urban contexts and spread through immigration, shaping, to a greater or lesser extent according to time and place, the economic, social, political and cultural life of alpine communities.

Similar considerations can be applied to the legislative sphere. Various studies have found that legislative norms in force in the Italian alpine area during the late Middle Ages are the result of the spread of customs and exogenous legal practices connected to common law and transmitted by notaries[39]. Many studies[40] exist which attest that statutory law (*jus proprium*) in alpine areas, and the pervasive presence of notaries in southern-alpine districts (observed and "denounced" by various witnesses since the sixteenth century) had been transplanted from the city. Not only that:

---

36 On this, see Pio Caroni, "Statutum et silentium", art. cit. p.147.
37 See for an example Francesca Chiesi, *Les Pedrazzini de Campo Vallemaggia: parcours commerciaux et intersections familiales d'une élite alpine (XVIIIe siècle)*, Genève, 2014 (Thesis unpublished Université de Genève, Fac. des lettres).
38 See Raul Merzario, *Anastasia ovvero la malizia degli uomini*, Rome-Bari, Laterza, 1992.
39 See Dionigi Albera, *Au fils des générations, op cit.*, pp. 241–263.
40 See for example Alessandro Lattes, *Gli statuti di Lugano e del suo lago*, Milano, Cogliati, 1908; Enrico Besta, "Gli statuti delle valli dell'Adda e della Mera", in *Archivio Storico della Svizzera Italiana*, a. XII, 1937, n. 3–4, pp. 129–156; Virgilio Gilardoni, "Gli statuti medievali di Brissago nelle volgarizzazioni del Sei e del Settecento: per una rilettura degli statuti rustici della Lombardia prealpina", in *Archivio Storico Ticinese*, 73–74, 1974, pp. 3–216; Claudia Storti Storchi, *Scritti sugli statuti lombardi*, Milano, Giuffré, 2007.

historians have proved that Roman law penetrated into Valais through students from the University of Bologna, which in the Medieval era was the center for the recovery of the Roman juridical tradition[41]. The population of Valais, in fact, included a significant number of jurists of Lombard and Piedmontese origin, who came to influence the local legal system[42].

Having established that historiography has accepted the diffusion of common law from the urban centres to the alpine valleys, what can be said about family practices in the broad sense? In this case too, the current situation is more complex and less clearly defined than it may at first appear, as exemplified by some of the Ladin valleys in the Dolomites. In Livinallongo, there was never any legal definition of *maso chiuso* (land which could not be divided through inheritance), but the influence of the Tyrolese economic system led people everywhere to develop the habit of considering the land as indivisible[43], and this eventually became the accepted rule. In practice, despite having a legal system of Roman inspiration, family practices seem to have assimilated Germanic patterns which applied to a substantially different social system.

Although it represents only a small part of the social framework, the case of Valtellina is, nonetheless, an interesting example on account of its annexation as a subject territory by the Grisons at the beginning of the sexteenth century. In effect, the spread of primogeniture and the practice of fidei-commissum among the aristocratic élites in the region from the seventeenth century does not seem to have been simply an imitation of the urban nobility, but was, rather, a response to new regulations imposed by the rulers in Grisons, granting exemption from public taxation for ecclesiastical property. This led many families to persuade sons who were not

41 Sven Stelling-Michaud, "Les étudiants valaisans à Bologne et la réception du droit romain au XIIIe siècle dans le diocèse de Sion", in *Vallesia*, 1951, pp. 59–85.

42 Louis Carlen, "Juristen und Jurisprudenz im Wallis zur Zeit des Kardinals Schiner", in *Blatter aus der Walliser Geschichte*, Bd. XIV, Jg. 2, 1967/68, pp. 99–114. On another level, it should also be pointed out that for many families belonging to the Haut-Valais élite, the profession of notary was an important step on the social ladder and one of the main ways of consolidating one's economic and social position. See Francine Fayard Duchêne, "Une famille au service de l'état pendant six siècles: les Kuntschen de Sion", in *Vallesia*, 48, 1993, pp. 269–366.

43 See Luciana Palla, "Maso chiuso ed economica montana nelle valli ladine dolomitiche", in Antonio Lazzarini, Ferruccio Vendramini (eds.), *La montagna veneta in età contemporanea. Storia e ambiente. Uomini e risorse,* Rome, Ed. di Storia e Letteratura, 1991, p. 95–114 (102).

the first-born to enter the priesthood, conferring the family inheritance on them by fidei-commissum, allowing the family to continue using their property beyond the reach of the Grisons tax office. This also effectively disguised the property of the nobility as Church possessions, leading to the extraordinary expansion of ecclesiastical mortmain (the basis of the *rentier* policy of the aristocracy in Valtellina)[44], helping to consolidate a family model which was also adopted by the élite of Grisons who had settled in the area. In brief, the phenomenon of the spread of family practices can take unexpected turns and can even arise from particular contingencies not strictly connected to the diffusion of the cultural matrix.

This brings us back to the question of the relationship between legislative models (particularly those regarding hereditary transmission) and the social models within which they occur. Notwithstanding the fundamentally social character of law, in that it provides functional solutions to the needs of the social groups who use it[45], the transmission of legislative models can give rise to somewhat diverse responses in terms of social order and family organisation. In this regard it has been observed that there are very few places in Europe where Roman Law and consuetudinary Germanic Law have not interacted and influenced each other[46]. There are indeed many examples which show how a change in political affiliation encourages contact between areas having different legislative cultures, resulting in the diffusion of legislative models, generally from dominant areas to politically subservient ones. The Italian valleys of the Grisons illustrate this quite well. With their integration into the territories of the Three Leagues, the three valleys of the Italian part of the canton (Bregaglia, Poschiavo and Mesolcina) took on various aspects of the Grisons system with its German framework. In Mesolcina, for example, under the control of the Grey League, common law was repealed and replaced by the laws of Grisons, which redefined formal testamentary law and the rules

---

44   Marino Berengo, "'La via dei Grigioni' e la politica riformatrice austriaca", in *Archivio storico lombardo*, n. 8, 1958, pp. 3–109. For an example, see Anna de Pietri, "Carriere ecclesiastiche e politiche familiari. Francesco Giani (1641–1702) e i suoi fratelli", in *Archivio Storico della diocesi di Como*, XIII, 2002, pp. 329–349.

45   Pio Caroni, "Quando la storia sociale inquadra quella del diritto", in *Archivio Storico Ticinese*, 135, 2004, pp. 125–137.

46   Lloyd Bonfield, "Gli sviluppi del diritto di famiglia in Europa", in Marzio Barbagli, David I. Kertzer (eds.), *Storia della famiglia in Europa. Dal Cinquecento alla Rivoluzione francese*, Rome-Bari, Laterza, 2001, pp. 121–175 (126).

of devolution of the inheritance and the legitimate portion[47]. Similarly, in Val Poschiavo where common law was more deeply rooted, progressive changes in legal principles led to the adoption of practices increasingly similar to those in use in the sovereign territories[48]. In Bregaglia, too, from the second half of the sixteenth century common law no longer had any influence on the patrimonial law governing married couples. The principle of legal equality between the sexes (present in Grisons law) came into force in the valley, prohibiting the exclusion of daughters from the inheritance of their parents and brothers, along with the custom of giving a dowry, and replacing them with the principle of reciprocal communal rights for both husband and wife.

It is worth remembering that "the law is not always a reliable barometer of the values of a certain culture"[49] and that it is principally the fruit and expression of political, economic and social balance and religious circumstances, and the Italian valleys of the Grisons were not entirely free of agnatic influence. This is suggested, for example, by the development of the *avantagium*, the practice which allows for the daughter to voluntarily relinquish her father's house, vegetable garden and household goods in favour of her brothers (there was no law prohibiting this). In the Calanca Valley, despite hereditary equality between the sexes, local regulations specify that "concerning the house in which the Father lives, the Male or Males shall have the right to two thirds, and the females to one third, wherewith however the females must cede it for its rightful value, but until they are married they have the right to live there, or the males at their own expense must find shelter for them in accordance with the status of the house, and the females must comply with this"[50]. In summary then, agnatic

---

47   Pio Caroni, *Einflüsse des deutschen Rechts Graubündens südlich der Alpen,* Koln-Wein, Böhlau, 1970. More specifically on the marital property system, see Id., "Le développement des régimes matrimoniaux dans la Suisse italienne du XVIe au XIXe siècle", in *Mémoires de la société pour l'histoire du droit et des institutions des anciens pays bourguignons, comtois et romands,* vol. 27, Dijon, 1966, pp. 39–64.

48   See for example, the increasing rarity of relinquishment of inheritance declarations on the part of daughters, or the transformation in the eighteenth century of dowries into a part of the inheritance. This evolution was formalised by the charters of Poschiavo in 1757, which seem to have been strongly influenced by Grisons laws. See Pio Caroni, *Einflusse, op. cit.*

49   Lloyd Bonfield, *Gli sviluppi, op. cit.*, p. 125.

50   Adriano Bertossa, *Storia della Calanca,* Poschiavo, Tip. F. Menghini, 1937, p. 306.

elements survive even within a bilateral normative framework, conferring considerable shades of difference on the juridical model in question.

Interesting parallels can be drawn between Grisons and Valais. Here, too, changes in political affiliation (between 1475 and 1536 the territory of Lower Valais came under the control of the *dizaines* of Upper Valais) brought about a gradual transformation in juridical terms. Initially, statutory law held out in the territory of lower Valais against episcopal Valais in 1474 and 1536[51]. Years later, the people of Upper Valais were required by the authorities to comply with the unified legal system introduced by the *Landrecht* of 1571. In the meantime, however, they were permitted to maintain some traditional local practices, in particular those regarding wills, substitutions, donations and inheritance[52]. This outcome prompted many civic authorities to enshrine these same rights within their own laws. Between 1571 and 1585 several communities[53] drew up new laws pertaining primarily to testamentary and *ab intestat* successions. The differences between the regulations of lower Valais and the *Landrecht* are mainly to be found in the degree of testamentary freedom, and some localities (Saint-Maurice, Entremont, Conthey, Leytron, Nendaz and Vouvry) took the opportunity to preserve the testamentary freedom enshrined in Roman law, with the sole restriction of the rightful share (*légitime*), which was fixed at one third of the inheritance[54].

It was only later, in the eighteenth century, that a turning point took place, bringing lower Valais closer to the inheritance model practised in upper Valais, when, as revealed in a study by S. Guzzi-Heeb, Lower Valais adopted the bilateral principle, thereby renouncing the agnatic principle of Savoyard law[55]. F. Fayard Duchêne also refers to this, noting that daughters from the de Torrenté family, who belonged to the Lower Valais élite, are mentioned regularly not only in wills, but also in inventories listing

---

51 Stéphane Abbet, "Influence et survivance du droit romain dans la rédaction des costume bas-valaisannes au XVIe siècle", in *Vallesia*, LXVI, 2011, pp. 125–149 (127).

52 *Ibid.*, p. 129.

53 These were Saint-Maurice, Nendaz, Entremont, Bagnes, Riddes e Saxon, Leytron, Hérémence, Conthey, Vouvry, Monthey. Other communities, such as Ardon-Chamoson and Martigny, were able, despite being subject to the Upper Valais *Landrecht*, to obtain dispensations regarding the law of succession and matrimony. See *Ibid*, p. 128.

54 *Ibid.*, p. 131.

55 Sandro Guzzi-Heeb, *Donne, uomini, parentela. Casati alpini nell'Europa preindustriale (1650–1850)*, Torino, Rosenberg & Sellier, 2007, pp. 243–276.

hereditary divisions[56]. Nonetheless, traces of the agnatic model can still be seen in Lower Valais. There was, in fact, never any true equality between daughters and sons inasmuch as the latter were often given precedence regarding certain goods. For example, the house, or *maison morative*, which was often home to several families, was not usually included in the will since it was automatically given over to the eldest son or passed undivided to all the heirs[57]. As in the case of the *avantagium* in Grisons, the household in Valais also plays an important part in the logic of family reproduction.

Family models and resistance

Undoubtedly, the Italian valleys of the Grisons and Lower Valais are examples of the "diffusion" of juridical culture when regions come into contact. However, with respect to other regions where a change in the political regime did not bring about an equivalent juridical change, we are dealing here with a more specific kind of evolution. The southern areas of alpine Lombardy (corresponding to the present-day Canton Ticino and the province of Sondrio), which became part of Switzerland at the beginning of the sixteenth century, are emblematic examples, for the change in political affiliation of the two regions, and their consequent subordination to, and political dependence upon, the sovereign Swiss cantons, did not lead to any real change of their position within the jurisdiction of the agnatic model, which continued to be their main reference throughout the Modern Era and into the nineteenth century. The persistence of this model is also shown by the local charters of Ticino as well as those of Valtellina and Valchiavenna, which would seem to confirm that the written form of legislative culture resisted the influence of customary law cultural models.

---

56 Jeannine Fayard Duchêne, "Du val d'Anniviers à Sion: la famille de Torrenté des origines à nos jours", in *Vallesia*, 61, 2006, pp. 1–299 (81). On the other hand, it should be pointed out that there was already a tendency towards bilateral inheritance at the end of the fifteenth century in the de Torrenté family. So the way in which Lower Valais belonged to the agnatic area before passing under the control of Upper Valais needs to be re-evaluated.

57 *Ibid.*, p. 79.

This, as D. Albera pointed out, appears to be something of a paradox since on the one hand the charters adopted in the Alps were generally copies of urban models, while on the other they were seen by the rural communities as emblematic of their freedom, their autonomy and their prerogative to govern themselves[58]. In the case of the southern Alpine territories, placed under the control of the Swiss cantons at the beginning of the sexteenth century, this apparent paradox must be read within a system of relations between subjects and rulers which, from a juridical point of view, has no clear defining characteristics. In this regard, P. Caroni has emphasised how it became apparent within the sovereign Swiss cantons that it was not possible to apply a universal approach to the different systems of statutory laws, to the point that they were obliged to implicitly recognise the *potestas statuendi* of their subjects[59]. Thus, the canton of Uri's attempt to introduce inheritance equality between sons and daughters in Leventina met with local resistance, as it was seen as a move on the part of the men of Uri to gain access to the family's wealth (such as dowries) by marrying the daughters of the wealthiest Leventine families[60]. We should, however, keep in mind that charters represent only a small part of all legal procedures, and any area not covered by common law could be dealt with in the regulations drafted by the confederate cantons. This was true for the charters of Bellinzona, Blenio and Riviera, where their subsidiary power was ratified by the regulations of their three sovereign cantons[61]. In other words, the local *jus proprium* did not provide total protection and cracks began to appear in the system, although it is impossible to tell what effects this had on family life.

In the territories of Valtellina, too, legal autonomy was not affected by the power of Grisons, and was confirmed by the charters drawn up in 1531 and 1548–49[62]. Regarding the territories of Ticino, the domination of

---

58   Dionigi Albera, *Au fils des générations, op. cit.,* p. 248.
59   Pio Caroni, "Sovrani e sudditi nel labirinto del diritto", in Raffaello Ceschi (ed.), *Storia della Svizzera italiana Dal Cinquecento al Settecento,* Bellinzona, Ed. Stato del Cantone Ticino, 2000, pp. 581–596 (590).
60   Carlo Pometta, *La successione legittima secondo gli statuti e i codici ticinese,* Lugano, Tipogr. luganese, 1921, p. 14.
61   Pio Caroni, "Statutum. Chiarimenti e prospettiva di ricerca", in *Scrinium,* Locarno, A. Dadò, 1976, pp. 55–72.
62   Diego Zoia, "Gli ordinamenti", in Guglielmo Scaramellini, Diego Zoia (eds.), *Economia e società in Valtellina e contadi nell'Età moderna,* t. I., *Dati, vicende e strutture economiche,* Sondrio, Fondazione Gruppo Credito Valtellinese, 2006, pp. 91–108.

Grisons in Valtellina was characterised by a significant penetration on the part of the Grisons élite into the local economy. Besides acquiring considerable tracts of land, some branches of prominent Grisons families transferred some of their economic and political interests into the area. One of the most visible results of this process was the widespread use of a form of agricultural emphyteutic lease known as the *livello,* under which farmers were granted possession and use of land owned by the Rhaetian and Valtellina gentry. In short, a kind of arrangement spread through Valtellina by this means which was based on dissociated ownership, and which was basically very similar to the one in force in neighbouring Tyrol, with the one difference that it did not lead to the *Bauer* type of domestic organisation found in that area, although transmission practices remained fixed to the agnatic principle and were, therefore, different from those of Tyrol as well as those of Styria and Carinthia. In these regions the governance of estates based on emphyteutic control went hand in hand with the welding of a social pact between the gentry and the *Bauer,* on the basis of a hierarchic model of joint possession[63], whereas in Valtellina there is no such pact and, domestic organisation preserved its typically agnatic nature. So, once again, the transmission of juridical models can give rise to quite different answers in terms of social structure and family organisation.

Conclusions

Far from answering all the questions surrounding the patterns of domestic organisation in the alpine area, the analyses put forward in these pages emphasise the heuristic nature of the internal diversity found in this agnatic area. Such variability can be read according to a "set of scales" which we can use to ascertain different degrees of coherence. At the same time, the variability highlights the complex structure of domestic organisation with regard to a particular pattern of inheritance, and within contexts (settlement, residence, society, economy, …) which in turn are extremely varied.

Besides establishing the "degree" of coherence present within agnatic domestic organisation, the interaction between the legal framework that

---

63   Dionigi Albera, *Au fil des générations, op. cit.*, p. 192.

defines inheritance practices and the social framework in which they take place can shed some light on the transversality of different ideal-types. Indeed, such instances of transversality suggest that the links between political structures, juridical models and forms of domestic organisation do not respond to casual mechanisms, but involve, rather, more subtle dynamics which are still difficult to understand without having recourse to microanalysis.

On a diachronic level, the rationale of the historical continuity shown by forms of organisation in response to the changes in the economic and productive frameworks of their time is still to be determined. To repeat a particularly apt metaphor which was suggested some years ago, the Alps can be described as the "European ceiling" of the agnatic model[64]. It can be considered, in other words, a space where those traits which appear late tend to remain unchanged for longer, far outlasting the social and economic frameworks which generated them. It would, of course, be convenient to trace the issue back to the conservatism and stagnation of alpine societies, but the present study suggests, rather, that agnatic domestic organisation was more persistent in places where the flexibility of hereditary practices allowed for the needs of different political, social and economic configurations of the time to be met.

---

64 Giovanni Kezich, "La soffitta d'Europa", in *Histoire des Alpes – Storia delle Alpi – Geschichte der Alpen*, 7, 2002, pp. 307–317. See also the comments of Pier Paolo Viazzo, *Comunità alpine, op. cit.*, p. 74.

MARGARETH LANZINGER

Patterns of Domestic Organisation: The Transfer of Goods and of Relatives

This paper aims to bring together two research topics which are crucial to any discussion of domestic organisation: transferral of goods and transferral of relatives. Specifically, the first section looks at the significance of marital property regimes, while the second part of the paper will focus on crisis situations caused by the death of a wife/mother. It examines the importance of relatives, particularly that of the sister of a deceased wife, in the context of male widowhood as representing an intersection at which affinal and consanguine relationships converged – insofar as the widower marries an in-law, at the same time an aunt of his children.

This study is based on the gender history of legislative structures, cultures and practices as well as on historical kinship studies. The two areas which we will examine, property regimes and kinship, appear to be closely interconnected, but even if we take this to be true we must still ask how, in practice, this interconnection expressed itself. What were the ideas underlying certain patterns, and what consequences did these patterns have? In the introduction to the volume they co-edited with Jon Mathieu, *Kinship in Europe,* David Sabean and Simon Teuscher propose a new chronology of kinship interactions in terms of "a succession of [...] two distinct major transitions". The first transition "leads from the late Middle Ages into the early modern period and is connected to local variations of the process of state formation and reconfiguration in property holding. The second begins in the mid eighteenth century and sheds new light on the processes of class formation, political modernisation, and the dynamics of capitalist productive relations"[1]. These two transitions are characterised by an important change in European kinship formation: during both the late Middle Ages and the early modern period, we can observe "a tendency

---

1   David W. Sabean, Simon Teuscher, Jon Mathieu, "Preface", in David W. Sabean, Simon Teuscher, Jon Mathieu (eds.), *Kinship in Europe. Approaches to Long-Term Development (1300–1900)*, Berghahn, New York – Oxford, 2007, pp. X–XIII (X).

to develop and maintain structured hierarchies within lineages, descent group, and clans and among allied families". This process "can be associated with an increasing stress on vertically organised relationships", whereas the second transition at the crossroads between the eighteenth and the nineteenth centuries brought about a stronger emphasis "on horizontally ordered interactions"[2]. This process of horizontalisation is characterised by intensified sibling relations and new marriage patterns: studies in this area have shown a considerable increase in first cousin and second cousin marriages[3]. Among the bourgeoisie, the tendency towards endogamous marriages coincides with social homogamy. This concept of two transitions and, at the same time, of two specific settings is very inspiring, and is useful as a framework for thinking about property arrangements, kinship relations and domestic organisation, and, last but not least, about their impact on power relations.

Concepts and approaches

In view of the recent concentration in the field of historical kinship studies on kinship networks extending beyond the household, Dionigi Albera's book emphasises the importance for kinship research of the "organisation domestique" which, he suggests, is a "dimension intermédiaire entre les

---

2   David W. Sabean, Simon Teuscher, "Kinship in Europe. A New Approach to Long-Term Development", in David W. Sabean, Simon Teuscher, Jon Mathieu (eds.), *Kinship in Europe, op. cit.*, pp. 1–32 (3).

3   See Gérard Delille, *Famille et propriété dans le Royaume de Naples (XVᵉ–XIXᵉ siècle)*, Rome/Paris, École Française de Rome, 1985; Ida Fazio, "Parentela e mercato nell'isola di Stromboli nel XIX secolo", in Renata Ago, Benedetta Borello (eds.), *Famiglie. Circolazione di beni, circuiti di affetti in età moderna*, Roma, Viella, 2008 pp. 141–181; Jean-Marie Gouesse, "Mariages de proches parents (XVIᵉ–XXᵉ siècle). Esquisse d'une conjoncture", in *Le modèle familial Européen. Normes, déviances, contrôle du pouvoir. Actes des séminaires organisés par l'École française de Rome et l'Università di Roma*, Roma, École Française de Rome, 1986, pp. 31–61; Raul Merzario, "Land, Kinship and Consanguineous Marriage in Italy from the Seventeenth to the Nineteenth Century", in *Journal of Family History* vol. 15, 1990, n. 2, pp. 529–546; David W. Sabean, *Kinship in Neckarhausen, 1700–1870*, Cambridge, Cambridge University Press, 1998.

liens de parenté et les structures familiales"[4]. Basically, he envisions a third phase in the history of the family as a comparatively intermediate path midway between "the old history of the family" and the new historical anthropology of kinship. At the same time, this third phase is situated on a meso-level between micro and macro perspectives[5]. Albera's study concentrated on a geographical area represented by the alpine region, and focused on domestic organisation, meaning every kind of relationship that is established in connection with cohabitation, production, distribution, transmission and reproduction. The author also places a great deal of emphasis on the legal context, the commons, settlement structures, social relations within villages and rural communities, and local political institutions, all of which are seen as interacting with domestic organisation. The underlying aim of his book is to establish a connection between history and anthropology, with a long-term perspective stretching from the fourteenth to the twentieth century. He defines his comparative approach as "dense, contextuelle, contrôlée et réflexive"[6].

There are clear differences between the concept of two transitions of kinship interaction and formation as developed in the volume *Kinship in Europe* and the third phase in the history of the family as proposed by Dionigi Albera, but there is also a common thread between the two: both approaches aim to integrate a wide variety of broadly contextualised relationships and aspects within the range of their studies. The main "technical" difference lies in their research methods: Dionigi Albera assembles, compares and reinterprets a broad range of studies published over the course of the past few decades, whereas David Sabean and Simon Teuscher formulate a research programme based on recent historical studies. Their programme is meant, first and foremost, "to provoke discussion between different schools of thought"[7]. Albera believes that the concept of two transitions is too generic, and is particularly critical of the first transition from the Middle Ages to the early modern period. He holds that the period of time taken into account is too long, pointing to the emergence

---

4   Dionigi Albera, *Au fil des générations. Terre, pouvoir et parenté dans l'Europe alpine (XIVᵉ–XXᵉ siècles)*, Grenoble, PUG, 2011, p. 7, pp. 47–48.

5   *Ibid.*, p. 49.

6   *Ibid.*, p. 53, p. 472.

7   David W. Sabean, Simon Teuscher, "Kinship in Europe. A New Approach to Long-Term Development", art. cit., p. 2.

of patrilineal tendencies as early as the Late Middle Ages. He also criti-
cises the suggestion of a strong interconnection between agnatic tendencies on the one hand and the succession of a single heir on the other – a
pattern that may well be particularly true of the nobility, the ruling classes
and urban societies. It is true, in fact, that a majority of the studies in the
volume *Kinship in Europe* are dedicated to these social groups rather than
other sections of society, like the rural communities[8] which are central to
Albera's book.

With regard to the second transition, the topics and objectives of both
approaches agree in emphasising the importance of marriage exchange,
patterns of inheritance, the transfer of property and wealth, and kinship relations. Additionally, the theoretical and methodological concepts of David
Sabean and Simon Teuscher have one objective in common with those of
Dionigi Albera: that of overcoming the limitations inherent in the field of
family history studies during the 1970s, centred as it was on typologies
and geographies of household formations (based on population registers,
and above all on *status animarum* records), resulting in over simplified and
excessively formulaic correlations and points of view. This approach, first
introduced by Peter Laslett and other researchers from the *Cambridge
Group for the History of Population and Social Structure,* remained at the
centre of international debate from the 1970s to the 1990s[9]. Studies from
the period tended to portray the family as autonomous, whereas some,
mostly Italian, historians[10] argued for a "relational approach that sees it as
a network of relationships within a constantly changing social context"[11].
Their criticism was, in part, related to the study having been limited to
persons present in the household at a particular moment in time, though
it was also connected to the fact that relationship networks beyond the
household – with neighbours, kinsmen, godparents etc. – were barely recognised or dealt with. As early as 1976 Edoardo Grendi called for a study
of the "reticolo di relazioni", or network of relationships, as an alternative
model to the formal household[12].

---

8   Dionigi Albera, *Au fil des générations, op. cit.,* pp. 44–46.
9   Peter Laslett, Richard Wall, (eds.), *Household and Family in Past Time,* Cambridge,
     Cambridge University Press, 1972.
10   Edoardo Grendi, "A proposito di 'famiglia e comunità': questo fascicolo di Quaderni
     storici", in *Quaderni storici,* 33, 1976, pp. 881–891 (882).
11   Jon Mathieu, *History of the Alps 1500–1900. Environment, Development, and Soci-
     ety,* Morgantwon, West Virginia University Press, 2009, p. 162.
12   Edoardo Grendi, "A proposito di 'famiglia e comunità'", art. cit., p. 883.

My study focuses on the region of South Tyrol, which is why its implicit dialogue with Dionigi Albera's book refers primarily to the chapters in which he speaks of the "peasant type", which is thought to be specific to Eastern Alpine communities,[13] and is one of three ideal types described by the author. Along with the peasant, or *Bauer*, type, his conceptual model also defined the "agnatique alpin" type and the "bourgeois" type[14]. The definition of the former is based on a famous study by John Cole and Eric Wolf, *The Hidden Frontier*[15]. Albera then paints a broader picture with a comparative study looking at other research on Austrian alpine communities. For his analysis of the *Bauer* type, he compares his findings to studies from the Eastern Alps, including South Tyrol, Austria and Slovenia. The characteristics of this type can be summarised as follows: social relations are focused on the farmstead and on the farmer ("*Bauer*") as the political and legal representative of the household; public life and local political issues are addressed mainly to heads of households; the village consists in well-defined farmsteads, often scattered across the landscape and somewhat isolated from each other; the predominant inheritance practice consists in the succession of one single heir, which, Albera states, leads to a decline in the social status of the other siblings, especially the brothers; a *Bauer*'s authority is based on his strong ties with the feudal lord and with territorial power. In terms of power structure and domestic relationships, the *Bauer*-type can be described as vertical, with the *agnatic alpine* type as an open pattern and the *bourgeois* type as a horizontal one.

The transfer of property

Themes of property and wealth have been studied, within the field of family history, mainly by looking at a number of different inheritance models and their consequences. Inheritance law and customs, as well as marital property regimes, had far-reaching effects on access to resources,

---

13 Dionigi Albera, *Au fil des générations, op. cit.,* pp. 83–99, 161–211.
14 *Ibid.*, pp. 152–155.
15 John Cole W., Eric R. Wolf, *The Hidden Frontier. Ecology and Ethnicity in an Alpine Valley*, New York, Academic Press, 1974.

and on marital, familial and other relationship structures[16]. This was particularly true in those places where daughters could inherit from their parents, as opposed to societies with a strict dowry system dictated by Roman
law, where they could not. While the position and agency of women under
the dowry system has been widely studied[17], the consequences of other
marital property regimes for gender, familial and kin relationships have
tended to receive relatively little attention. This is also true for Eastern
Alpine societies. This section looks at how joint and separate ownership
marital property regimes affected the social position of both spouses. Our
observations are based on the results of a comparative analysis between
four different regional, social or legal contexts including Lower Austria
and Tyrol, areas which will be the main focus of our study throughout.[18]

---

16   Susanne Rouette, "Erbrecht und Besitzweitergabe: Praktiken in der ländlichen
      Gesellschaft Deutschlands, Diskurse in Politik und Wissenschaft", in Rainer Prass
      et al. (eds.), *Ländliche Gesellschaften in Deutschland und Frankreich, 18.–19.
      Jahrhundert*, Göttingen, Vandenhoeck & Ruprecht, 2003, pp. 145–166.
17   See for example *Clio. Histoire, Femmes et Sociétés*, 7, 1998, special issue "Femmes,
      dots et patrimonies"; Giulia Calvi, Isabel Chabot, (eds.), *Le ricchezze delle donne.
      Diritti patrimoniali e poteri familiari in Italia (XIII–XIX)*, Torino, Laterza, 1998;
      Ida Fazio, "Le ricchezze delle donne: verso una ri-problematizzazione", in *Qua-
      derni storici*, 101, 1999, pp. 539–550; Simonetta Cavaciocchi (ed.), *La famiglia
      nell'economia europea, secc. XIII–XVIII. The Economic Role of the Family in the
      European Economy from the 13th to the 19th Centuries. Atti della "Quarantesima Set-
      timana di Studi", 6–10 aprile 2008*, Firenze, Firenze University Press, 2009; Barbara
      B. Diefendorf, "Women and Property in *Ancien Régime* France. Theory and Practice
      in Dauphiné and Paris", in John Brewer, Susan Staves (eds.), *Early Modern Con-
      ceptions of Property*, London/New York, Routledge, 1995, pp. 170–193; Martha C.
      Howell, *The Marriage Exchange. Property, Social Place, and Gender in Cities of
      the Low Countries, 1300–1550*, Chicago, University of Chicago Press, 1998; Diane
      Owen Hughes, "From Brideprice to Dowry in Mediterranean Europe", in *Journal of
      Family History*, Vol. 3, 1978, n. 3, pp. 262–296, 1978; Margareth Lanzinger, "Varia-
      tionen des Themas: Mitgiftsysteme", in Margareth Lanzinger, et al., *Aushandeln von
      Ehe. Heiratsverträge der Neuzeit im europäischen Vergleich*, Köln/ Weimar/Wien,
      Böhlau, 2010, pp. 469–492.
18   The book project "Negotiating Marriage" presented a comparative study of marriage
      contracts. It consisted of four detailed studies carried out in different territories and
      covering different models of marital property: community of property, community
      of acquired property and separation of property, and different social classes: rural/
      peasant, artisan, urban/merchant and nobility. The core period encompasses the
      eighteenth and nineteenth centuries. The studies are based on a shared framework
      of research questions and themes. Margareth Lanzinger, et al., Aushandeln von Ehe,
      op. cit.

Our main objective was to examine interconnections between inheritance practices, marital property regimes and power relations between the sexes and across generations. For the purposes of this study, the most important data come from comparisons between rural fiefdoms in Lower Austria, particularly those of Friedau-Weißenburg, an agricultural area which first exhibited preindustrial characteristics in the mid-eighteenth century. Gertrude Langer-Ostrawsky looked at these themes in our joint project, as did my own research on two Tyrolean court districts: Innichen, a court and market town with a strong artisan and trade component, and the Welsberg court district, which covered several villages and valleys, and was of a more rural and agricultural nature, despite the presence of a smattering of artisans and traders. In contrast to most other Austrian crown lands (including Lower Austria) where the preference was for a community of property regime, the marital regime which prevailed in Tyrol was that of separate property. Although impartible succession was customary in both areas, the consequences of the community of property system in Lower Austria differed dramatically from those of the separation of property system in the area of Tyrol covered in our research,[19] and this information proved to be decisive for the interpretations presented in our study.[20]

Marriage contracts constitute a particularly useful source material for understanding the aforementioned distinctions and the impact of marital property regimes, because a significant proportion of wealth changed hands or was negotiated within the context of marriages.[21] Such contracts can also provide us with an idea of how the surviving spouse was

---

19   In some areas of Tyrol the main system involved partible inheritance, while in other areas property was typically passed on to one heir only. See Paul Rösch, "Lebensläufe und Schicksale. Auswirkungen von zwei unterschiedlichen Erbsitten in Tirol", in Paul Rösch (ed.), *Südtiroler Erbhöfe. Menschen und Geschichten*, Bozen, Raetia, 1994, pp. 61–70. The dominant form in Innichen and Welsberg was one of undivided succession with preference given to the eldest son or daughter.

20   The following paragraphs are based on Gertrude Langer-Ostrawsky, "Vom Verheiraten der Güter. Bäuerliche und kleinbäuerliche Heiratsverträge im Erzherzogtum Österreich unter der Enns", in Lanzinger, et al., Aushandeln von Ehe. op. cit. pp. 27–76; Margareth Lanzinger, "Von der Macht der Linie zur Gegenseitigkeit. Heiratskontrakte in den Südtiroler Gerichten Welsberg und Innichen 1750–1850", in *ibid.,* pp. 205–326.

21   With regard to the economic relevance of marriage, see Erickson Amy Louise, "The Marital Economy in Comparative Perspective", in Maria Ågren, Amy Louise Erickson (eds.), *The Marital Economy in Scandinavia and Britain 1400–1900*, Aldershot, Ashgate, 2005, pp. 3–20.

provided for after the death of their husband or wife. Formal agreements like marriage contracts and intergenerational property transfers, or contracts agreed between an heir and his widowed mother, can also reveal the presence of potential sources of tension and conflict, and provide a picture of the opposing parties in such conflicts, such as a widow against her deceased husband's relatives, or children from a former marriage against their stepfather, or simply a battle between children and their surviving parent, especially their mother. Marriage contracts stipulated the inheritance claims of a couple's offspring as well as giving instructions on the entitlements of the surviving spouse and how they were to be provided for. The contracts also specified the entitlements of the next of kin and outlined the arrangements to be made for reserved property (*Vorbehaltsgut*), assets that had been kept outside of the conjugal fund. Differences in the transferral and management of property and wealth had particularly pronounced effects on the positions of widows and widowers, as well as on children as heirs and, in a broader sense, on wider kinship.

The two territories being compared in our study each had quite different manorial systems, but they also shared common traits. In both territories we find peasants working on the land, and we find the landlords who owned it and passed it on through the hereditary system that had developed during the Middle Ages. Peasants were free to sell or bequeath their property as long as they managed their farms competently and paid their fees and duties. In Lower Austria, the rights of peasants were limited; they were obliged to seek permission from their landlords to leave the region or district or to marry, and to submit all contractual agreements including sales, donations and marriage to the seigneurial offices. This tightly controlled system has provided us with a large body of documentation pertaining to all social groups, in the seigneurial archives of Lower Austria[22]. The material includes thousands of marriage contracts, which even the poorest prospective husbands and wives were required to produce. In Tyrol, on the other hand, peasants were free, tenure of land did not involve subjugation to a landlord, only the obligation to pay fees and taxes, and there was no legal obligation to create written marriage contracts. Couples were free to decide whether or not they wished to document their prenuptial agreements by writing them down in court.

---

22 Helmuth Feigl, *Die niederösterreichische Grundherrschaft*, St. Pölten, Verein für Landeskunde von Niederösterreich, 1998[2], pp. 49–50.

As mentioned above, the principle of impartible succession of a single heir or heiress predominated in both territories.[23] There was no legal discrimination against daughters in either territory and they had the same entitlement as males to inheritance and succession, although in practice daughters took over the tenant farm or the trade only if there was no male heir or if her brother was either uninterested or incapable of running the farm or trade. In practice, therefore, access to property via intergenerational inheritance was distributed unequally between men and women.

The impact of different marital property regimes

The concept of community of marital property prevalent in Lower Austria meant that marriage led to a joint and indivisible estate.[24] The marital couple held all property in common ownership, and both their names were entered into the land register (*Grundbuch*). This common ownership took no account of the respective amounts contributed by the bride or the bridegroom[25]. Neither spouse could sell or otherwise dispose of any part of the property without the agreement of their partner. Both shared fully in the legal obligations of their spouse, meaning that a wife bore full responsibility for any risk or debt incurred by her husband. This kind of marital property regime generally meant that the partner who married into the estate came to occupy a powerful position irrespective of their gender or of the value of their contribution to the marriage.

---

23 The Archduchy of Lower Austria did not possess a uniform legal framework until the Josephine Civil Law Code of 1786. Before that the prevailing system had been one of customary law, the *Landsbrauch*, which dated back to the Middle Ages. In Tyrol the legal basis for property claims made before 1786 was the sixteenth-century *Tiroler Landesordnung* (Tyrolean Law Code) in its final version of 1573.

24 In certain cases – for example, where a remarriage involved a significant age gap and/or difference in social status between spouses – a partial community of property system was followed, under which only a part of the assets of one or both spouses became jointly owned.

25 Wilhelm Brauneder, *Die Entwicklung des Ehegüterrechts in Österreich. Ein Beitrag zur Dogmengeschichte und Rechtstatsachenforschung des Spätmittelalters und der Neuzeit*, Salzburg, München, Fink, 1973.

With the separation of marital property system, prevalent in the rural areas of Tyrol, the opposite was true: marriage had no impact on the property rights of either spouse, and whatever wealth they brought to the union was kept separate throughout the marriage. Nonetheless, during the early modern period a husband had the right to access and manage the dowry, or marriage portion (*Heiratsgut*), and all other property owned by his wife. The partner who married into the estate – in most cases the wife – tended to occupy a position of weakness that was dependent on the value of their contribution to the marriage. The right to purchase half of the property afforded primarily in-marrying men the opportunity to improve their social position – but limits were applied to the right of property succession, especially for the children of a subsequent marriage and for his own relatives[26].

In Lower Austria the community of property regime meant that the surviving spouse, regardless of sex, was entitled to one half of the joint patrimony, while the other half was to be divided equally between the surviving spouse and their children. In any case, the widow or widower was entitled to a majority share of the family's property, allowing them to occupy a rather strong position. Remarriage was, as a result, quite common, and could even lead to a number of successive remarriages. In practice this led children from previous marriages to lose any claim to their parent's estate. In addition they were usually expected to accept postponement of their portion of the inheritance, sometimes for many years and generally until they themselves married. This system clearly benefitted surviving spouses, and subordinated the interests of children and other relatives to those of the household rather than favouring the deceased's lineage. Furthermore, the portion that children did inherit was for the most part rather small[27].

The opposite was true for the Tyrolean system of separation of marital property. Marriage was not intended to result in the permanent transferral of money or property from one line to another, thereby interrupting the paternal line of descent. If a husband brought a house or a farm into the marriage (as was often the case, though by no means always), his property

---

26   Margareth Lanzinger, "Paternal Authority and Patrilineal Power: Stem Family Arrangements in Peasant Communities and Eighteenth-Century Tyrolean Marriage Contracts", in *The History of the Family*, Vol. 17, 2012, n. 3 pp. 343–367.

27   Gertrude Langer-Ostrawsky, "Vom Verheiraten der Güter. Bäuerliche und kleinbäuerliche Heiratsverträge im Erzherzogtum Österreich unter der Enns", art. (art.) cit. pp. 27–29, 72–75.

did not, upon his death, pass to the widow, but to one of the children. The Tyrolean court districts included in this study tended to give precedence to the male offspring of the first marriage, with peasant societies in particular specifying that the successor should be the eldest son. If no children survived, a close relative was designated as heir or heiress; a nephew or niece, for example. The *Tiroler Landesordnung* (Tyrolean Law Code) of 1573 stipulated that the wife's personal wealth (her contribution to the marriage and her part of the inheritance, etc.) was to be paid to her immediately on the death of her husband. She had no legal right to maintenance (*Leibzuchtrecht*), and was entitled for one year only to room and board in the household of her husband's family. Nonetheless, it must have been difficult in practice to ensure that widows received the wealth that they had contributed to the marriage. For this reason marriage contracts appear to have contained an alternative solution: the so-called *Herberg,* something like a rent-free lodger who could claim the right to subsistence and the use of the kitchen and garden and other basic necessities. This arrangement allowed a woman's wealth to remain part of her deceased husband's property. The *Herberg* model was an arrangement almost exclusively intended for widows, whereas widowers were granted lifelong access to the wealth of their wives.

By the end of the eighteenth century there was a marked shift towards mutual access to the entire wealth of both husband and wife. A widow who had obtained right of usufruct did not become owner of the property, but neither was she required to withdraw to the *Herberg*[28]. A widow's usage of her husband's wealth brought with it the obligation to provide for the upbringing and education of their children. The widow, for example, was obliged by the terms of the marriage contract to: "obtain for the children the necessary nourishment and clothing, see to it that they learn to read, write and do arithmetic, and that the boys learn a trade, and the girls sewing, so that they will be capable of earning their bread."[29] The usufructuary model could, at times, give rise to tensions, particularly when adult children were involved, since it obstructed their chances of inheriting the property. Many

28 Margareth Lanzinger, "Women and Property in 18th Century Austria. Separate Property, Usufruct and Ownership in Different Family Configurations", in Beatrice Moring (ed.), *Female Economic Strategies in the Modern World*, London, Pickering & Chattoo, 2012, pp. 145–159.

29 Tiroler Landesarchiv (TLA) Innsbruck, Verfachbuch Innichen (VBI) 1784, fol. 708–708'.

marriage contracts, therefore, placed limits on mutual usufruct in cases
where the couple had children. The surviving spouse's usufructuary rights
were to last only until the children had reached a certain age – in most
cases 18, 20 or 24 years: "Fourthly and lastly, both spouses would like
to promise each other lifelong usufruct of their respective wealth in such
a way that it should cease only if children be present, and should in this
case last only until all children have reached the age of 18."[30] Moreover,
widows were faced with the loss of their usufruct or maintenance rights in
the case of remarriage. As a result, the remarriage rates of widows were
particularly low. The legal position of widowers who had once married
into a household (*einfahrende Gesellen*) was similarly weak, although in
practice they benefitted from more comprehensive rights of usufruct and
purchase options.

As shown by the preceding comparison, the feuds of Lower Austria
and the two Tyrolean court districts shared the same general principle of
inheritance, that of impartible succession, but the legal systems governing
the transfer of property and wealth during and after marriages were at opposite ends of the scale. Inheritance practice and marital property arrangements did, in fact, influence each other, and they were tightly intertwined.
In this way, the two different marital property regimes each developed their
own dynamics and rationale within one and the same inheritance model.
Consequently, power structures and, particularly, conflict dynamics were
not determined solely by inheritance practices, but also by marital property practices. Marital property relationships played a decisive role in the
distribution and transfer of property; they affected relationships between
generations, and also profoundly shaped gender relations because such
property relationships revolved around marriage (like in Lower Austria) or
the line of descent (like in Tyrol). Our study found that property appears to
be a more significant factor than gender. Property and power took a more
horizontal form in Lower Austria, while in Tyrol they followed a rather
vertical orientation. In contrast to those of Lower Austria, marital property
customs and laws in Tyrol generally gave precedence to the husband and
to the children of the first marriage. In this way agreements documented
in marriage contracts not only secured and protected the patrimony which
a woman contributed to the marriage, but they also provided for the widow's needs after the death of her husband. At the same time, they served

---

30   TLA Innsbruck, VBI 1795, fol. 354.

to guarantee a thoroughly "dynastic" style of lineal succession.[31] Are we dealing here with the *Bauer* type? First of all, it is important to stress that each community presents us with a broad and diverse array of transfers, ownership structures, property arrangements and usage agreements stipulated between prospective spouses and, in some cases, between their parents, with contexts varying according to social, economic, or marital status, gender, etc.[32] Aside from the transferral of goods, another revealing area of investigation is related to the importance of consanguineous and affinal relatives.

The presence of relatives

From the findings presented in John W. Cole and Eric R. Wolf's study, *The Hidden Frontier*, on kinship as a support network in the context of the labour market, we learn that: in the German-speaking village of St. Felix in South Tyrol, kin were employed only to a limited extent, selectively, and in exchange for immediate compensation, while in the neighbouring Ladin-speaking Tridentine village of Tret, the authors observed a continuous reciprocity between relatives, which also allowed for temporary one-way exchanges. Cole and Wolf make reference to a concept suggested

---

31 Indeed, changes did take place in the nineteenth century, but the main features outlined here tend to have continued or even to have been reinforced. This continuity, especially among the peasantry, of *ancien régime* inheritance practices and marital property regimes into the nineteenth century had been enshrined in law. The *Josephinisches Gesetzbuch* of 1786 (the General Civil Code published under Emperor Joseph II), like the General Civil Code of 1811, defined the separation of goods as the default marital property regime. Under Joseph II, a special inheritance law for the peasantry was promulgated which established the legal successor as the oldest son, although subsequently a more relaxed approach had to be taken in areas with different, deep-rooted, traditions.

32 Margareth Lanzinger, "Marriage Contracts in Various Contexts: Marital Property Rights, Sociocultural Aspects and Gender-specific Implications. Late-Eighteenth-Century Evidence from two Tirolean Court Districts", in *Annales de démographie historique*, 1, 2011, pp. 69–97 (75–76).

by the anthropologist Marshall Sahlins[33], and speak of two models – one of "balanced reciprocity" and another of "generalised reciprocity" – placing them in the context of a variety of inheritance practices and their consequences[34]. In St. Felix the predominant inheritance custom was that of undivided succession, which in Cole and Wolf's view led to a "monolithic family" consisting of the main heirs and property owners, while in Tret partible inheritance was the most common form, along with a "segmented" family-type, characterised by dependencies amongst the inheriting siblings.[35] According to these findings, diverse patterns of kinship relations would also depend on different forms of organisation within the household and on the resulting differences in inheritance practices and property structures.[36]

Much merit should be given to the two anthropologists for their analysis of kinship relations and how they affected daily life. Naturally, their results (obtained from research carried out in the field) describe the situation as it was in the 1950s and 60s, and there are obvious limitations when applying them to past societies. Studies on the importance and dynamics of kin relationships – in the Anglo-Saxon and German academic worlds, unlike in France and Italy did not appear until the mid-1990s. Nonetheless, other suitable source material can be found through an understanding of day-to-day household organisation practices in order to reveal how relatives may have acted as a social network[37].

---

33 Marshall Sahlins, "The Sociology of Primitive Exchange", in Michael Banton (ed.), *The Relevance of Models for Social Anthropology*, London, Tavistock, 1965, pp. 139–236.

34 John W. Cole, Eric R. Wolf, *The Hidden Frontier, op. cit.*, p. 169f.

35 The dependence of the siblings not paid out (as well as of their descendants) who had immigrated to South America, was expressed, for example, through the fact that property was only allowed to be sold or mortgaged with the agreement of all involved. Decisions were therefore easily blocked.

36 On this basis, moreover, varying degrees of ties to markets and external relationships of different strengths could have an influence on the what kinds of relationships were established with relatives and in-laws. See Gérard Béaur et al. (eds.), *Familles, Terre, Marchés. Logiques économiques et stratégies dans les milieux ruraux (XVIIe–XXe siècles)*, Rennes, Presses universitaires de Rennes, 2004.

37 Jon Mathieu, „Ein Cousin an jeder Zaunlücke". Überlegungen zum Wandel von Verwandtschaft und ländlicher Gemeinde, 1700–1900", in Margareth Lanzinger, Edith Saurer (eds.), *Politiken der Verwandtschaft. Beziehungsnetze, Geschlecht und Recht*, Göttingen, V&R Unipress, 2007, pp. 55–71; David W. Sabean, *Kinship in Neckarhausen, op. cit.*

When speaking of the *Bauer* type, Dionigi Albera describes relationships based on kinship and neighbourhood as altogether not very consistent[38]. Sandro Guzzi-Heeb, reviewing Albera's book, sees problems with an approach that evaluates the social importance of relatives according to the formal structures involving marriage alliances and descendants: "en simplifiant un petit peu, dans le type Bauer la dévolution suit un modèle dynastique, donc seule la descendance est importante, la parenté élargie n'étant pas très influente du point de vue social».[39] He cites, as an example, the highly regarded study on the inhabitants of Gévaudan and environs by Élisabeth Claverie and Pierre Lamaison. This community also favoured a single heir, although this was in connection with bilateral succession – similar to Albera's *bourgeois* type. Bilateral kin relationships, within this formal structure, are supposedly more important than any other, but Claverie and Lamaison, conversely, observed high levels of competition and rivalry between the two *maisons*. In such situations relatives played a key role in establishing an equilibrium: they were decisive in creating solidarity and in mediating conflicts[40]. If, then, we can describe kinship as a network, then it must be assumed that the extent and kinds of practices that took place within this network of relatives by blood and by marriage could be highly varied.

Another look at the comparisons between premarital agreements in the two Tyrolean courts of Innichen and Welsberg and those in certain seigneuries in Lower Austria reveals the important position held by relatives in Tyrol, which is particularly true of nephews and nieces of childless couples. They also show a distinct difference between the two areas regarding the frequency of relatives' physical presence in court and/or at the manorial office. In Lower Austria the bride and bridegroom usually attended the signing of the contract alone, with no other family members formally present, an arrangement that may be connected to the fact that the majority of newlyweds set up their own household. The contracts did have to be signed by witnesses for both parties, but the names of these

---

38   Dionigi Albera, *Au fil des générations, op. cit.*, p. 153.
39   Sandro Guzzi-Heeb, Review: Albera Dionigi, "Au fil des générations. Terre, pouvoir et parenté dans l'Europe alpine XIVᵉ-XXᵉ siècles)", in *Schweizerische Zeitschrift für Geschichte / Revue suisse d'histoire / Rivista storica svizzera*, vol. 63, 2013, n. 1 pp. 165–169 (168).
40   Élisabeth Claverie, Pierre Lamaison, *L'impossible mariage. Violence et parenté en Gévaudan, 17ᵉ, 18ᵉ et 19ᵉ siècles*, Paris, Hachette, 1982.

witnesses suggest that they were not closely related to the married couple. In addition, women in Lower Austria were not subject to guardianship (*cura sexus, Geschlechtsvormundschaft*) during the early modern period, meaning one less reason for the involvement of relatives. In Tyrol, on the other hand, there were a number of pretexts for the involvement of relatives, particularly that of fathers and brothers. This could be the case when the marriage contract was part of a more comprehensive agreement that also affected the circumstances of fathers, mothers, uncles and aunts; or when either one of the spouses moved to a different community as a result of the marriage. Legal requirements also came into play, for example in the rather rare cases when the bride or bridegroom were underage, but more often in the context of guardianship over women. The role of guardian was usually assumed by fathers, brothers or close relatives, rather than important members of the local community.[41] These latter, or paternal uncles can be seen acting as guardians to children whose widowed mothers were remarrying, representing their interests before the court as well as those of their paternal lineage. Generally, the presence of relatives in court could be motivated by a wish to supply guidance, support and assurance, but might just as well stem from the exercise of power and control, though, could similarly be seen as expressing a social relationship of belonging[42].

The transfer of relatives

Domestic organisational structures were marked by a certain amount of competition between different groups with conflicting interests regarding property arrangements and the transfer of goods. We also find evidence of

---

41   See TLA Innsbruck, VBI 1783, fol. 364; fol. 477'; fol. 528'; *Ibid.,* VBI 1784, fol. 693'; fol. 698; fol. 703; fol. 706'; *Ibid.,* VBI 1785, fol. 1'; fol. 34.

42   See TLA Innsbruck, VBI 1780, fol. 493–494. In his book on Valais, Sandro Guzzi-Heeb examined cases showing very large delegations of relatives at the conclusion of marriage contracts. A marriage contract from 1664, for example, was signed by "decine di famigliari", or "dozens of relatives" (Sandro Guzzi-Heeb, *Donne, uomini, parentela. Casati alpini nell'Europa preindustriale (1650–1850)*, Torino, Rosenberg & Sellier, 2007, pp. 152–154). Margareth Lanzinger, "Paternal Authority and Patrilineal Power" art. cit., pp. 350–353.

a pacifying influence from those who attempted to bring about an agreement between the opposing parties[43]. As well as being a fertile terrain for conflict, kinship can also provide a support network in times of crisis. Another type of source document, the marriage dispensation application, allows us to define relatives as making up a social network of the 'exceptional normal' variety, to use a term coined by Edoardo Grendi[44]. These documents do not represent ordinary marriages, since such dispensations were required to allow a wedding to take place between couples who were related within the fourth degree of affinity or consanguineity, as such a union was usually forbidden under canon law. Marriages of this kind, which had to be approved by the Pope, naturally left more evidence in the archives than other more straightforward weddings. Despite their exceptional nature, they provide useful information on the overall structural aspects and the different varieties of domestic organisation. My study is based on an analysis of marriage dispensation applications relating to the closer degrees of affinity and consanguineity between prospective spouses in the diocese of Brixen, which included large parts of old Tyrol and Vorarlberg, covering the period between 1831 and 1890.[45] Applications for papal dispensation were not strictly formal documents, as noted disparagingly by André Burguière[46], but they often contain detailed descriptions of the situation in question and the arguments put forward by applicants, giving us an intimate glimpse of a certain aspect of family life, although it must be remembered that these are a highly strategic kind of document.

---

43 Margareth Lanzinger et al., "Étude comparative des antagonismes et des stratégies de compensation: dispositions en faveur de conjoints, enfants ou parents dans les contrats de mariage de différents espaces juridiques aux XVIIIe et XIXe siècles", in *Austriaca. Cahiers universitaires d'information sur l'Autriche*, 69, 2009, pp. 13–42.

44 Edoardo Grendi, "Micro-analisi e storia sociale", in *Quaderni storici*, 35, 1977, pp. 506–520 (512).

45 This material has been studied alongside other examples from the neighbouring dioceses of Chur, Salzburg and Trento. See Margareth Lanzinger, *Verwaltete Verwandtschaft. Eheverbote, Dispenspolitik und Dispenspraxis 1780–1890*, Böhlau, Wien/Köln/Weimar, 2015. The research project was financed by a Hertha Firnberg Postdoctoral Fellowship (2005 to 2007) and an Elise Richter Postdoctoral Fellowship (2008 to 2011) granted by the Austrian Science Fund (FWF).

46 André Burguière, using French source material from the eighteenth century, notes that the arguments presented in these documents are primarily stereotypical, and are closely aligned with official *canonical reasons*. See André Burguière, „Cher Cousin": les usages matrimoniaux de la parenté proche dans la France du 18e siècle", in *Annales. H.S.S.*, Vol. 52, 1997, n. 6., pp. 1339–1360 (1346f).

Dispensation records show patterns of social and spatial proximity between consanguineous and affinal relatives at a household level: proximity tended to be a result of shared working environments, where relatives were employers or housekeepers, servants, carers, day labourers, etc., of other relatives. In addition, we find young or middle-aged women joining the household of their married sister or aunt, often after the birth of her first child, or to help out in the family business. Family members and close relatives, then, were figures of trust and were influential both in terms of work and of mobility. They guaranteed better treatment of invalid parents and sick or disabled siblings, and we often come across the assertion that a relative was a better carer than a 'stranger' could be. It was often to relatives that one turned in times of hardship, like financial difficulties and other domestic crises.

This support became particularly important when one of the spouses died young, for example in childbirth or after an illness or accident, tearing a young man or woman away from their family. A sister, cousin, or niece of the deceased wife, or a brother of the deceased husband would have been present in the household to care for or support the family during a period of illness or after a death. The support of in-laws could be crucial for both the widower and for the widow. Sisters-in-law and cousins, etc., worked mostly as housekeepers and assumed a position of some responsibility within the household. Several documents mention relatives working as housekeepers or servants, who were often willing to work for low wages or even without being paid. Some of them even invested their own small savings to support the household if it faced a precarious financial situation. It is much less common to see a deceased husband's male relative running a farm or a business in the widow's household than it is for a deceased wife's female relative to be seen running the widower's household and caring for other family members. Again and again these dispensation requests made explicit reference to 'blood ties' as a way to guarantee particularly close and reliable relationships characterised by a caring regard for the welfare and education of nephews and nieces, selfless participation in family affairs, etc. Those who were not blood relatives, 'strangers', were seen in a negative light: a maidservant who was a 'stranger' was depicted as 'unreliable', and stepmothers were characterised as 'wicked'.

Extended cohabitation ran the risk of being seen as morally questionable by neighbours and local clerics, meaning that marriage was often a practical and obvious solution. However, papal policy on dispensation had become more rigid, and hardly any marriages of this kind between first-degree affinal relatives were approved in the 1830s and 1840s. Added to this was the high financial cost of papal dispensations. These factors contributed to the particularly dramatic situations described in source documents related to repeated attempts to obtain approval for these kinds of union. We find a particularly high incidence of requests for marriages between a widower and his sister-in-law in the German speaking world, far higher than that, for instance, in Mediterranean countries. Domestic organisation in response to a crisis caused by bereavement, therefore, came to represent the point at which affinal and consanguine relationships became highly important, at the same time, especially in cases where there were small children to be cared for. Upon closer examination, we find that many dispensation requests portray their households as inhabited by consanguineous and affinal relations extending beyond the nuclear family and, at the same time, pointing to a wider network.

Conclusion

The transferral of both goods and of relatives took place within a structure that was influenced by a patrilineal and/or lineage-based rationale. This was the case not only in the early modern period, but also during the nineteenth century. However, it is also important to consider other axes of influence that interacted and interfered with the predominant, vertically oriented line. This applies to marital property regimes as well as to kinship relations, which could also be horizontally organised[47]. So in order to trace and reveal the situated interplay, we should conceptualise domestic organisation as highly interlaced social processes, and examine them with a multi-perspective approach. Multiperspectivity is a concept of society that is not based on rigid, schematic structures, and instead recognises variety and decentralisation, various options for actions, and informality in social relationships. We do, therefore, need to employ microhistory as a research method.

---

47   Elisabeth Joris, "Kinship and Gender: Property, Enterprise, and Politics", in David W. Sabean, Simon Teuscher, Jon Mathieu (eds.), *Kinship in Europe, op. cit.*, pp. 231–257 (242f).

SANDRO GUZZI-HEEB

The Uses of Kin. Kinship, Social Networks and Identities in the Swiss Alps (Eighteenth-Nineteenth Centuries)

Structure, Networks and Identities in the History of Kinship

The role and function of kinship have been subjected to a certain amount of critical revision over the past two decade[1]. Comprehensive research projects have demonstrated that kinship structures are not a historical constant, and have revealed a very different picture. A highly stimulating recent publication by Dionigi Albera proposed that kinship organisation in the Alpine region could be divided into three fundamental types. Although the author sees specific models as being made up of a wide range of variables, he focuses fundamentally on structural characteristics, like alliances and devolution, which thought of as representing the foundation of social organisation[2]. In this regard, Albera puts forward and reconceptualises the "hidden frontiers" proposed by John Cole and Eric Wolff, where structural

---

1   See for example Franco Ramella, *Terra e telai. Sistemi di parentela e manifattura nel Biellese dell'Ottocento*, Torino, Einaudi, 1984; Giovanni Levi, "Family and Kin – a few thoughts", in *Journal of Family History* 15, 1990, pp. 567–578; Gérard Delille, *Famille et propriété dans le Royaume de Naples (XVIᵉ–XIXᵉ siècle)*, Paris et Rome, Ecole française de Rome, 1985; Martine Segalen, *Quinze générations de Bas-Bretons; parenté et société dans le pays bas-bigouden sud 1720–1980*, Paris, P.U.F., 1985; Osvaldo Raggio, *Faide e parentela. Lo stato genovese visto dalla Fontanabuona*, Torino, Einaudi, 1990; Barry Reay, "Kinship and the Neighborhood in Nineteenth-Century Rural England: The Mith of the Autonomous Nuclear Family", in *Journal of Family History*, vol. 21, 1996, n. 1, pp. 87–104; David W. Sabean, *Kinship in Neckarhausen, 1700–1870*, Cambridge, Cambridge University Press, 1998; Janet Carsten (ed.), *Cultures of Relatedness. New Approaches to the Study of Kinship*, Cambridge, Cambridge University Press, 2000.
2   Dionigi Albera, *Au fil des générations. Terre, pouvoir et parenté dans l'Europe alpine (XIVᵉ-XXᵉ siècles)*, Grenoble, PUG, 2011.

distinctions are made between different types of social organisation in the Alpine region[3]. From a methodological point of view, however, rules of devolution and alliance structures in rural societies are not the same as the practice and form of kinship networks; thus the relationship between structure and process, or between structure and social practice, cannot be taken for granted but must be studied and interpreted with caution.

With a new focus on the high rate of marriages between cousins and between kin in general, David Sabean proposed that a major transition took place in the history of kinship during the eighteenth and nineteenth centuries, resulting in a "kinship hot society" in Western Europe[4]. Sabean's affirmation implies the presence of a network-level phenomenon in so far as it suggests that, on the whole, kinship relations increased at this time: in his analysis of "*Vetternwirtschaft*" as a political topic, and in studying individual cases, Sabean makes a more explicit case for the presence of this phenomenon. His central thesis, however, rests largely on structural factors like alliance patterns and, above all, the spectacular increase in marriages between close relatives.

The evidence of a profound structural change in the nature of kinship during this period is confirmed by further studies, some of which were carried out in the Alpine area, which is also the subject of this study[5]. This interpretation, however, has recently been contested. On the basis of sources from Westphalia, Christine Fertig has argued that the numerical

3   John Cole, Eric Wolf, *The Hidden Frontier: Ecology and Ethnicity in an Alpine Valley*, New York, Academic Press Inc., 1974.

4   David W. Sabean, *Kinship in Neckarhausen, op. cit.*; see also David W. Sabean, Simon Teuscher, Jon Mathieu (eds.), *Kinship in Europe: Approaches to the Long-Term Development (1300–1900)*, New York and Oxford, Berghahn Books, 2007; François-Joseph Ruggiu, "Histoire de la parenté ou anthropologie historique de la parenté? Autour de Kinship in Europe", in *Annales de Démographie historique*, 1, 2010, pp. 223–256.

5   Dionigi Albera *Au fil des générations, op. cit.*; Jon Mathieu, "Verwandtschaft als historischer Faktor. Schweizer Fallstudien und Trends, 1500–1900", in *Historische Anthropologie* 10, 2002, pp. 225–244; Sandro Guzzi-Heeb, *Donne, uomini, parentela. Casati alpini nell'Europa pre-industriale (ca. 1650–1850)*, Torino, Rosenberg & Sellier, 2007; Jon Mathieu, "'Ein Cousin an jeder Zaunlücke'. Überlegungen zum Wandel von Verwandtschaft und ländlicher Gemeinde, 1700–1900", in Margareth Lanzinger, Edith Saurer (eds.), *Politiken der Verwandtschaft. Beziehungsnetze, Geschlecht und Recht*, Göttingen, V&R Unipress-Vienna University Press, 2007, pp. 55–71; Luigi Lorenzetti, Raul Merzario, *Il fuoco acceso. Famiglie e migrazioni alpine nell'Italia d'età Moderna*, Roma, Donzelli editore, 2005.

increase in cousin marriages could simply be the result of a demographic evolution that made alliances between related persons statistically more likely[6].

Fertig's criticism is important for a quantitative, structural analysis of alliances, but her arguments are not relevant to the qualitative transformations that several authors have identified as taking place during the eighteenth and nineteenth centuries. Some recent publications have attempted to bring the discussion forward by studying actual cases or with theoretical reflections on kinship, anthropology and history[7]. As it stands today, however, the debate is still characterised by a lack of theoretical precision regarding the concepts used, often leading to a fatal confusion between kinship *structures* and kinship *networks*. Kinship structures can be defined as formal patterns of alliances and relatedness within a defined group (for example the high statistical rate of "cousin marriages" or, say, of cross cousin marriages); kin networks, on the other hand, indicate more fluid patterns of informal social relations between kin, including a wide range of social interaction or cooperation. Kinship networks, then, must be seen as a part of wider social networks[8].

---

6   Christine Fertig, *Familie, verwandtschaftliche Netzwerke und Klassenbildung im ländlichen Westfalen (1750–1874)*, Stuttgart, Lucius & Lucius, 2012; cf. Guzzi-Heeb, *Donne, uomini, parentela, op. cit.*, pp. 347–351.

7   Dionigi Albera, *Au fil des générations, op. cit.*; David W. Sebean, Simon Teuscher, Jon Mathieu (eds.), *Kinship in Europe, op. cit.*; Joseph-François Ruggiu, "Histoire de la parenté", art. cit.; Simon Teuscher, *Bekannte – Klienten – Verwandte. Soziabilität und Politik in der Stadt Bern um 1500*, Köln, Weimar, Wien, Böhlau, 1998; Gérard Delille, "Réflexions sur le 'système' européen de la parenté et de l'alliance", in *Annales H.S.S.*, 2, 2001, pp. 369–380; Bernard Derouet, "Parenté et marché foncier à l'époque moderne: une réinterprétation", in *Annales H.S.S.*, 2, 2001, pp. 337–368; Jon Mathieu, "Verwandtschaft als historischer Faktor. Schweizer Fallstudien und Trends, 1500–1900", in *Historische Anthropologie* 10, 2002, pp. 225–244; Sandro Guzzi-Heeb, *Donne, uomini, parentela, op. cit.*; David W. Sabean, Christopher H. Johnson (eds.), *Sibling Relations and the Transformation of European Kinship 1300–1900*, New York-Oxford, Berghahn Books, 2011; Michael Mitterauer, *Historische Verwandtschaftsforschung*, Wien/Köln/Weimar, Böhlau Verlag Wien, 2013.

8   See for example, Stanley Wasserman, Katherine Faust, *Social Network Analysis: methods and applications*, Cambridge, Cambridge University Press, 1999; Emmanuel Lazega, *Réseaux sociaux et structures relationnelles*, Paris, P.U.F, 2007²; Vladimir Batagelj, Andrej Mrvar, Wouter de Nooy, *Exploratory social Network analysis with Pajek*, Cambridge, Cambridge University Press, 2005. On kinship, family and networks, see Claire Lemercier, "Analyse de réseaux et histoire de la famille: une rencontre encore à venir?", in *Annales de démographie historique* (numéro spécial

From this point of view, Sabean's book shares a certain ambiguity with recent studies by Albera and others in that they all speak about complex transitions in time, encompassing important changes both in kinship structures and in the nature of kin-centred social networks. I believe that three different spheres should be carefully defined. Two are of a *structural* nature:

1. An increase in the number of marriages between blood relatives, a phenomenon which could be observed in different parts of Europe;
2. A qualitative reorientation of alliances and social cooperation which at the end of the early modern period were, for example, moving away from a somewhat agnatic and vertical rationale towards more cognatic and horizontal preferences. This evolution implies the presence of a structural as well as a network-based context, since an evaluation of agnatic or cognatic tendencies is not based on the study of kinship patterns alone, but also takes account of social and economic interactions.

Another is related to networks:

3. The increasing importance for kin of social relations was referred to by Sabean with what has now become a well-known term, the "kinship-hot" society. This network context is probably the most difficult to define and to analyse; from this point of view it is not surprising

---

Histoire de la famille et analyse de réseaux), 1, 2005, pp. 7–31; John Padgett, Christopher Ansell, "Robust Action and the Rise of the Medici, 1400–1434," in *American Journal of Sociology*, 98, 1993, 6, pp. 1259–1319; Juan Luis Castellano, Jean-Pierre Dedieu, *Réseaux, familles et pouvoirs dans le monde ibérique à la fin de l'Ancien Régime*, Paris, CNRS, 1998; Michel Bertrand, "De la familia a la red de sociabilidad", in *Revista Mexicana de Sociología,* vol. 61, 1999, n. 2, pp. 107–135; Cyril Grange, "Les réseaux matrimoniaux intra-confessionnels de la haute bourgeoisie juive à Paris à la fin du XIXe siècle", in *Annales de démographie historique* (numéro spécial *Histoire de la famille et analyse de réseaux*) 1, 2005, pp. 131–156; Carola Lipp, "Kinship Networks, Local Government and Elections in a Town in Southwest Germany, 1800–1850", in *Journal of family History*, vol. 30, 2005, n. 4, pp. 347–365; Douglas R. White, Thomas Schweizer (eds.), *Kinship, Networks and Exchange*, Cambridge, Cambridge University Press, 1998.

that Sabean's definition, along with those of more recent studies, is less precise and open to a great deal of confusion with structural elements[9].

The problem is that the majority of studies tends to draw conclusions on social networks basing only on kinship structures, implicitly adopting a structuralist point of view without verifying, for instance, whether an increase in marriages between cousins is actually an indicator of an equivalent increase in the importance of overall social relations between relatives. In fact, a substantial increase in "cousin marriages" in different Europeans societies does not automatically mean that such alliances are socially more important than other interactions such as, for instance, class solidarity or professional cooperation. In the Alpine regions of which I will speak in this paper, kinship during the eighteenth and nineteenth centuries was (or became?) a fundamental factor in local conflicts, influencing the emergence of political factions and parties; this was despite the fact that the role of close cousin marriages remained rather marginal and their frequency, as in the Valley of Bagnes, decreased after 1750[10]. Spiritual kinship and political identities seem to be just as influential in forming political networks as biological kinship[11].

From another point of view, the theme of kinship identities is a very important, although somewhat neglected, factor. In 1980 Peter Laslett published an influential article on the history of illegitimacy: Laslett described how a tendency for illicit sexual intercourse could be observed in certain families, tending to create a "bastardy-prone sub-society". With

---

9   According to Sabean and Teuscher, for example, cousin marriages form the basis of dense social networks and milieus, but the relationship between social structures and the nature of social networks is not defined with precision. David W. Sabean, Simon Teuscher, "Introduction", in David Warren Sabean, Simon Teuscher, Jon Mathieu (eds.), *Kinship in Europe, op. cit.*

10   In Bovernier, kin marriages up to the 3rd degree of consanguinity and 1st of affinity represented 3.5% of all marriages in the eighteenth century and 14.4% in the nineteenth century according to our database (see footnote 12). In Liddes they represented 3.34% in the eighteenth century and 11.4 % in the nineteenth century.

11   Sandro Guzzi-Heeb, "Spiritual Kinship, Political Mobilization and Social Cooperation: A Swiss Alpine Valley in 18th and 19th Century", in Guido Alfani, Vincent Gourdon (eds.), *Spiritual kinship in Europe, 1500–1900*, Houndmills (Basingstoke), Palgrave Macmillan, 2012, pp. 183–203. Of course, we could see spiritual kinship as being another formalized structure; nevertheless, it remains partly independent from alliance and devolution.

this concept, Laslett and and his co-author Karla Osterveen shed light on the problem of social or cultural continuities within close kin groups, like the transmission of values and attitudes through kinship ties. Through this image of a particular sub-society, Laslett implicitly evoked the network-related aspect of kinship which was also implicit in the concept of the milieu proposed by Sabean and Teuscher. Unfortunately, this approach was not very popular among historians of the following generations, despite the fact that the transmission of values and identities was clearly within the scope of classical family history studies.

Thus, "cousin marriages", or the transformation of formalised kinship structures in general, are only one of many indicators of the social role of relatedness. In order to understand its true significance for social life, we need to analyse at least three different aspects of the kinship network:

1. The different social practices between relatives and the concrete use of kinship networks; what exactly are the consequences of the growth in the importance of kinship relationships? Which concrete relationships were changing and, perhaps, increasing between the eighteenth and the nineteenth century?
2. The role of the kinship network as a social group in which behaviour patterns, values and identities are, to a certain extent, shared and transmitted to the following generations. In this sense we could say that kin groups play a cultural role as units that promote solidarity, cooperation and identity, although they can also be subject to divisions and conflicts.
3. To what extent can such kinship networks be seen as a foundation for wider social or political networks? A debate on the importance of kinship relations always implies an evaluation of non-kin relations as well as of the interaction between these intertwined groups.

From this point of view, the study of social cooperation and conflict in everyday life will shed more light on the social relevance of kinship. Such an analysis, however, is only possible at a micro-historical level, because kinship relations need to be laboriously reconstructed using local genealogical data mostly derived from local parish records[12]. My paper will

---

12 Since 1975 a group of six researchers has been working on classifying all available information on the families in the community with the help, above all, of parish registers dating from between 1639 and 1900. For the Val de Bagnes, we have detailed information on 25,000 baptisms, 10,000 deaths and about 8,000 marriages.

focus on Alpine communities in Western Valais (Switzerland), for which we can rely on extremely detailed genealogical databases (Map 1).

The uses of kin: which kind of network?

Many authors in the field of social history assume that a kinship tie is a social relation *per se*, but this is not the case[13]. We all have kin we do not know, or with whom we have no contact. In this sense only *active* kinship is socially relevant, or kinship between relatives who know and interact with each other[14].

The problem, here, is one of identifying which kind of relationships link relatives together and what kind of network they build. Pierre Bourdieu, in his study of a Kabyle community, distinguished between *official* kinship and *everyday* kinship (*parenté officielle* and *parenté usuelle*), suggesting different ways of using the kin network. Bourdieu's distinction is important, as it shows how different kinds of networks can be built on the basis of kinship. All the same, I believe that it is necessary to define the different kinds of social networks more carefully by specifying the different ways one can make use of one´s relatives, forming networks which are largely independent of the underlying alliance structure.

The research was carried out under the authority of the Centre d'études des populations alpines (CREPA) in Sembrancher (Valais), and their findings were published in Maurice Casanova, Jean-Michel Gard, Alfred Perrenoud, *Familles de Bagnes du XIIe au XXe siècle. Généalogie, histoire, étymologie, armoiries*, 5 vol., Le Châble, Commune de Bagnes, 2005–08. CREPA has, in the meantime, produced similar genealogies for other villages in the area, like Bovernier, which have been integrated into a larger database, the "Répertoire historique de la population du Valais" (RHPVS).

13 I will not linger on the important discussion about biological kinship and kinship as a cultural construction: cf. Janet Carsten (ed.), *Cultures of Relatedness, op. cit.*; Sylvia Yanagisako, "Bringing It All Back Home: Kinship Theory in Anthropology", in David W. Sabean, Simon Teuscher, Jon Mathieu (eds.), *Kinship in Europe, op. cit.*

14 Pierre Bourdieu, "La parenté comme représentation et comme volonté", in Pierre Bourdieu, *Esquisse d'une théorie de la pratique, précédée de trois études d'ethnologie kabyle*, Paris, Seuil, 2000, pp. 83–187.

I will attempt to illustrate this problem with a concrete case. In the small village of Bovernier (Valais) in the Swiss Alps, the notary Jean-Léonard Bourgeois drew up a series of contracts between 1791 and 1793 which reveal the existence of a dense kinship network centred on the Florin, Pont and Rebord families, including Claude Florin, an important member of the community council during the republican era (1798–1803). Marriage contracts and other documents show that there was close cooperation between individuals and families on the basis of heritage, transactions and mutual help: a set of social and economic interactions embedded in a kinship network structured around the families of four sisters belonging to the Pont family (Fig. 1).

Fig. 1: Economically interdependent kin group.

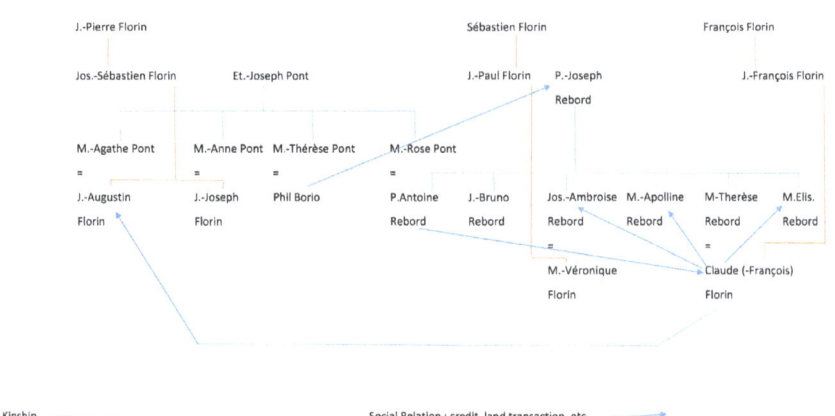

These kinds of close interactions constitute a group we can define, though not very elegantly, as the *economically interdependent kin group* of Claude Florin: most transactions within this network can be explained by the fact that its members have inherited or will inherit from others belonging to the same network and share economic interests with them.

Often, economic interdependence and close relatedness justify very important social interactions which, within an even closer group, I would define as *"primary kinship"*, meaning the tightly interconnected group of kin on which one relies for primary necessities, for instance if young children are left orphaned by the death of both parents they would need to be raised and educated by relatives[15]. Detailed information about these kind of interactions is available particularly from families of the local elite: I have studied, for example, the primary kinship relationships in the family of Charles-Emmanuel de Rivaz, a prominent local politician between 1790 and 1830, where maternal cousins played a crucial role, substituting the absent parents of young related children[16]. In this sense, primary kinship depends largely on structural factors, which in the case of our study were above all bilateral devolution patterns, that encourage close relations with maternal kin and in-laws.

However, primary kin are not automatically the same relatives as those who can be solicited in search of political or, more generally, strategic support. The aforementioned Claude Florin was also a member of the new republican elite which took control of the communal council in the 1790s and during the republican era. In this role he cooperated closely with other relatives, and with spiritual kin, especially with affines (blood relatives of his wife) not belonging to his "primary" or interdependent, kinship. In this case it is possible to speak of Florin's "*strategic kinship*" to describe related persons able to provide political or strategic support in order to achieve a goal[17] (Fig. 2).

---

15 Sandro Guzzi-Heeb, "Close Relatives and Useful Relatives. Welfare, Inheritance and the Use of Kinship in an Alpine Dynasty (1650–1800)", in David R. Green, Alastair Owen (eds.) *Family Welfare: Gender, Property and Inheritance since the Seventeenth Century*, Westport-USA, Grenwood, 2004, pp. 97–120.

16 Sandro Guzzi-Heeb, *Donne, uomini, parentela, op. cit.*, pp. 107–137.

17 The history of local political and religious conflicts between 1796 and 1806 reveals the existence of a fundamentally different cooperation network around the figure of Claude Florin; primary kinship is influential rather than crucial from this point of view, and well-to-do relatives play a central role. We could define other types of cooperation between kin, like that involving "instrumental kin" who provide practical support with work, administration, or the practical needs of individuals or families. Cf. Sandro Guzzi-Heeb, *Donne, uomini, parentela, op. cit.*, pp. 79–103.

Fig. 2: Relations between the Republican officers of Bovernier, 1792–1806.

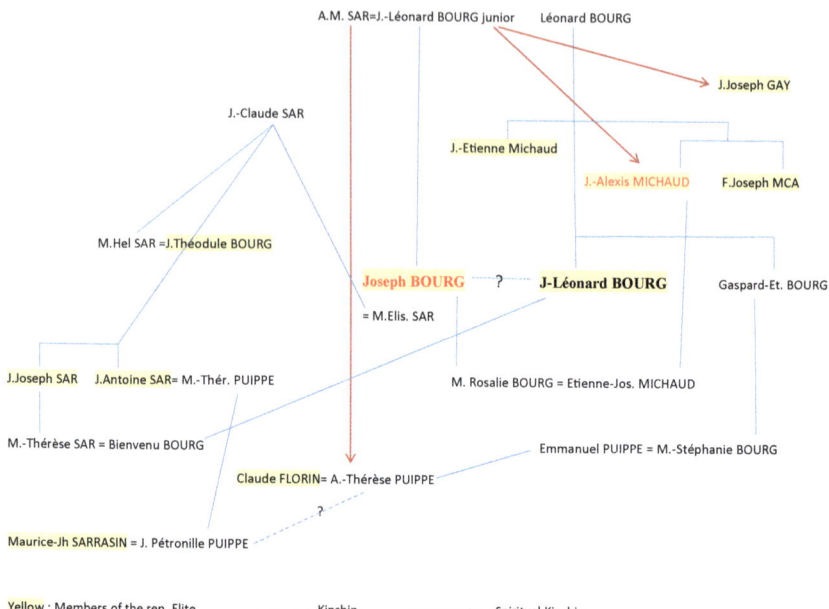

Two provisional conclusions are important at this point: the first is that relationships between kin can be part of very different networks, and it is crucial to analyse the nature of the relationship in order to formulate conclusions on the nature of their influence. The second conclusion is that kin networks are partly if not entirely, independent of alliance structures. In particular, strategic and instrumental kinship are not automatically determined by household or kinship structures, but rather by the wider social networks to which one attains through social interactions. The hidden structural frontiers between different types of household organisation and devolution patterns do not automatically determine different kinds of networks. In order to unravel the mechanisms of alliance and kinship reproduction we must study a concrete example, analysing the political, social and religious conflicts that shape the lives of the individuals involved.

Alliance and kinship: the political factor

In 1806, Nicolas Cavé, the parish priest of Bovernier (Map 1), was forced to temporarily leave his parish, a small village in the Entremont region of the Swiss Canton of Valais.

Map 1: Valais, Bovernier, Bagnes.

Over the previous 10 years relations between the community and the priest had become increasingly tense: the civil authorities contested the money due to the parish, attempted to free themselves from church control and to administer the village school and parish property autonomously. Similar conflicts took place during the same period in other nearby parishes under the influence of the French Revolution and the creation of the Helvetic Republic in 1798 under pressure from French troops. Documentary sources of the time contain clear references to Republican ideas on the role of the clergy, education, and culture, as well as to questions of popular culture like dancing.

What is interesting for our study is the way social networks can shape opposing groups and factions. Nicolas Cavé himself named his bitterest adversaries, prominent among whom were **Joseph Bourgeois**, officer (*métral*) of the hospice of Grand St-Bernard until 1797 and then member of the Republican municipality and **Jean-Léonard Bourgeois**, President of the municipality from 1798 to 1806. The documents written by Cavé mention several other local officers who were in conflict with him, providing us with a very clear picture of the republican authorities at that time[18]. If we look at kinship as well as at godparenthood relationships between these men and their families, we quickly see that they form a dense network around the powerful "métral" Joseph Bourgeois, and Jean-Léonard Bourgeois (Fig. 2)[19].

We must, as a result, recognise the presence of a republican, anticlerical, faction, identifiable in a dense network which, since the 1790s, had been cooperating with the aim of reorienting the political direction of the community. We can see the same phenomenon at work in the larger neighbouring community of Bagnes where a similar, reform-minded, communal elite took power at the end of the eighteenth century. Its members were the protagonists of a faction which had opposed the local feudal lord, the Abbot of Saint-Maurice, throughout the eighteenth century[20]. In Bagnes, family and descent shaped local factions and ensured their long term continuity, although there was certainly no increase in the number of marriages between cousins at this time.

This comparison is interesting because we know that Bovernier became an openly radical community in the second half of the nineteenth century, and in 1856 another bitter conflict broke out with the priest. It is true, in fact, that the anticlerical network that appeared during the Republican era would have a clear influence on the rise of anticlericalism and radicalism in nineteenth century Valais. From this point of view, kinship as a social network contributed to the continuity and stability of political

---

18   Specifically, Cavé names J.-Théodule Bourgeois, the communal Church goods manager in the years 1798–99, Jean-Alexis Michaud, mayor (syndic) 1796–97, Jean-Joseph Sarrasin, who held several communal offices; J.-Antoine Sarrasin, mayor 1802–03, Maurice-Jh Sarrasin, as well as Claude Florin, J.-Joseph Florin, J.-Emmanuel, François-Joseph et J.-Etienne Michaud, J.-Baptiste Terrettaz, all members of the Republican municipality. I omit some other individuals because the degree of their involvement in the struggle is unclear. Archives de la paroisse de Bovernier (APBo), C1-C14.

19   According to our genealogies (Database RHPVS), these two wealthy men were not related, but the two groups seem to have been close socially and politically.

20   Sandro Guzzi-Heeb, *Passions alpines. Sexualité et pouvoir dans les montagnes suisses (1700–1900)*, Rennes, Presses universitaires de Rennes, 2014.

factions, although inter-cousin marriages also remained relatively rare in the nineteenth century and, as we will see, they mostly occurred in a particular social and ideological context.

In Bovernier the tensions between the local population and the clergy did not come to an end after the "Restoration" of 1815. On the contrary, there were regular conflicts even after the arrival of Pierre-Daniel Abbet as parish priest in 1817. On various occasions the priest complained about the local population, saying that adults were working on Catholic holidays, that they did not attend Sunday mass, and that the children were "impudent and impious" (*effrontés et impies*)[21]. Like his predecessor, he wanted to prohibit dances which were, he believed, opportunities for unruly and sinful behaviour. In the 1830s conflicts arose around the election of the local schoolmaster and the introduction of mixed classes for boys and girls at the school; as we have seen, teaching at the school had been a bone of contention since the republican era[22].

Nonetheless, the political context was changing rapidly. A large liberal-radical movement grew up in the canton of Valais during the 1830s and obtained a majority of the seats in the Cantonal parliament in 1839. The region of Martigny and Entremont was at the core of this evolution: at this time radicals controlled the local administrations of several communities or represented strong and very active minorities. Several sources provide useful information about the composition and the development of an influential radical movement in Bovernier. For the year 1844 we can rely on membership lists of the radical association "Young Switzerland" (*La Jeune Suisse*), mostly made up of militant young men inspired by the ideas of the Italian agitator Giuseppe Mazzini. In 1847 the community faced yet another serious conflict with the priest, Pierre-Daniel Abbet, when forty-one men signed a petition urging the local authorities to petition for the replacement of the priest, refusing to contribute to his upkeep or that of the parish church.[23] Several members of "Jeune Suisse" had signed the letter. As far as we know, Abbet remained in Bovernier during the following years, but tension still remained high. In 1857 a new petition, this time

---

21   Jean-Marc Michaud, *Histoire de la paroisse de Bovernier*, Sierre, Ed. à la carte, 2005, pp. 103–108.
22   *Ibid.* pp. 103–105.
23   "Pétition des ressortissants de Bovernier pour obtenir le remplacement du curé Abbet". 17.12.1847. Archives d'Etat du Valais (AEVS), Sion, DI 6.8, Bovernier, N. 10.

signed by seventy men of the community, urged the Bishop to withdraw the parson and his servant from the village, threatening to look for a Protestant replacement if their request was not satisfied. The petition was successful and, after a difficult interregnum, Bovernier got its new priest.

Although seventy men represented a substantial proportion of the community's male population (we counted 76 households and 373 inhabitants in 1864), they did not represent all of the families in the village. This, thanks to the aforementioned documents, means that we can distinguish between radical families and those who did not support the petitions or who supported only one of them. In fact, since we know the names of the militant radicals, as well as those of some conservatives, we are able to investigate to what extent it is possible to observe familial continuities within the factions, and to what extent the nineteenth century radicals were the descendants of the republican, anticlerical elite active during the years 1796–1806. In order to perform a more detailed analysis, however, we must define the different genealogical and kin groups present in the village, as in Table 1[24].

We should, however, be careful when doing this because some branches are larger than others. The groups Bourgeois 2 or Michaud 1A, for instance, gave huge support to the radical faction, but not all men belonging to these groups signed the radical petitions of 1847 and 1857, for whatever reason. Hence, we must try to estimate the "radical intensity" of the various groups by calculating what proportion of all males known to be alive in 1857 is represented by individuals who participated in radical actions at the time of the second anticlerical petition. This can only be an estimate, because dates of death are not always available. Despite this uncertainty, the table shows not only that the "degree of radicalism" was very different from one group to another, but we can also distinguish between clearly radical kin groups and conservative ones, whereas other kin groups were not politically homogeneous.

---

24   We can do so thanks to the genealogical database produced by CREPA, the RHPVS (cf. footnote 10).

Tab. 1: Radical "intensity" of selected kinship branches. Radical activists in 1844, 1847 and 1857 as a percentage of all men of the same branch known to be alive in 1857.

Political orientation	Branches with more than one man known to be alive in 1857						% of radical males
radicals	Puippe /1B	Florin /1A	Sarrasin /2	Rebord /1B	Michaud /1A	Arlettaz /1A	51–100
	Bourgeois /1	Bourgeois /3	Rebord /0				
mixed-rad.	Dely /1B	Michaud /1B	Bourgeois /2	Florin /1B			35–50
mixed-consv.	Dely /1A	Gay /1A	Aubert /3	Sarrasin /4	Rouiller /1		20–34
conserva-tives	Gay /1B	Arlettaz /1B	Bourgeois /5	Chambovey /1	Terrettaz /1A	Pellaud /1A	0–19

This table enables us to distinguish four groups of branches, according to the political orientation of their members: in those cases where 51–100% of all active men were radicals, we can speak of clearly radical branches; between 31–50% can be described as mixed branches with an important radical component; between 20–30% denotes mixed, rather conservative branches; and from 0 to 19% can be seen as representing conservative branche[25]. Among the larger groups, with the sole exception of Rebord/1B, the radical families were descendants of republican men involved in the conflict with the parish priest. The seven most prominent republican branches constituted the bulk of the radical faction in the nineteenth century. We can underscore the crucial role of the influential Bourgeois 1 and 2 groups, going back to Joseph and J.-Léonard Bourgeois at the beginning of the nineteenth century, as well as of the Michaud (1A and 1B, descendent of Alexis Michaud) and Sarrasin 2 groups, who played a leading role in the years 1796–1806; the Florin 1 group (descended from the aforementioned Claude Florin) also played a significant role. These kin groups seem to have represented the core of an anticlerical, reform-oriented, faction in Bovernier from the 1790s until the second half of the nineteenth century.

---

25 However, we must be careful with regard to the smallest branches, where only one male is known to have been alive in 1857, including the Aubert 1, Sarrasin 1 and 3 and Fournier 1: in these cases ranking is dependent on the individual choices of one (or two) persons.

Radical and conservative networks

Long term continuities in families can easily be detected in the patrilineal line, through which the name and a certain collective identity are passed down, but these factors are not absolute; it is, in fact, crucial to consider the evolution and restructuring of kinship networks over time. The radical network that we examined above suggests that kin groups belonging to the same political circles tended to form privileged alliance networks. In the case of Bovernier, we can attempt an analysis of such alliances within the families of the young adherents to the radical "Young Switzerland" movement in 1844.

We see, for example, that nearly all spouses from Bovernier originated from the same branches as the radical activists; in other words the radical "Young Swiss" married into the same kin groups to which they themselves belonged (especially Michaud 1A)[26].

Fig. 3: The network of Young Switzerland.

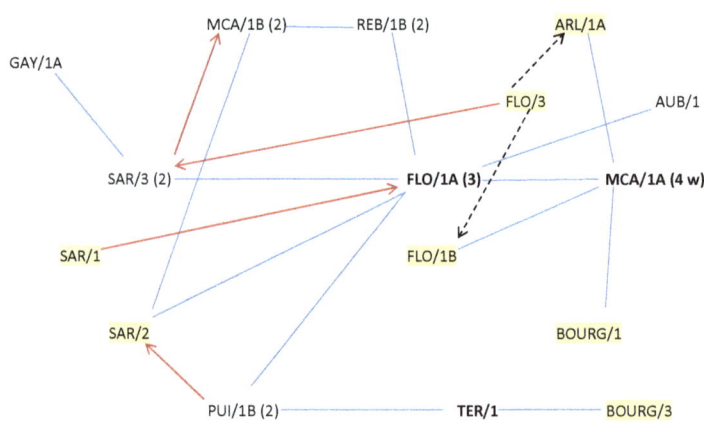

Yellow: one member of the group belongs to Young Switzerland (YS);   Turquoise: more than one member of the group belongs to YS

———— Alliance

———→ Mother →   - - - -→ Father's mother

---

26 This group is fairly wide, but the main relationships of the radical faction are concentrated within the families of Joseph-Clément Michaud and his uncle, Cyprien (the two men were virtually brothers-in law as well, as we will see, since they had had children with two sisters, Anne-Madeleine and Anne-Rosalie Maillard).

From a network point of view (Fig. 3), the Florin Group was evidently at the core, with seven links: this is the group that stretches back to Claude-François Florin, who was involved in the conflict with the parish priest in 1806. The same is true for the other central groups, especially the Michaud 1A-group. Radical activists built a privileged political network or a radical faction. This picture confirms what we already knew from Bagnes: the members of a radical faction show a strong tendency to marry the close relatives of other radicals or to marry into the same families[27].

Kinship, spiritual kinship and social groups

Family and kinship history have often focused strongly on alliances as a basic structure of relatedness. But the network-building role of alliances should not be overestimated: alliances do not always have the same significance and the same social consequences.

In fact, godparents can represent politically stronger allies than blood relations or in-laws; in the Alps, spiritual kinship seems to be extremely important as a channel for political solidarity. In Bagnes, spiritual kinship had a clear political nature: radicals tended to choose godparents for their children who belonged to other radical families, and conservatives chose from their own politically allied families[28].

In Bovernier the godfathers and godmothers of radical activists do not appear to have played any significant network building role. More important in this respect are the godparents of the activists' children, who were the men and women with whom the radical activists actively established social relations. Let us consider those who were chosen by the radical *Jeune Suisse* as godparents for their children. In many cases the spiritual kin were relatives, but most of them were not: in 80 out of 109 baptisms at least one of the godparents has no recognisable kinship tie with the parents of the baptised child.

---

27 Sandro Guzzi-Heeb, *Passions alpines, op. cit.*, pp. 155–163.
28 *Id.*, "Spiritual Kinship, art. cit.; see also Guido Alfani, *Padri, padrini, patroni. La parentela spirituale nella storia*, Venezia, Marsilio, 2006; Françoise Héritier-Augé, Elisabeth Coupet-Rougier (éds.), *La parenté spirituelle*, Paris, Ed. des Archives contemporaines, 1995.

From a merely quantitative point of view, spiritual kinship does not seem to have played a crucial political role; but if we look at it in the context of networks, we observe that many non-related godparents provided a significant link to radical groups. Godparents from the Michaud/1A group provide, for example, a link to other radical families, like the Michaud/1B group, the Arlettaz/1, the Rebord/1B and the Florin/1B; godparents from the Borgeois/2 branch to the Borurgeois/3, Puippe/1B, and Rebord/1B. Spiritual kinship built a social bridge between politically allied families.

In order to obtain more significant results, we can compare this network to families from the same generation who did not belong to the radical network, for whom we observe significant differences in the orientation of spiritual kinship. The main groups of this conservative network are Bourgeois/5, Aubert/1; Sarrasin/4, Pellaud/1, Rebord/1A and Puippe/ 1A; interestingly, the great majority of masses held in the parish church during the nineteenth century was sponsored by these families[29].

The spiritual kinship network of these conservative families was much more restricted than that of radical families – a pattern which depends partly on a tendency for frequent alliances between close relatives; the few exceptions to this rule, like alliances with the radical branch Florin/1A, were established before 1830 when political allegiances had not yet become polarised.

In summary, not only alliances, but spiritual kinship too were essential factors in the construction of a coherent radical milieu after 1830, although close cousin marriages were rare. It is not the alliance structure within the kinship group which matters, but the social relationship with active and spiritual kin.

Political Milieus and Sexuality

In the second half of the nineteenth century a particular phenomenon can be observed in Bovernier: eight cohabiting couples bore several children before or out of marriage, living together for several years without

___

29   APBo, 15 and 17.

being married. Other men and women had several illegitimate children, (probably) with different partners.

Open cohabitation was highly unusual in this deeply Catholic region. We do not find significant evidence of this phenomenon in other communities of the region until the twentieth century. In this regard we can presume that cohabitation was a strong indicator of popular radicalism, or at least of popular dissent, in the countryside. In fact, the majority of the eight unmarried mothers and fathers were closely related to core radical branches:

Tab. 2: Unmarried couples in Bovernier and kinship.

n	unmarried mother	unmarried father	branch mother	branch father	mother's mother
1	ARL-AUBERT, Marie Brigitte	GROSS, Francois	ARL/1	**ex**	ARL/1
2	ARL-AUBERT, Marie Joseph	MATHEY, Pierre Joseph	ARL/1	**ex**	?
3	ARL-AUBERT, Marie Joseph	CHAMBOVEY, Joseph Daniel	ARL/1	CHAMB/1	ARL/1
4	BOURGEOIS, Marie Helene	DELY, Louis Emmanuel	BOURG/1	DELY/1	FLO/3
5	GAY, Adeline	REBORD, Francois Joseph	GAY/1AB	REB/1B	SAR/2
6	GAY, Marie Louise	BOURGEOIS, Louis Gaspard	ex	BOURG/2	ex
7	PELLAUD, Marie Rosalie	ROUILLER, Etienne Valentin	PLA/1	ROU/1A	MCA/1A
8	TERRETTAZ, Valerie	SARRASIN, Jerome Louis	TER/1A	SAR/2	(f)MCA/1A

yellow: core radical branches

ex: foreigners

The case of the Aubert-Arlettaz women is unique, because these unmarried mothers were all related to Thérèse Arlettaz (born 1789), who had an illicit relationship with J-Joseph Aubert; Thérèse was cousin to several nineteenth century radical men.

For the other unmarried couples, one of the parents was closely related to at least one radical activist: here it is possible to highlight the crucial role played by the Bourgeois-group (/1and /2) as well as that played by

Sarrasin/2, which I have already highlighted as core radical groups. Furthermore, other illicit couples were closely related to core radical groups like Michaud/1A through their mothers or their grandparents. The list of unmarried parents includes direct descendants of the Republican leaders Joseph and Jean-Léonard Bourgeois, as well as close relatives of members of the Young Switzerland movement, like the Rebord brothers and Maurice Arlettaz. In other words, illegitimacy in these kin groups was no coincidence, it was an expression of social and political dissent.

But what is the nature of this social group? It is interesting to examine the social network of the unmarried couples, starting with spiritual kinship: who were the men and women willing to act as godparents to children consciously conceived out of wedlock? The sources leave us in no doubt: our analysis showed the existence of a strong solidarity network between and around unmarried couples, which included other radical families. Around half of the godparents in question were chosen among close relatives, but many interesting relationships were established between families who were not closely related.

Fig. 4: Spiritual kin of unmarried couples in Bovernier, 1845–1900 (Branches).

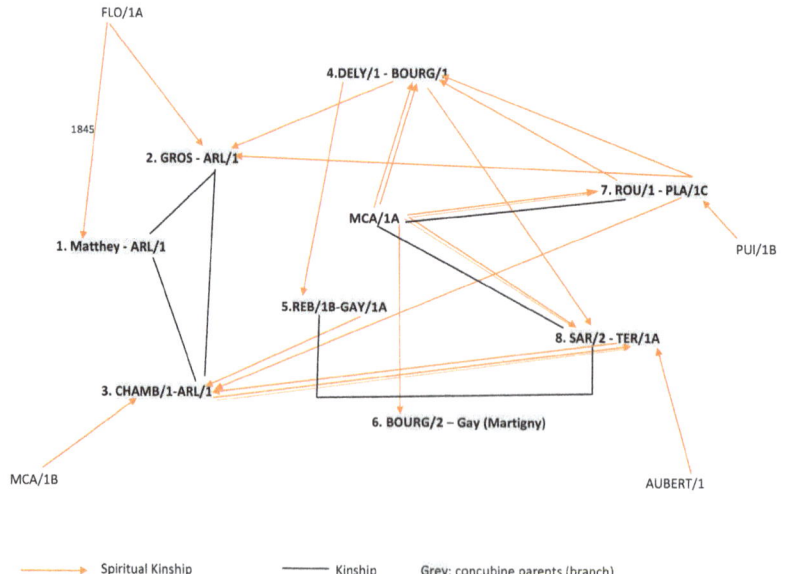

As we can see in fig. 4, the network is strongly interconnected; only couple 2, the first to live together out of wedlock, is slightly separate. The chronological factor is important: before 1870 the solidarity network did not yet exist; unmarried parents were forced to choose kin or strangers as godparents for their children. After 1875 the network began to take shape, and local solidarity networks tied the families of the unmarried parents together, including a few radical groups like the Michaud/1A (related to several unmarried men and women) Florin/1A, Puippe/1B, Michaud/1B.

The best men and bridesmaids at the weddings of these couples generally came from the same groups. The Michaud/1A group, however, had a central role, just like at the time of the *Jeune Suisse*: this group, and particularly the family of Joseph-Clément Michaud, appears at the core of the radical faction from the 1840s, although none of the family belonged to Young Switzerland and the group as a whole was not one of the most radical.

This pattern raises an interesting question: did the sexual and family lives of the local elites and activists have any influence on their political positions?

Previous research focused on the neighbouring valley of Bagnes suggests that a tendency towards illicit sexual relations was clearly linked with the development of criticism against the Church, later with open anticlericalism and radicalism. Was this the case in Bovernier and other regions? Unfortunately, historical kinship and network studies have rarely paid attention to the sexual variable; even studies based on systematic genealogical data and the reconstruction of kinship networks did not make sexuality a focus of their analyses[30].

Obviously, when dealing with sexuality in past societies we are confronted with substantial methodological problems in that we only have fragmentary information to rely on. Nevertheless, local studies exploiting systematic genealogies could shed new light on the influence of kinship in the transmission of sexual attitudes and identities.

With regard to networks, illegitimate children are not interesting as such, but as a symptom of an underlying sexual attitude within the kin group. It is, in fact, quite evident that illicit relations are concentrated within particular branches or kin groups, forming what Peter Laslett and

---

30   For ex. David W. Sabean, *Kinship in Neckarhausen, op. cit.*; Dionigi Albera, *Au fil des générations, op. cit.*; Christine Fertig, *Familie, verwandtschaftliche Netzwerke und Klassenbildung, op. cit.*

Karla Osterveen called a *"bastardy-prone sub-society"*. We can approach the problem in Bovernier by looking at the 40 branches that are found residing in the village throughout the whole of the nineteenth century. 50% of all confirmed illegitimate parents (78) originated from only eight kin groups: I counted the parents and not the children so as to take account of unmarried mothers and maternal lines as well.

Tab. 3: Unmarried parents and kin groups in Bovernier (1700–1900).

Name	Branch	Illicit. Rel.	Political orientation
Sarrasin	SAR/2	11	core radicals
Michaud	MCA/1A	10	core radicals
Arlettaz	ARL/1	7	core radicals
Bourgeois	BOURG/2	6	mixed with strong radical component
Bourgeois	BOURG/1	6	core radicals

Although illegitimacy was a widespread phenomenon in nineteenth century Bovernier, the five branches with the highest number of illegitimate children were core radical groups or mixed groups with an important radical component component (Tab. 3).

These were not only marginal impoverished groups, as Laslett suggests, Bourgeois/1, Michaud/1A and Sarrasin/2 belonged to the village elite and held important local offices; some of their members were notaries, mayors and presidents of the community, other men from these families were well-to-do members of society.

Can we be sure that illegitimacy was connected to the spread of radicalism in Western Valais? Evidence from the neighbouring community of Bagnes suggests that the correlation is significant. Of the twenty-six families with the highest number of visible illicit relations (i.e. illegitimate children and prenuptial conceptions) in this valley, at least seventeen were core radical families, and some others are politically mixed. The nineteen groups we can identify as belonging to the radical core are responsible for over 63% of all illegitimate births in nineteenth-century Bagnes. The figures for Bovernier are less exhaustive, because we have as yet been unable to quantify prenuptial conceptions there, but an interesting picture does appear.

As mentioned above, the case of the Arlettaz women is an unusual one; their connections to radical elements are less close than they are in the other branches. Other core radical groups, like Florin 1A or Sarrasin 3, however, include a smaller number of illegitimate children; but the interesting element of these cases, is the close kinship between illicit parents and radical activists (up to the 2nd degree). A closer analysis shows that most Young Switzerland radicals, for example, could count illegitimate children within their close kin group, even though illicit relations in their wider branch were not always particularly common.

Table 3 highlights once again the structurally central role of sexual attitudes within particular family traditions, especially within the leading kin-groups of the Republican era, namely Bourgeois/1 and /2, Michaud/1 and Sarrasin/2, …. These groups seem to be at the center of anticlericalism and sexual and political dissent throughout the late eighteenth and nineteenth centuries. From this point of view, family traditions formed the basis for specific political, religious and sexual identities which influenced the shape of social networks but were not closely dependent on kinship structures or devolution patterns.

The function of "cousin marriages": kinship, love and politics

Before reaching the conclusion of this paper it is important to touch upon the question of the function of "cousin marriages", which David Sabean and his collaborators identified as the most important indicator of a "kinship hot" society[31]. Were close kin marriages a general structuring social factor, or were they the consequence and the manifestation of close political and sexual interactions?

Alexis Michaud, who according to our sources was the protagonist of the first sexual scandal in Bovernier in 1793, had an illicit affair with his cousin, Elisabeth Sarrasin[32]. Surprisingly, many of the alliances between close relatives involved illicit sexuality to some extent: the case

---

31   David W. Sabean, *Kinship in Neckarhausen, op. cit.*; David W. Sabean, Simon Teuscher, "Introduction", in David Warren Sabean, Simon Teuscher, Jon Mathieu (eds.), *Kinship in Europe, op. cit.*

32   We are able to systematically detect close kin marriages in our database thanks to PUCK (Program for the Use and Computation of Kinship data), an interesting software which allows us to analyse different types of alliance patterns in a genealogical corpus. Further information can be found at www.kintip.net.

of Joseph-Clément Michaud is illuminating in this regard. As mentioned above, Joseph-Clément had an illicit relationship with Anne-Rosalie Maillard, the sister of his paternal uncle's wife, which produced a daughter, Anne-Marie. A couple of years later Anne-Rosalie Maillard married Joseph-Clément's brother, Jean-Augustin. This story suggests that close kin marriages were often linked to illicit sexual relations with kin and with arrangement which had to be made afterwards.

A similar story involved Valérie Terrettaz, the illicit daughter of Marie-Ursule Terrettaz and Etienne Michaud (Michaud/1A). Valérie first married Joseph-Marie Bourgeois (Bourgeois/5), who was from a rather conservative group, but the two soon became separated, probably because the husband left the village to work in France. Valérie then had an illicit relationship with Jerôme-Louis Sarrasin to whom she bore a child; some years later she is found living together with Jerôme's brother, Pierre-Joseph (Sarrasin/2). This is not an exceptional situation.

Etienne-Félicien Michaud (/1A, *1866) married his relative, Marie Esther Michaud (3th-4th degree,) in 1891; they were descendants of Joseph-Clément Michaud and his cousin, Joesph-Florentin Michaud (both from Jean-Etienne Michaud/1A *1750, both liberals in 1857). Marie-Esther was the daughter of a cousin of Valérie Terrettaz, the unmarried mother mentioned above. This marriage was not preceded by any illicit relationship, as far as we know, but it took place within a radical kinship milieu where the tolerance for illicit sex was high: Jean-Théodule Michaud, Joseph-Clément's cousin, had an illegitimate child in 1850, and his daughter Julienne Caroline would go on to have three illegitimate children.

In fact, not all families shared the tendency for marriages between cousins or close relatives. On the contrary: most cousin marriages involved the members of a small number of families, above all the Michaud/1A group, Bourgeois/1, Aubert/1 and Rebord/1B, which account for 50% of all men and women involved in close cousin marriages throughout the nineteenth century (out of a total of 58).

It is interesting to observe that, with one exception, these were core radical groups with a very high rate of illegitimate children and which included unmarried parents during the second half of the nineteenth century. In other groups, like Michaud/1B, Bourgeois 3 or Dely/1, we find only sporadic instances of marriages with close relatives, or none at all. In fact, most cousin marriages are concentrated within a few families: in the Michaud/1A group, for instance, they took place among the descendants of Cyprien Michaud and his nephew Joseph-Clément, a key figure in Bovernier's radical network[33]. In the Bourgeois/1 group they are concentrated among the descendants of Hyacinthe Bourgeois, the son of the leader of the republican movement at the end of the eighteenth century[34].

Most close cousin marriages seem, therefore, to confirm the solidarity that existed within a specific, homogeneous political and sexual context. The conservative Bourgeois 5 group reveals a particular family strategy: in the nineteenth century the members of this group often married close kin, most of them belonging to the same patrilineal branch. We do not know exactly why this was; the fact is that this conservative branch was more and more isolated, becoming part of a small conservative minority. We can therefore suppose that political isolation forced this group to adopt a selective close kin strategy; we can, in fact, observe a similar tendency for the rather conservative Aubert 1 branch. From this point of view the increasing frequency of cousin marriages was (also) a consequence of a growing polarisation between opposing political and ideological factions, particularly after 1825 and up to the bitter conflicts of 1856–57.

Conclusions: Kinship, identities and social milieus

The analysis of kinship and devolution structures has been a crucial pillar in the fields of anthropology and historical anthropology. Its importance was part of a structural approach which aimed to reconstruct basic elements of the social system; as Dionigi Albera has recently demonstrated, it still remains a useful instrument with which to analyse different societies and different development paths. The study of social networks, on the other hand, was conceived of as providing an opportunity to reveal social

---

33   As we have seen above, the two men had sexual relationships with two sisters (footnote 26).

34   Hyacinthe first married two relatives from the Aubert 1 and the Sarrasin 4 groups; after that he married Mélanie Chappot, a woman connected to the Sarrasin 4 group through her mother, who had more illegitimate children and was accused of infanticide. Hyacinthe's family and that of his brother, Germain, contain a high number of illicit sexual relations.

dynamics which are partly independent of structures like kinship or class. Consequently, there are two different methodologies and approaches, each of which provides different pictures of kinship and social transformation. How compatible are the two approaches? The question of the relationship between kinship structure and network remains largely open.

The important theoretical conclusion is that (kinship) networks are not simply derived from structures, like the degree of kinship between married persons or devolution patterns. The detailed study of marriages in Bovernier suggests that alliance structures are, conversely, deeply influenced by personal and familial networks, particularly when those involved belong to the same political or ideological group and to a sexually permissive network. Cousin marriages in Bovernier often take place between partners belonging to a similar ideological and sexual milieu; they are the consequence, and not the cause, of social networks.

The logic of social, political or sexual networks can, therefore, partly determine structures like alliance patterns, as well as the way in which women and men choose the relatives with whom they wish to cooperate, their *active kinship,* through roles such as spiritual kin, political allies or sexual partners.

Of course, structure does matter. We may suppose that there is a rather close relationship between the rules of inheritance and what I have called "primary" kinship, based on economic interdependences; but this is not the case for other "uses" of active kin like sexual relationships and political cooperation, and is only partly the case for spiritual kin. The choice of partners at these levels is, rather, determined by network dynamics, or in other words by shared political, religious or sexual backgrounds.

The network logic of the social group can be more important for the political or social organisation of a community than the structure of kinship: in order to understand the social conflicts and the formation of political factions and parties in nineteenth century Bovernier it is more important to examine the practical involvement of kin, of spiritual kin and of "friends" than it is to study the bilateral structure of kinship and inheritance, where no particularly dramatic changes can be detected after 1700.

Part 3:
Towards Europe

ÉLIE HADDAD

Times and Spaces of Noble Kinship (France, Sixteenth-Eighteenth Centuries)[1]

After two decades dominated by micro-type approaches, with close attention paid to the strategies of social actors, recent works in kinship history are now returning to overall interpretations of changes in family organisation in Western Europe between the Middle Ages and the nineteenth century. They propose both a renewed chronology and an explanation for the changes in the European kinship system. We will focus on three main analyses.

According to Gérard Delille, the Western Christian system of kinship took shape and developed between the thirteenth and the sixteenth centuries (depending on the region), as a result of the Lateran Council (1215) and the gradual triumph of the new patrilineal onomastics (first name/ Christian name and surname) to identify people. Such a system was based on the unwritten tacit rules that there could not be any marriage within the same name, nor within the names of the mothers (i.e. the wives of the male ancestors in the direct line). For Delille, both rules were flanked by a systematic search for cycles of alliances as close as possible to kinship prohibitions (the 4th degree as stated by the Lateran Council) by means of some exchanges among alternating lines. This system experienced some crisis in the eighteenth century before it collapsed in the nineteenth century. The most crucial part in this process was probably played by the construction of territorial States and their concern to control the populations. Contrary to what Maurice Godelier thought, this kinship system should have resulted in accelerating economic exchanges and the development of capitalism.[2]

The editors of *Kinship in Europe* propose another chronology, based on two crucial changes. The first one took place in the fifteenth and

---

1   Many thanks to Cécile Soudan who translated this article.
2   Gérard Delille, "Parenté et alliance en Europe occidentale. Un essai d'interprétation générale", in *L'Homme*, 193, 2010, pp. 75–136.

Élie Haddad

sixteenth centuries. They consider that the development of States and the formalization of social hierarchies led to a growth in the vertical relations in society. As far as kinship is concerned, this resulted in the reinforcement of patrilineages and agnatic relations, with preference given to male primogeniture, in order to enable families to form corporate groups capable of maintaining leading political and social positions reached in the State or town apparatus. The second change began in the middle of the eighteenth century, when endogamous lines increased, based both on class and milieu and on inbred kinship. Such change was related to the formation of social classes and to the new gendered differentiation of roles within ownership groups. It also reflected various reconfigurations: institutional (for the service of the State), legal (for ownership) and economic (for capital circulation) reconfigurations. Contrary to what is usually said, the nineteenth century was not characterised by a decreasing relevance of family links but by a "kinship-hot society".[3]

The third analysis is produced by Dionigi Albera. From the Alpine perspective, he proposes a chronology based on three major shifts – historical and spatial – in the history of the European domestic organisation: the medieval creation of communities of inhabitants about 1200, the formation of territorial States from the 16th century and, finally, the contemporary legal, political and economic changes around 1900. Of course these are main trends which operated in various ways according to the region and which may have oscillated diversely over several centuries. According to Albera, discrepancies resulted from segmented historical processes and from local specificities as the orientation towards such or such a type of domestic organisation produced a path dependency which would account for long-term phenomena, although also allowing more rapid changes. This could be an explanation for both regional similarities and differences. Though he did not neglect economic or social factors, Albera focused on the distinctive political developments of regions to explain why and how the Alpine area followed different paths within the general European history. "Political" must be taken in the broadest sense of the term: of course the construction of more or less centralised States did play a part. However, beyond the changes of sovereignty (in the Italian Alps) or the

---

3   David W. Sabean, Simon Teuscher, "Kinship in Europe. A New Approach to Long Term Development", in David W. Sabean, Simon Teuscher, Jon Mathieu (eds.), *Kinship in Europe. Approaches to Long-Term Development (1300–1900)*, New York, Berghahn Books, 2007, pp. 1–32.

linguistic differences between populations with distinct origins (in the Austrian Alps), different domestic orders might also have been shaped by the presence, to a greater or lesser extent, of the feudal system and of seignoiries, by the degree of importance of communities or of peasant political organisation in the management of communal fields, or by the influence of the written Law in the Italian Alps.[4]

The three chronologies do not coincide with each other and do not offer exactly the same explanations of the transformation of Western European societies, even if they all consider the construction of the States and political factors to be key elements of this change. All three analyses attend to the spatial and temporal differences; however Albera examines more thoroughly these variations. Indeed, he explains that the three main stages of change did not occur everywhere in a similar way, neither at the same time nor with the same consequences – and this produced different histories within the general process.

Following this third path, and through an examination of the evolution of transmission within the French early modern nobility, I would like to introduce further considerations concerning developments within particular social groups. The issue is whether the nobility underwent a specific domestic reorganisation, or perhaps transformation, different from that experienced by other social groups; or whether there is intrinsic diversity, dependent upon the social position of the noble family. More importantly, I aim at proposing some elements to explain changes in the noble domestic organisation in relation to the more general social and political evolution of the kingdom. Thus, it will be possible to consider how such changes took place within the broader models of European kinship. My arguments are mainly based upon the analysis of families of the middle and upper nobility who often owned land or houses in several provinces and who lived partly at Court or in the army. In the following pages, I will present propositions that are to be confirmed. In addition, further research will be necessary to validate these assumptions also for the lower nobility. This is a work in progress.

---

4   Dionigi Albera, *Au fil des générations. Terre, pouvoir et parenté dans l'Europe alpine (XIVᵉ–XXᵉ siècles)*, Grenoble, PUG, 2011.

Not an obvious spatial diversity

Legal diversity and practices of transmission

In early modern France, transmission was ruled by several written or customary laws. Did these laws have any influence on noble domestic organisation?[5] In matters of transmission and community of property, the real
character of customs should have induced the provisions of marriage contracts to follow the custom of the place where the property and domicile of
the spouses were respectively located. Yet in certain cases, some departure
from the custom was accepted by the law for special circumstances,[6] especially for marriage contracts which held a specific position as "favourable
acts"[7]. Families thus had real latitude in the organisation of the devolution
of a part of their estates. Donations of present and future property, which
were usually prohibited, were allowed in marriage contracts, as were the
refusal of an inheritance to come and donations on condition of survival
or, on the contrary, due to death, otherwise prohibited due to the rule that
"giving or retaining has no worth". In the same way, it was possible to
waive local custom on some points or to adopt another custom to govern
all or part of the clauses of a marriage contract. In fact, except in cases of

---

5   The influence of customs on transmission is much discussed. For two different per-
     spectives: Bernard Derouet, "Territoire et parenté. Pour une mise en perspective de la
     communauté rurale et des formes de reproduction familiale", in *Annales H.S.S.*, 50,
     1995, 3, pp. 645–686, and Jérôme-Luther Viret, *Valeurs et pouvoir. La reproduction
     familiale et sociale en Île-de-France. Écouen et Villiers-le-Bel (1560–1685)*, Paris,
     Presses Universitaires de Paris-Sorbonne, 2004. On special provisions in customs
     concerning noble distribution of estates, see Laurent Bourquin, "Partage noble et
     droit d'aînesse dans les coutumes du royaume de France à l'Époque Moderne", in
     L'Identité nobiliaire. Dix siècles de métamorphoses (IXe*–XIX*[e] *siècles)*, Université
     du Maine, Publications du Laboratoire d'Histoire Anthropologique du Mans, 1997,
     pp. 136–165.
6   Joseph Nicolas Guyot, *Répertoire universel et raisonné de jurisprudence civile, cri-
     minelle, canonique et bénéficiale; ouvrage de plusieurs jurisconsultes*, Paris, Visse,
     1784–1785, t. 5, p. 145.
7   *Ibid.*, t. 4, p. 611. See also Jean-Baptiste Denisart, *Collection de décisions nouvelles
     et de notions relatives à la jurisprudence actuelle. Septiéme édition. Revue et con-
     sidérablement Augmentée*, Paris, Veuve Desaint, 1771, t. 1, p. 708 and François Bour-
     jon, *Le Droit commun de la France et la coutume de Paris réduits en principes*, Paris,
     Grangé et Cellot, 2e édition revue et augmentée, 1770, t. I, p. 506.

express prohibitions, customary law tried less to impose a common norm than to provide solutions that would apply *"in the absence* of contracts between individuals"[8].

Finally, it must be added that most often in middle and upper noble families, the transmitted properties were governed by different customs because of their high number. In practice, these families highly favoured the Paris custom in their contracts of marriage, wherever the location of their lands[9]. This custom seems to have had the advantage of flexibility, making it possible both to create a community of property that worked as a dynamic structure for the couple's family economy, and to protect the personal wealth of women[10]. Contrary to what has long been thought, the system of transmission among the nobility gave women a central position in the devolution of property, of seigniories, offices and rents[11]. At the same time, the possibility of keeping inherited property separate (*garder les biens en propre*) allowed the woman's paternal lineage to preserve or retrieve the property if the alliance was childless. The flexibility of Paris custom made it possible for families to organise the devolution of property in a relatively precise way.

We must insist on the fact that these arrangements and derogations from the jurisdiction of customs or from their rules depended upon good relations among the heirs: conflicts could invalidate clauses that were too far removed from social and legal norms. However, the legal pluralism of the Ancien Régime and the conception of marriage as a favourable act did allow the social actors, and particularly those who had the capacity, to play with the norms. The domestic organisation and transmission practices of these families did not depend exclusively on local custom.

---

8   Bernard Derouet, "Les pratiques familiales, le droit et la construction des différences (15e-19e siècles)", in *Annales H.S.S.*, vol. 52, 1997, n. 2, p. 372.

9   Élie Haddad, "Faire du mariage un acte favorable. L'utilisation des coutumes dans la noblesse française d'Ancien Régime", in *Revue d'Histoire Moderne et Contemporaine*, vol. 58, 2011, n. 2, pp. 72–95.

10   Robert Descimon, "La fortune des parisiennes: l'exercice féminin de la transmission (XVIe–XVIIe siècle)", in Simonetta Cavaciocchi (ed.), *La Famiglia nell'Economia Europea Secc. XIII–XVIII*, Firenze, Firenze University Press, 2009, pp. 619–634.

11   Claire Chatelain, *Chronique d'une ascension sociale. Exercice de la parenté chez de grands officiers (XVIe–XVIIe siècles)*, Paris, Éditions de l'EHESS, 2008; Élie Haddad, *Fondation et ruine d'une "maison". Histoire sociale des comtes de Belin (1582–1706)*, Limoges, Presses Universitaires de Limoges, 2009.

A practice of replicating alliances independent from location

The practice of replicating alliances with distant relatives, related by descent or by marriage, (*renchaînements d'alliances*), was not dependent on geographical location: the same forms can be observed in all the families analysed, whatever their provincial origin. To appreciate this practice, it is necessary to look at both feminine and masculine lines since it occurred indifferently on both sides. Replicated alliances with distant relatives by descent or by marriage through feminine lines or through cycles of alliances passing through collaterality were numerous and deeply rooted in genealogy. Let us take the example of the Phélypeaux de Pontchartrain[12]. This family is a remarkable example of networks built up through alliances among the Ancien Régime elites. It highlights the crucial character of the pairing of lines by alliances that can be considered both from the male and female points of view without any great change in the logic. The idea that alliance is equivalent to descent and descent equivalent to alliance is fully operative: as others, the Phélypeaux replicated alliances by descent without any direct exchange between lineages and without necessarily any exchange through a patriline (Fig. 1).

Fig. 1: *Alliances in collaterality (close to the Pontchartrains).*

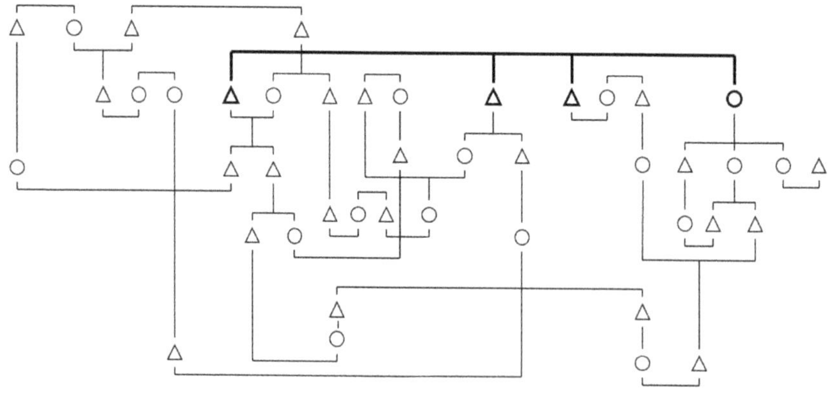

---

12   The following graph was drawn from genealogical data found by Charles Frostin, *Les Pontchartrain, ministres de Louis XIV. Alliances et réseaux d'influence sous l'Ancien Régime*, Rennes, PUR, 2006.

Marked in bold (Figure 1), the incomplete siblings (2 brothers and 2 sisters are not mentioned) of the Phélipeaux advanced this lineage among the elites of the Ancien Régime. Figure 1 only shows one of the possible paths in the genealogies proposed by Ch. Frostin. It would be possible to show many other examples of such replication of alliances between collateral relatives, and of the practice of restoring alliances through collaterality and sometimes through women. On the basis of a very different example (the Etoros of New Guinea studied by Raymond Kelly[13]), François Héran makes a comment, the logic of which can be applied to what happened most often within the context of French early modern nobility:

> From a structural point of view, the direct exchange of sisters was less efficient than indirect exchange: it only strengthened a link of alliance between two lines with an already acquired identity. The indirect exchange did better: either it moved together two branches of a single line that were separating by giving them a common ally, or went so far as introducing a third line that was matched to one of the two others. In this enriched formula, alliance contributes to reshaping descent.[14]

In early modern France, the rationale behind these practices of replicating alliances was not only transmission. There was no cycle of alliance strictly speaking since, most often, there was no end to the women exchange cycle and so no end to dowry transmission. In addition, as these alliances concerned families of differing wealth and status, they created "chains of allies moving down the hierarchy" ("*chaînes descendantes d'alliés*")[15] and, more generally, bonds of dependency or solidarity which were potentially available.

The case of remarriages is also enlightening. A quick glance at genealogies shows how they were frequent on both the female and on the male side. Remarriages highlight particular alliances among descendants that can be presented as follows (Figure 2).

---

13 Raymond C. Kelly, *Etoro Social Structure: A Study in Structural Contradiction*, Ann Arbor, University of Michigan Press, 1977 [1974].

14 François Héran, *Figures de la parenté. Une histoire critique de la raison structurale*, Paris, PUF, 2009, p. 278.

15 Michel Nassiet, *Parenté, noblesse et États dynastiques XVᵉ–XVIᵉ siècles*, Paris, Éditions de l'EHESS, 2000, p. 166.

Fig. 2: Alliances derived from remarriages.

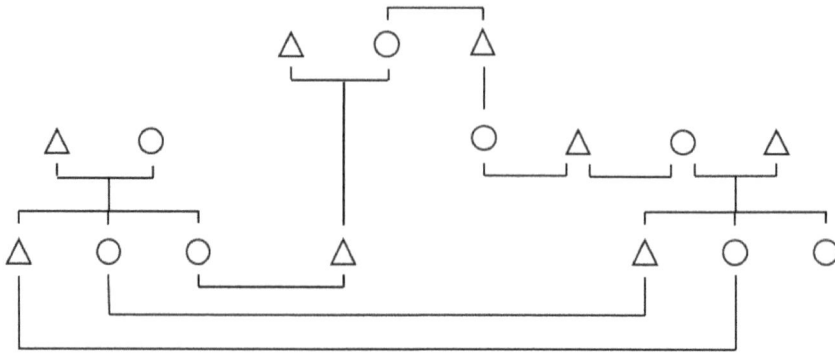

Work on several genealogies of noble families and their allies shows how important these types of alliances were in which one or several remarriages played a pivotal role, interweaving links between different lines or lineages united directly or by contiguity with other lines or lineages; and these alliances were renewed again and again later on.

The practice of replicating alliances occurred over several generations through men as well as women, and most often both. From this point of view, the construction of purely patrilineal genealogies – a predominant exercise in the historiography of the nobility – has hidden this fundamental phenomenon in the functioning of kinship in French early modern society.

These kinds of practices became increasingly unusual in the seventeenth century and, above all, in the eighteenth century. The smaller number of children who married within the nobility fostered this trend since it limited the potential practice of replicating alliances later on. The change in the demographical behaviour of elites necessarily induced a change in the functioning of kinship. Primogeniture and the decreasing number of children made the constitution of patrilineages impossible, and resulted in isolated and fragile lines.[16] Several studies have shown this

16   See Gérard Delille, "Échanges matrimoniaux entre lignées alternées et système européen de l'alliance: une première approche", in Jean-Luc Jamard, Emmanuel Terray, Margarita Xanthakou (eds.), *En substances. Textes pour Françoise Héritier*, Paris, Fayard, 2000, pp. 219–252, as well as *Le Maire et le prieur. Pouvoir central et pouvoir local en Méditerranée occidentale (XVᵉ–XVIIIᵉ siècle)*, Paris, Éditions de l'EHESS, 2003, and *Id.*, "Réflexions sur le 'système' européen de la parenté et de l'alliance (note critique)", in *Annales H.S.S.*, vol. 56, 2001, n. 2, pp. 369–380.

major transformation of the European kinship system;[17] and it affected the majority of the French nobility whatever its geographical location.

"Topolines" ("topolignées"), "Houses" and relationship to the land

A further element common to the whole French nobility, at least the land-based nobility, was the relation to property, especially to seigniories and titled fiefs (the administrative nobility was built on a different relation to office[18]). It is necessary to go back to the eleventh and twelfth centuries to find the bases of the system governing the nobility in the sixteenth century. This is the moment when "aristocracy" (as Joseph Morsel calls a specific power-domination relation) transformed its relation to space, as shown by the first castles. The aristocracy settled and organised themselves spatially. "This spatial organisation is ensured by relevant practices of succession, converted into genealogical continuity through anthroponymic practices and narratives concerning the past"[19]. "Topolines" arose from the spatialisation of a domination. This expression (*topolignées*) was created by Anita Guerreau-Jalabert to designate lines of heirs "formed by those who successively owned the most important part of the estate – the separate inherited property (*les "propres"*) –, each heir seeking, in a mainly homeostatic system, an identical reproduction or an increase of the material or symbolic items of a social position based above all on domination over the land and people of a place".[20]

If the phenomenon includes the acknowledgement of a head of household in charge of the complex of kinship powers, rights, properties and

17   Gérard Delille, "Représentation, généralisation, comparaison. Sur le système de parenté européen", in *Annales H.S.S.*, vol. 62, 2010, n. 1, pp. 137–157; David W. Sabean, Simon Teuscher, Jon Mathieu (eds.), *Kinship in Europe*, op. cit.

18   Robert Descimon, Élie Haddad (eds.), *Épreuves de noblesse. Les expériences nobiliaires de la haute robe parisienne (XVIᵉ–XVIIIᵉ siècle)*, Paris, Les Belles Lettres, 2010.

19   Joseph Morsel, *L'Aristocratie médiévale Vᵉ–XVᵉ siècle*, Paris, Armand Colin, 2004, p. 104.

20   Anita Guerreau-Jalabert, article "Parenté" in Jacques Le Goff, Jean-Claude Schmitt (eds.), *Dictionnaire Raisonné de l'Occident médiéval*, Paris, Fayard, 1999, p. 865. See also by the same author "El sistema de parentesco medieval: sis formas (real/ spiritual) y su dependencia con respecto a la organización del espacio", in Reyna Pastor (ed.), *Relaciones de Poder, de Produccion y Parentesco en la Edad Media y Moderna*, Madrid, CSIC, 1990, pp. 85–105.

relations involved in a name that ensures perpetuation in terms of kinship and descent, it can be analysed in terms of "house", with the anthropological meaning given to this notion by Claude Lévi-Strauss.[21] "House"[22] is a process of transmission with a patrilineal bias based on property. This provides kinship with a real character in the framework of the feudal system – which may be described, according to Alain Guerreau, as power over land and people.[23] More generally, this relation to estate is crucial to understand the modes of transmission. The wealth of noble "houses" was made up altogether of their estate, name and titles, containing symbolic as well as supernatural properties. The fiction that the name of a lineage might come from the name of a seigniory and the temptation to add "de" before the name are directly related to the fact that a "house" is altogether made of an estate and a name with its titles and prerogatives. As for the symbolic or supernatural properties, they were rooted in the sacred places founded by the seigniors on their land (chapels, for example) that structured their space of power, relating them fictively through the communion of the living and the dead to their ancestors buried in the land. Some movables might also become part of the identity of the "house" (and not be included in the inventories after death).[24] At the end of the Middle Ages, *house* meant specifically a group of people living in a space, some of them sharing kinship links, and dedicated to its reproduction. The organised domestic economy induced by the *house* is an illustration of its real nature. Female transmissions, in the absence of males, illustrated this system: indeed, in the residence / descent dialectic (constituting the "house"), residence won over male descent in the absence of the latter, since the

---

21 Claude Lévi-Strauss, "Nobles sauvages", in *Culture, science et développement: contribution à une histoire de l'homme: mélanges en l'honneur de Charles Morazé*, Toulouse, 1979, republished in *La voie des masques* with the new title "L'organisation sociale des Kwakiutl", Paris, Presses Pocket, 1988, pp. 151–152.
22 In order to clearly mark the different meaning of the term, I will use quotation marks when I use the anthropological meaning and italics when I use it with the meaning it had in the Middle Ages or in early modern France. The other anthropological terms likely to be misleading (e.g. "Lines" or "Lineages") will be in italics when used in their vernacular sense.
23 Alain Guerreau, "Fief, féodalité, féodalisme. Enjeux sociaux et réflexion historienne", in *Annales E.S.C.*, vol. 45, 1990, n. 1, pp. 137–166.
24 I analyzed the organisation and history of a noble "house" in *Fondation et ruine d'une "maison", op. cit.*

seigniory that provided the name was the first property of a "house" and the basis of continuity.

"House" was a social process that was not necessarily fulfilled in all dominant families, since some properties (whatever their nature) might be lacking to ensure its perpetuation. However, this domestic organisation was independent of customs. B. Derouet stated that for peasantry, there was no mechanical relation between law and kinship system.[25] The same applied to nobility. However, the overall functioning of the French nobility's kinship underwent transformation in the early modern period, as part of the overall changes which the second order was then experiencing.

Chronological inflexions of noble kinship

Changes in kinship terminology

The first indication of change in attitudes to noble kinship is found in the development of its terminology. Up to the fifteenth century, the term *lineage* (*lignage*), that appeared in the eleventh century[26], referred to every kinship line according to the use of the suffix – age, which designated a collective at the time.[27] In Medieval Latin as in Old French, *lines* (*lignes*) referred to any descent or ancestral relationship between several persons in a strictly linear representation. However, these lines could be composed of men as well as women and most often excluded collateral relatives. The term *lineage* (*lignage*) as a set of kinship lines did not refer to the patrilineage (*patrilignage*) according to the anthropologists, since it had a cognatic nature.[28] Thus it is an anachronism to think that *lignage*, when accompanied by a qualifying adjective as in the French expressions *Haut lignage* or *Grand lignage*, would mean patrilineage. Probably, the term *lineage* finally designated not only kinship but also a quality specific to a family

---

25 Bernard Derouet, "Les pratiques familiales", art. cit.
26 About 1050 according to *Dictionnaire historique de la langue française* directed by Alain Rey, Paris, Le Robert, 1993.
27 I thank Anita Guereau-Jalabert for the information on this issue.
28 Anita Guerreau-Jalabert, "La désignation des relations de parenté en latin médiéval", in *Archivum Latinitatis Medii Aevi*, t. 96–97, 1986–1987, pp. 65–108.

that had to be transmitted among its members. Several texts included the word *lineage* in a list of virtues. However, the attributive adjective "noble" rarely refers to *lineage*, but most often to *line* (*lignée*).[29] *Line* (*ligne* or *lignée*) is thus associated with the transmission of noble status. And if it designated first of all the succession of generations coming from a shared ancestor, it also referred to the ancestry of one individual, and especially to paternal ancestry. This development from the Old French may assumedly be related to the transmission of the noble status in the male line, because fiefs were preferentially devolved upon male heirs.

In the early modern period, the terms *lines* (*lignées*) and *lineages* (*lignages*) gradually fell into disuse,[30] giving way to the term *house*. Now it remains to be understood what this change in vocabulary meant in social terms, as well as regarding the conception of kinship. The use of the word *house* goes back to the fourteenth century and continued up to the end of the Ancien Régime. However, it was only in the 1420s that it started to be used to designate a form of kinship – and this use did not spread before the second half of the fifteenth century. This term held a high level of distinction; it can be seen in the way in which the alliance of a *house* to another *house* was used to enhance the honour of relatives through marriage. As for the terms *lines* and *lineages*, *house* was often accompanied by social qualifications, and great princely families were designated as *houses* that took the name of their kingdom or principality, e.g. the *house of France*.

Most often, *house* refers to domestic space or political organisation within princely and upper noble families – as designating a dwelling place – and does not allow us to know whether it was used specifically in its kinship-related meaning. The association between property, residence, domestic space and family group was so strong that, frequently, both meanings were possible and equally applicable. At the beginning of the sixteenth century, the term *house* kept a very concrete meaning and the idea of property, and of residence attached to the name, remained. The continuity of the *house* through the female line was common, although it

---

29   According to the *Dictionnaire historique de la langue française, op. cit.*, the French term *lignée* appeared about 1120.

30   Jean-Louis Flandrin had already mentioned this fact in *Familles. Parenté, maison, sexualité dans l'ancienne société*, Paris, Seuil, 1995 [1976]. He noticed that though the word *lignage* was still used in the sixteenth century, with the broad sense of kinship, in the following century it simply remained a legal term.

resulted generally from the marriage of a woman to someone below her condition. However it was not considered socially discreditable.

The meaning of the word *house* evolved from the second half of the sixteenth century. Without losing entirely its solid reality, the *house* was gradually identified with the patronimic name, inducing a clear patrilineal bias. In addition, it was gradually assimilated to the notions of *race* and *blood*.[31] With titles such as "history of the house of ...", the blossoming genealogical literature of the time detailed the various branches of what corresponded to patrilineage. In the end, the term *house* finally meant only patrilineage, divided into different branches, i.e. different patrilines.

Disappearance of the practice of restoring names and arms (reprises de noms et d'armes)

Along with these changes in kinship vocabulary, other practices also evolved. As the patronym became important, so "house" embraced a more strictly patrilineal form of kinship. The expressions *paternal house* (*maison paternelle*) or *father's house* (*maison du père*) appeared in the 16th century and became very important thereafter. Conflicts arose in relation to the definition of *house* as an interplay between name and property, and concerning how such a complex had to be devolved. The provisions in marriage contracts and last wills, with conditions to restore name and arms, often related to *fideicommissum*, were occasions of conflict about *house* devolution. For instance in the case of the succession of the Laval house at the end of the 16th century, which was the subject of a judgement by the court of parliament,[32] two conceptions collided: the first one considered the *house* as an indivisible whole that included names and material and immaterial properties, the transmission of which was likely to pass to women who could bear the inheritance (in other words: women were likely to become successors); for

---

31 These notions have been widely discussed, often anachronistically. Arlette Jouanna gave a contextual definition of the notion of *race,* though it interpreted it in the light of later conceptions. See: *L'Idée de race en France au XVIᵉ siècle et au début du XVIIᵉ siècle*, Montpellier, Presses de l'Université Paul Valéry, 1981 [1976], 2 vol. On the notion of *blood*, see Christopher H. Johnson, Bernhard Jussen, David W. Sabean, Simon Teuscher (eds.), *Blood & Kinship. Matter for Metaphor from Ancient Rome to the Present*, New York, Berghahn Books, 2013.

32 Julien Pelée, *Les Œuvres de Mᵉ Julien Peleus, Advocat en parlement*, Paris, Pierre Billaine, 1638, pp. 98–105.

the second, name and heredity or name and property were dissociated. This latter conception rejected any practice of restoring names and arms even if it was a way to avoid that property falling into the hands of a foreign *house*. The verdict delivered on 9th April 1595 by the Paris Parliament favoured such dissociation between name and property.

As a consequence, the practice of restoring names and arms disappeared gradually during the first half of the seventeenth century and became extremely rare, except for political reasons. One of the final examples is of a Grimaldi female successor whose husband – a Thorigny – restored the name of his wife's *house* using a royal warrant (*brevet de retenue*) granted by the king in 1715. One of the results of the functioning of the "house" system was a great confusion among the name of the fief and the name of the family. This was now harshly criticised by genealogists, who sometimes condemned former times when a female heir was able to force her less wealthy husband to lose his name. Thus, practices of transmission amongst the nobility correlated with changes in the vocabulary to designate kinship, especially with regard to the term *house*.

Written evidence and nobiliary genealogies

The final change impacting the representations, as well as the practices, of transmission amongst the nobility was the gradual verticalisation of the concept of the *house* through an increasing focus on genealogical depth.[33] At the beginning of the sixteenth century, noble status was above all determined locally, according to the different customs, and by social acknowledgement.[34] It was based on traditional criteria, as emphasised by Ellery Schalk[35]: the profession of arms, deeply rooted as a mark of nobility, even

---

33   For a thorough analysis of the ideas presented in this part, see Fanny Cosandey, Élie Haddad, "Temps de la noblesse, temps de la monarchie (XVIe–XVIIe siècles)", in Pierre Bonin, Fanny Cosandey, Élie Haddad, Anne Rousselet-Pimont (eds.), *Des usages du temps: approches d'histoire juridique, politique et sociale*, Rennes, PUR, 2016, pp. 73–100.

34   Jean-Marie Constant, *La Noblesse française aux XVIe et XVIIe siècles*, Paris, Hachette, 1985, p. 8. Robert Descimon, "Sites coutumiers et mots incertains: la formation de la noblesse française à la charnière du Moyen Âge et des Temps modernes", in Thierry Dutour (ed.), *Les Nobles et la ville*, Paris, Presses universitaires de Paris-Sorbonne, 2010, pp. 343–360.

35   Ellery Schalk, *From Valor to Pedigree,* Princeton University Press, 1986.

if it did not correspond to reality in some provinces[36]; virtue, that is the necessary and intrinsic noble quality which gave the ability to command; the way of life and the possession of a fief – this last criterion was often of critical importance, since the difference between seignior and nobleman was often blurred in local life;[37] and finally, a noble status beyond memory (*noblesse immémoriale*) passed down through the bloodline. The notion of "beyond memory" is to be understood in a literal sense: i.e. exceeding the oral memory of the older people of the place, who were asked in case of contention. Indeed, royal courts did not intervene in matters of nobility except in cases of dispute[38]: the king did not claim to pronounce in general on who was and who was not noble[39], and only occasionally did he resort to his power to confer a title of nobility[40]. But even in the case of a trial challenging someone's nobility, witnesses who were nobles themselves were summoned and, in accordance with customs, they testified that the defendant's ancestors had lived as nobles for two or three generations, or for a hundred years at least (that was the case in Brittany). The progressive and silent integration to nobility (*anoblissement taisible*), the importance of which was pointed out by Jean-Marie Constant, resulted logically from this local and beyond-memory definition of nobility,[41] based on the way of living. In the Ancien Régime, depth of time was not given precedence

---

36   Jean-Marie Constant, *Nobles et paysans en Beauce aux XVIe et XVIIe siècles*, Lille, Service de reproduction des thèses Université Lille III, 1981.

37   See an example in Auvergne developed by Anne-Valérie Solignat, *Les Noblesses auvergnate et bourbonnaise, pouvoir local, stratégies familiales et administration royale (vers 1450-vers 1650)*, PhD thesis under the supervision of Nicole Lemaître, université Paris I, 2010, 3 vol.

38   Étienne Dravasa, "'Vivre noblement'. Recherches sur la dérogeance de noblesse du XIVe au XVIe siècles", in *Revue juridique et économique du Sud-Ouest*, vol. 16, 1965, n. 3–4, pp. 135–193, et vol. 17, 1966, n. 1–2, pp. 23–129.

39   Françoise Autrand points out the importance of the noble reputation in obtaining letters patent of nobility in the 15th century: the king only validated a pre-existing social acknowledgement. "L'image de la noblesse en France à la fin du Moyen Âge. Tradition et nouveauté", in *Comptes rendus de l'Académie des Inscriptions et des Belles Lettres*, 1979, pp. 340–354.

40   On letters conferring nobility in early modern France, see Jean-Richard Bloch, *L'anoblissement en France au temps de François Ier. Essai d'une définition de la condition juridique et sociale de la noblesse au début du XVIe siècle*, Paris, F. Alcan, 1934 [1906].

41   Jean-Marie Constant, "La mobilité sociale dans une province de gentilshommes et de paysans: la Beauce", in *XVIIe siècle, La Mobilité sociale au XVIIe siècle*, ed. by Roland Mousnier, 122, 1979, pp. 7–20.

in the pedigree, though it was a stated value and a quality that improved nobility. Keeping the Charter records was above all aimed at defending the rights related to the possession of a seigniory.[42] As "topoline" or "house" continuity was not based on genealogies and written evidence, it was subject to the handling of names and arms.[43]

However, recently ennobled families were gradually targeted, whether they had become nobles by arms, by their progressive and silent integration to nobility (*annoblissement taisible*), or by ennobling venal offices placed in circulation by the Crown. The transmission of nobility through blood was called into question during the Wars of Religion, especially by some ultra-Catholics. As a consequence, many nobles argued for the closing of the second order.[44] The notion of antiquity (*ancienneté*) was proposed as the criterion of true nobility. Thus, as early as the 1570s, the notion of *house* (with the noble family defined in relation to the ownership of properties, especially fiefs) was commonly found in texts accompanied with qualifiers such as *noble* or *ancient*, never used before. The promotion of antiquity can also be found in books dealing with nobility published in the last third of the sixteenth century[45], and these finally placed the stress on the idea of *race* which, though it was not new, became increasingly important and more relevant than before.[46] The race-based definition gradually disconnected the transmission of nobility from the possession of fiefs and allowed room for doubts about the origins, leading to a new focus on families' instabilities and to a temptation to seek family titles in order to prove the antiquity of the noble status. This rhetoric of antiquity versus ennoblement was strengthened in the first half of the seventeenth century, as is seen in the 1614 *Etats généraux*.[47] It culminated in the large-scale investigations into titles of

---

42   Philippe Contamine, Laurent Vissière (eds.), *Défendre ses droits, construire sa mémoire. Les chartriers seigneuriaux XIIIᵉ–XXIᵉ siècle. Actes du colloque international de Thouars 8–10 juin 2006*, Paris, Société de l'Histoire de France, 2010.

43   See an example in Michel Nassiet, "Un cas de manipulation de la parenté: la maison de Derval", in *Bulletin de la Société archéologique et historique de Nantes et de Loire-Atlantique*, 131, 1996, pp. 59–68.

44   Ellery Schalk, *From Valor to Pedigree, op. cit.*

45   E.g., François de L'Alouete, *Traité des Nobles et des Vertus dont ils sont formés*, Paris, Robert le Manier, 1577.

46   François de Thierriat, *Trois Traictez. Sçavoir, 1. De la noblesse de Race, 2. De la noblesse Civile, 3. Des Immunitez des Ignobles*, Paris, Lucas Bruneau, 1606.

47   Roger Chartier, "La noblesse et les États de 1614: une réaction aristocratique?", in Roger Chartier, Denis Richet (eds.), *Représentation et vouloir politiques. Autour des États-Généraux de 1614*, Paris, Éditions de l'EHESS, 1982, pp. 113–126.

nobility initiated in the first years of Louis XIV's personal reign.[48] By imposing 1560 as the limit for the proofs certifying the nobility of one's family, the
monarchy acknowledged tacitly that there was prescription before this date.
In other words, anyone tacitly ennobled before 1560 without any royal Act
was not questioned. The length of time necessary to pretend to *immémorial-
ité* that was ordinarily accepted (three generations, including *ego*) was then
extended. Above all, the monarchy fixed a time limit that was used later as a
reference for most of the second order. The very logic of customary *immé-
morialité* was demolished further, since investigations into nobility were
now based only on written and authenticated proofs, and oral testimonies
were no longer accepted.

In addition, these investigations established doubt as a valid principle
when considering the nobility of those who pretended to be noble. And
this doubt quickly became effective in the practice of power since ennobled
families were thereafter constantly required to provide certificates of their
noble antiquity when they aimed to acquire certain titled offices, military
offices, abbeys or honours. The reinforcement of patrilineary ideology and
monarchical control over nobility soon had broad social implications. It
became impossible for families ennobled after 1560 to claim to *immé-
morialité*. As for the others, the requirement to provide proofs confronted
them with an "instability of their antiquity"[49] since genealogists sought
precise ennobling traces. The conception of time carried by this suspicion
logic was mainly a relation of imprescriptibility in the acquisition of nobility, even if the investigators and genealogists commissioned by the king
did not agree on this issue.[50] In other words, a nobility whose origin was

---

48 Jean Meyer, *La Noblesse bretonne au XVIIIᵉ siècle*, Paris, Éditions de l'EHESS, 1985
    [1966], 2 vol.; Jean-Marie Constant, "L'enquête de noblesse de 1667 et les seigneurs
    de la Beauce", in *Revue d'Histoire Moderne et Contemporaine*, vol. 21, 1974, n. 4,
    pp. 548–566; Valérie Piétri, *Famille et noblesse en Provence orientale de la fin du
    XVIIᵉ siècle à la Révolution*, PhD thesis under the supervision of Francis Pomponi,
    Université de Nice-Sophia Antipolis, 2001, 3 vol.

49 The expression was forged by François-Joseph Ruggiu, "Ancienneté familiale et con-
    struction de l'identité nobiliaire dans la France de la fin de l'Ancien Régime", in
    Josette Pontet, Michel Figeac, Marie Boisson (eds.), *La Noblesse de la fin du XVIᵉ au
    début du XXᵉ siècle, un modèle social?*, Anglet, Atlantica, t. I, pp. 309–325.

50 Élie Haddad, "The Question of the Imprescriptibility of Nobility in Early Modern
    France", in Charles Lipp, Matthew Romaniello (eds.), *Contested Spaces of Nobility
    in Early Modern Europe*, Farnham, Ashgate, 2011, pp. 147–166.

unknown was only a presumed nobility, always likely to be questioned if an evidence of common rank was found in ancient records.

Thus over a period of a century, the conception of kinship, the domestic organisation and the transmission practices of the French nobility underwent a transformation involving a clear patrilineal orientation, generating the successful ideology of *patrilineage* in the second half of the seventeenth century. This was a general process since it occurred at the crossroads of correlated changes in the monarchical power, in the second order and in the social and economic development of the kingdom.

How to consider the development of noble kinship

Changes in monarchical power and developments of nobility

Changes in monarchical power and its relations to nobility were of great importance in the evolution of the second order and of noble kinship.[51] My aim here is not to explore the details of the changes in the construction of absolute monarchy. Thus I will limit myself to outlining the main elements of this process.

We have seen that noble kinship was forged in relation to feudalism and seigniorial organisation. Seigniorial power changed as monarchy aimed at building a political space of regal sovereignty out of feudal hierarchy. Indeed, monarchy drew upon the legal elaboration of feudality (created by sixteenth century jurisconsults) as well as the weakening of feudal structures. When under the spotlight of royal justice, the seigniorial power is at best a simple delegation, at worst an usurpation, of the royal power.[52]

---

51 For an overview of these changes, see Robert Descimon, "Chercher de nouvelles voies pour interpréter les phénomènes nobiliaires dans la France moderne. La noblesse, 'essence' ou rapport social ?", in *Revue d'Histoire Moderne et Contemporaine*, vol. 46, 1999, n. 1 pp. 5–21 and "*Nobles* de lignage et *noblesse* de service. Sociogenèses comparées de, l'épée et de la robe (XVᵉ–XVIIIᵉ siècle)", in Robert Descimon, Élie Haddad, *Épreuves de noblesse, op. cit.*, pp. 277–302.

52 Robert Descimon, "La royauté française entre féodalité et sacerdoce. Roi seigneur ou roi magistrat?", in *Revue de synthèse*, IVᵉ série, 1991, 3–4, pp. 455–473; Fanny Cosandey, "Instituer la toute-puissance? Les rapports d'autorité dans la France d'Ancien Régime", in *Tracés*, vol. 17, 2009, n. 2, pp. 39–54; Fanny Cosandey,

The monarchy also worked towards a stronger reinforcement of the ideology of *patrilineage*, with the objective of reforming the second order and controlling it socially and politically. As has been shown, such a control involved a clear legal delimitation of nobility. The legal practices at the heart of large-scale investigations from Colbert onwards were very different from the science of law characterising treaties in the previous century – with their high level of refinement and subtlety.[53] However, the investigators had to make compromises due to the outcry unleashed by the first wave from 1661. It appeared necessary to work with local forms of nobiliary acknowledgement that had always prevailed. Thus, investigations into nobility resulted in a compromise that took the nobiliary ideology of race seriously into account in order to subvert it with the idea of nobility of service.[54] And the fact that the monarchy resumed the traditional discourse on antiquity as a way to legitimate membership of the second order extended the related genealogical activity, since it was based on the idea of an historical continuity.[55] This production of purely patrilineal genealogies contributed to impose a general conception of nobiliary kinship over the patronymic and thus over the model of *patrilineage*.

The social organisation of the fief was also impacted by the partial dissociation of the title from the ownership of titled lands. Under the reign of Louis XIV, the king started to create titles of marquis by royal warrant, i.e. a title without any fief attached as a marquisate. This affected the real character of the dignity. Even earlier, the creation of a *noblesse de robe* based on some ennobling venal office and definitely confirmed by the establishment in 1604 of the *"paulette"* (a type of insurance based on the transmission of an office owned by a father in favour of one of his children) contributed significantly to the redefinition of the second order and its relationship to the accompanying dignities.

Monarchy also played an important role in the introduction of forms of credit that irrigated the elites' estates and contributed to turning money (sometimes paper money) into a universal operator that could utilise

---

Robert Descimon, *L'Absolutisme en France. Histoire et Historiographie*, Paris, Seuil, 2002.

53   Robert Descimon, "Élites parisiennes entre XVᵉ et XVIIᵉ siècle. Du bon usage du Cabinet des Titres", in *Bibliothèque de l'École des chartes*, 155, 1997, pp. 607–644.

54   See Robert Descimon, "Élites parisiennes ", art. cit., as well as "Chercher de nouvelles voies", art. cit.

55   Roberto Bizzocchi, *Genealogie incredibili. Scritti di storia nell'Europa moderna*, Bologna, Il Mulino, 1995.

properties as well as dignities. Hence, finance became the crux of the political *praxis* of absolutism;[56] it reshaped the elites and their increasingly money-based practices of transmission, as can be seen in the development of money-dowries in the eighteenth century.[57] This monetisation, as well as credit extension, accelerated the circulation of property outside the kinship area.

Finally, let us mention the part played by the monarchy in widening the gap between the domestic and the public spheres and, as a corollary, in facilitating the gradual emergence of the concept of a "private" sphere.[58] These royal policies encouraged the bloodline and patrilineage as the models organising nobiliary kinship and, at the same time, weakened the ideological basis for domination by the second order.

Separating kinship from the transmitted estate

As a consequence of the strengthening of this patrilineal inflexion, residence – namely seigniory – became of secondary importance in naming practices and in the domestic organisation compared with male filiation. In other words, from the second half of the sixteenth century and, above all, in the seventeenth century, noble kinship underwent a de-spatialization trend, opposite to what happened in the eleventh and twelfth centuries. This weakened the original "topolines" and the "house" model. Due to the shift in the naming system in Louis XIV's reign, mentions of names of seigniory (as "*sieur de*" or "*seigneur de*") gradually disappeared and were directly integrated into patronymic names (e.g. the Compain de l'Etang) without any relation to the effective possession of seigniory.[59] This change went hand in hand with the inflationist granting of feudal titles by the monarchy, also partially disconnected from any real possession, while titles were put at the service of differentiation inside kinship sets (especially among siblings) without any relation whatsoever to the ownership

56 Robert Descimon, "*Nobles* de lignage", art. cit.
57 Mathieu Marraud, *La Noblesse de Paris au XVIIIᵉ siècle*, Paris, Seuil, 2000.
58 Roger Chartier (ed.), *Histoire de la vie privée 3. De la Renaissance aux Lumières*, Paris, Seuil, 1999 [1985].
59 Robert Descimon, "Un langage de la dignité. La qualification des personnes dans la société parisienne à l'époque moderne", in Fanny Cosandey (ed.), *Dire et vivre l'ordre social en France sous l'Ancien Régime*, Paris, Éditions de l'EHESS, 2005, pp. 71–72.

of a titled fief. The process of the untying of kinship from any transmitted estate also contributed to untying "houses".

This structural fact made possible the development of land circulation, under the combined pressure of economic changes and the crisis of the "house" model when confronted by the rise of patrilineal ideology. The increasing monetisation and use of credit, when associated with the strengthening of blood over estate in the conception of noble kinship, tended to reduce the attachment of men to land or of nobles to their seigniory, and thus to increase the circulation of estates and to endow property merely with a market price. In this respect, it is noticeable that between the sixteenth and the eighteenth centuries, the way seigniories were described in the acts changed thoroughly: their value was gradually monetised, including in-kind fees whose money-equivalent was systematically given – an unknown practice in the sixteenth century. The weight of rents (of different natures, either active or passive) in estates, the drastic drop in land dowries, the boost to seigniories sold outside kinship circles (including through small adverts placed countrywide) are all elements tending toward the same direction, with a dislocation of the link between status, estate and power. More thorough research is required to establish whether these changes occurred at different times, either in different provinces or at different levels of the nobility. Nevertheless, the general character of the shift cannot be questioned.

Was noble kinship an exception in French society?

Is it possible to compare the changes in noble kinship to what happened in the rest of French society? At that time, as the noble complex referred to the family and domestic group living under the same roof, to the dwelling itself and to the economic estate embracing the whole, its management was considered in terms of political governance. It was a commonplace to draw a parallel with the political organisation of the kingdom, to praise the prince's quintessential "paternal qualities" or to speak of him as the master in his *house*.[60] The political-domestic articulation was based on a fundamental organisation of monarchy, the *maison royale*. The comparison between *house* governance and the governance of the kingdom was easier

---

60   Aurélie Du Crest, *Modèle familial et autorité monarchique (XVIe–XVIIIe siècle)*, Aix-en-Provence, Presses universitaires d'Aix-Marseille, 2002.

since the French monarchy was established on the double basis of private property and public realm, combining dynastic and political strands, due to the consequences of the Salic law and the monarchy's specific developments between the fourteenth and seventeenth centuries.[61]

Does this mean that the *maison royale* acted as a social model for the French nobility? It is not easy to answer that question. The idea of a top-down influence, especially with regard to kinship, is common among historians of the family. Of course Ernst Kantorowick showed that the notion of *maison royale* was forged in the 14th century with reference to *universita*[62]. It might have become a benchmark for kinship continuity, strongly acknowledged in the fourteenth century succession crisis: a kinship structured around the possession and transmission of property was likely to create some ideal corporate unity. The *maison royale* became a commonly used expression in the fifteenth century, when this term was increasingly used to designate families of the upper nobility.

However, it could also be asked why the "house" system that prevailed in parts of the French peasantry was not one of the roots for kinship social organisation in the traditional society of medieval and early modern France. Noble *house* referred to a name that was not simply a land-based name. Though it was based on a principal seigniory, i.e. with real landed origins, it could become detached from it. And this was never possible in peasant "houses". In other words, a noble "house" was a milder form of "house" anthropologically speaking: only part of the estate was mobilised in it; another part circulated through selling and purchasing, both within and between families.

Yet one question remains: why did peasants not undergo the same transformation in domestic organisation? According to the area, either the *parentèle* model or the lineage model prevailed.[63] In both cases, the transmission practices were organised around a logic of descent, while in the

---

61 Fanny Cosandey, "De lance en quenouille. La place de la reine dans l'État moderne (14ᵉ–17ᵉ siècles)", in *Annales H.S.S.*, vol. 52, 1997, n. 2, pp. 799–820; "'La maîtresse de nos biens': pouvoir féminin et puissance dynastique dans la monarchie française d'Ancien Régime", in *Historical Reflections / Réflexions historiques*, vol. 32, 2006, n. 2, pp. 381–401.

62 Ernst Kantorowicz, *Les Deux corps du roi. Essai sur la théologie politique au Moyen Âge*, Paris, Gallimard, 2000 [1957], p. 880.

63 See Georges Augustins, *Comment se perpétuer? Devenir des lignées et destins des patrimoines dans les paysanneries européennes*, Nanterre, Société d'ethnologie, 1989 and Dionigi Albera, *Au fil des générations*, *op. cit.*

"house" case the prevailing logic was that of residence. In the former case, the right to inherit was strictly determined by kinship. In the latter case, this right was related to the material, natural and finally "sociological" links between the domestic group and the property involved in the transmission issue; inheriting necessarily meant being a successor – the notions cannot be dissociated here[64]. According to B. Derouet, the linear and vertical structure of kinship is always based on social exogenous processes depending on the kind of property (either offices, fiefs, or land) or on how property was empowered through immobilization. As for D. Albera, he implicitly relates the model of domestic organisation he called *Bauer* to feudality, and the appearance of agnatic or bilateral orientations to the weakening of the feudal yoke. Obviously noble "houses" were entwined with the seigneurial system: "topolines" and nobles "houses" were established before the notion of *maison royale,* which appeared as a specific way of institutionalising the domestic basis of the king's power. From this point of view, though this institution may have influenced the way nobles conceived their own *house* and domestic organisation from the fifteenth century, it cannot be the origin of it. Noble kinship was cognatic and based on the same principles as the whole of medieval Western Christianity. On the other hand, the forms of domestic organisation in the nobility were proper to the *dominium* relationship settled by the seigneurial system through the possession of landed estates.

Conclusion: How to consider the development of French noble kinship within the context of changes within European kinship?

The reason for the untying of "house" from transmitted estate is due to the convergence of several different factors. Among them we may mention the loss of the real character of noble titles and dignities, as a consequence of royal policies, as well as the insistence on the antiquity of nobility and male line transmission that stressed the patrilineal bias of domestic organisation, through a social process that began in the second half of the

---

64   Bernard Derouet, "Territoire et parenté", art. cit., p. 655.

sixteenth century and was confirmed by Colbert's reforms. We must also add the increasing mobility of seigniories – which was a sign of a new conception of the relation to land possession – and the expansion of credit. The seigneurial system, which was an integral part of the French monarchical structure, thus lies at the root of changes in noble kinship and, more generally, in concepts of nobility. However, the process of the untying was never complete as long as the seigniory existed as a fundamental structure of property. Likewise the French monarchy could never divorce itself from its feudal and domestic origins.

The particular path of French noble domestic organisation was due to the specific political and social history of the Kingdom within an inherited structure – the feudal and seigneurial system which was destroyed only by the Revolution. This trend towards a domestic organisation founded on "houses" produced a path dependency which allows us to understand many long term specificities of nobility. It had important social effects, even if it did not prevent transformations during the Early Modern period. D. Albera's interpretation of the spatial variations of domestic organisations is thus relevant in order to understand the specific history of the domestic organisation of a social group.

FABRICE BOUDJAABA

Changes in the Norman Inheritance System: a Legal Revolution or an Anthropological Evolution of Kinship in the Eighteenth and Nineteenth Centuries?

In the last ten years several important publications linking family organisation with systems of transmission and social and family reproduction have revitalised both fields and provided new avenues of research. In contrast to previous decades' sometimes excessive reliance on case studies, these new studies by David Sabean, Jon Mathieu and Simon Teuscher on kinship in Europe[1] and by Dionigi Albera on kinship in alpine Europe[2], have reintroduced a systematic framework as well as a long-term approach into the field. These two new works certainly do not reject the case-study approach; indeed, they often make use of it, but with the intention of placing it within a larger frame of reference on kinship systems in Europe. As a result, they are bound to encourage further case studies of a new kind which will likely confirm or invalidate what have until now been considered the main trends in family organisation in Western Europe between the end of the Middle Ages and the beginning of the twentieth century. Sabean's book, in particular, shows the change from a mainly patrilineal kinship system to one favouring agnatic relationships and the nuclear family from the eighteenth century on.

This hypothesis is stimulating, but it needs to be examined with the help of new empirical methods. François Joseph Ruggiu, in a very interesting note, emphasises that it is based on a series of studies that mostly concern elite groups and may not be valid for the entire population, being

---

1   David W. Sabean, Simon Teuscher, Jon Mathieu (eds.), *Kinship in Europe: Approaches to Long-Term Development (1300–1900),* New York – Oxford, Berghahn Books, 2007.

2   Dionigi Albera, *Au fil des générations. Terre, pouvoir et parenté dans l'Europe alpine (XIVᵉ-XXᵉ siècles),* Grenoble, PUG, 2011.

particularly unrepresentative of peasant communities[3]. Dionigi Albera's work, which shares many of the influences that appear in that of Sabean, looks at all inhabitants of the Alps and thus indirectly answers this criticism, at least in part. However, mountain societies have their own unique geographic and economic characteristics, and it is therefore useful to examine other areas too. Though mountain zones and the stem family have clearly been at the heart of kinship studies in modern Europe[4], Sabean's hypothesis can be just as relevant when examining other areas and other types of family organisation.

From this point of view Normandy offers an interesting opportunity to examine the second phase of long-term changes in the kinship system as proposed by Sabean *et al.* Unlike close-knit communities in mountainous areas or elite groups within the aristocracy, the main type of living arrangement in Normandy was the nuclear family. It was, however, a region where customary family law in the early modern period had a strong patrilineal component throughout the whole population, because virtually all daughters were excluded from inheritance and were married under the dowry system. Normandy, therefore, provides a testing-ground for the hypothesis, put forward by Sabean and his colleagues, that there was a second long-term shift in kinship systems across a rural society in what was mostly plains country, and where the system of transmission was patrilineal, but households were based on the married couple.

Because of its system of inheritance, which was rather specific to Northern France, the Norman case allows us to raise questions about family reproduction from a perspective somewhat similar to that of Albera, that is, in a regional and changing context, but in a region where family structures were very different.

This article will consider two relatively simple questions. How did the Normans, who for several centuries had used a system of customary law which very clearly favoured descent in the male line – since custom excluded daughters from succession – react to the introduction

---

3 François-Joseph Ruggiu, "Histoire de la parenté ou anthropologie historique de la parenté? Autour de *Kinship in Europe*", in *Annales de démographie historique* 1, 2010, pp. 223–256.

4 Dionigi Albera, *Au fil des générations, op. cit.*, pp. 57–68. The case of Cerdagne, which has been studied over the long term, shows that the system of devolution was not static but underwent great changes during the early modern period (Marc Conesa, *D'herbe, de terre et de sang. La Cerdagne du XIVe au XIXe siècle*, Perpignan, PUP, 2012).

of the 1804 Civil Code, which brought in perfect equality of inheritance between sons and daughters? And how did peasants and small artisans respond to this change, which was, above all, political and legal? If they accepted it, were they imitating the other social classes, or were they anticipating that the law would change anyway? In other words, was the nineteenth-century trend towards a family founded on the married couple the result of the institutional change signalled by the introduction of the Civil Code, or did the change originate in earlier developments in the Norman family dating from before the legal transformations of the Revolutionary era?

It is often difficult for the historian to carry out a study encompassing both a large geographic area and a long period of time, because the shifting legal relations that, in practice, indicate changes in the Norman system of kinship, can only be identified in the details of notarial acts and in the clauses of wills or marriage contracts. This would mean finding comparable sources over several centuries for the same area, and would require a great deal of research encompassing a wide range of secondary sources in order to cover the longest possible period and widest possible area. That in turn would make valid comparisons very difficult, since each researcher would follow his own method. That is why we have chosen to concentrate on the period of the implementation of the Civil Code.

Unless we argue that the acceptance of the new family law was only a sign of a legalistically-minded population[5] – and surely if that were the case we should speak only of legal systems and not of family systems – the implementation of the Civil Code allows us to conduct an *in vitro* experiment, a kind of laboratory test. The way in which individuals agreed, or did not agree, to break with a system of male privilege and female exclusion which stretched back centuries, should help us better understand both the nature of the changes within the Norman family system and the legal concepts used by historians interested in the subject of transmission.

For this study I have relied on the analysis of wills from the eighteenth century and of marriage contracts from the first third of the nineteenth century. The documents come from two areas of Normandy: Vernon, a rural region in the Paris-Rouen corridor, on the edge of the Île-de-France,

---

5   Jérôme Viret, *La famille normande. Mobilité et frustrations sociales au siècle des Lumières*, Rennes, Presses Universitaires de Rennes, 2013, pp. 331–337.

with wheat fields on the plateau and vines in the Seine valley[6]; and the region around Beaumont, near Pont-l'Évêque, which lies to the west, in the heart of Normandy, and specialises in cattle farming[7].

I shall describe the main features of Norman customary law and then look at the reception the Normans gave to the Civil Code. Since, as we shall see, the new rules that overturned the existing rules of transmission were easily accepted, I shall then return to look at the way in which eighteenth-century Normans drew up their wills and marriages in order to understand their changing attitudes towards the patrilineal principle. Is it possible at that period to discern signs of a new balance favourable to women in transmissions and to see it as a sign that the masculine and vertical conception of kinship was yielding to a conception based on the nuclear family?

The main patrilineal principles in the Custom of Normandy as compared to the Civil Code

Among customary laws, the Custom of Normandy is generally considered to belong to the egalitarian type. Jean Yver thought that it belonged to the category of "Customs of strict equality"[8]. More recent legal historians agree with this[9]. However, this equality only held for some of the children, that is the male heirs. The daughters were not, strictly speaking, excluded from the succession, but rather, they would be disqualified in cases where one or more brothers were present[10]. As compensation they had the right to a *légitime* [money towards their dowry]. Under the Custom, particular attention was paid to the transmission of property down the paternal

---

6   Fabrice Boudjaaba, *Des paysans attachés à la terre? Familles, marchés et patrimoines dans la région de Vernon (1750–1830)*, Paris, Presses Universitaires de la Sorbonne, 2008.

7   Jacques Renard, *Pont-l'Évêque et ses campagnes aux XVIIIe et XIXe siècles: des veaux et des hommes, un exemple d'oliganthropie anticipatrice*, Paris, SPM, 2011.

8   Jean Yver, *Essai de géographie coutumière, égalité entre héritiers et exclusion des enfants dotés*, Paris, Sirey, 1966.

9   Jacqueline Musset, *Le Régime des biens entre époux en droit normand du XVIe siècle à la Révolution*. Caen, Presses Universitaires de Caen, 1997.

10   Article 235 of the Custom of Normandy.

line; and equally among all male heirs, which is why bequests were not encouraged. Another main characteristic of the Norman Custom was "the distinction, emphasised more than in other Customs, between personal property (*biens propres*) and the movables and acquisitions obtained by the couple during the marriage (*meubles et acquêts*) in order to give a clearer structure to the succession of the personal property"[11]. The desire to preserve the family line meant that the Custom paid great attention to the fate of the *propres* and limited the possibility of bequests. Article 427 of the Custom thus forbade all bequests of *propres*, even when the individual had no children[12]. Not only did the Custom not allow one particular son to be favoured, it also strictly limited the power to make bequests, even when the individuals had no direct heirs; this must have affected a large number of inheritances, since the dowry system was enforced by the Custom, and so limited the possibility of the patrimony being mixed in with community of property. The *propres* were excluded and went to the collateral heirs in the paternal line; when the direct male line died out, the patrilineage took over[13].

It was also the case that disguised bequests, such as the sale of property at well below market value, were also problematic, since the *retrait lignager*, which allowed relations to recover at will goods sold, applied not only to an individual's *propres,* but also to the *acquêts*. The rights in the male line were reinforced still further by the *retrait lignager*, which is discussed at length in Articles 468 to 477 of the Custom.

Overall then, though the Custom of Normandy included an egalitarian principle, it also had a strong patrilineal character because of its exclusion of daughters from the succession and the provisions for keeping the *propres* in the male line.

This orientation of the Custom was reinforced by matrimonial law. Unlike many regions with so-called egalitarian division of property, Normandy did not recognise, and even prohibited, community of property. The "legal" matrimonial regime was the dowry. This, whether drawn up by

---

11   Charles Lefebvre, "L'ancien droit matrimonial en Normandie", in *Nouvelle revue historique de droit*, Paris, A. Picard, 1911, p. 77.

12   Even for property acquired in the course of marriage (*acquêts*), the Custom sought to avoid breaking up the inheritance since the possibility of making a bequest was limited to a third of these goods when there were no children.

13   The possibility of a bequest was strictly framed and limited. Article 427 forbade all bequests of personal property (*propres*) even for someone with no descendants.

a notary or not, applied to everyone; Article 389 of the Custom explicitly forbade the community of property. The daughters could claim their right to a *légitime*, that is a dowry (*dot*). However, the obligation of fathers to provide a dowry for their daughters was only a moral one. The legal obligation rested on the brothers when the father had died before their sister's wedding. The Custom strongly protected the *biens propres* from dispersion. The dowry came from the father's *propres* but could amount to no more than a third, and it was always less than the brothers' share. But the Custom also offered the possibility of giving a "*don mobil*", a gift of money or furniture, to the husband, to avoid encroaching on the *propres* and so protecting the patrilineal estate. If the wife was widowed, she had a right to a dower portion (*douaire*), either the amount set by the Custom ("*coutumier*"), which was more generous and corresponded to the usufruct of a third of the husband's *propres*, or a "set amount" (*préfix*), always less than a third. In addition, she had a right to a third of the movables (*meubles*) in full ownership and the usufruct of a third of her husband's *acquêts*.

The Civil Code called the principles of the Custom into question and its application implied a profound transformation of the patrilineal principles regulating the mechanisms of transmission in the *ancien régime* of Normandy. It imposed egalitarian division between all the children, including the daughters, but left a portion free with which to give an advantage to one child. The Code also provided for the common property of *biens meubles* and *acquêts* as part of the legal framework. The dowry system was still permitted, however, as long as the marriage contract was drawn up by a notary (Article 1387).

The "Civil Code moment" is a particularly favourable time to examine how family systems evolved in relation to the law. The text changed the common rules of transmission but the old practices could be maintained, if individuals wished, by the use of different legal tools such as donations, wills or marriage contracts. Examining how people made use of the notaries services ought to tell us how Normans reacted to the introduction of the Civil Code and how attached they remained to certain modes of operation in the family domain. However, this is only possible where there was easy access to the law, either on a financial or on an intellectual level, for whatever social group is being studied. In other words, we can only observe the attachment or otherwise of small peasants and artisans to the patrilineal principle in circumstances where they were able to use the tools the law offered. A quick survey of evidence from notarial archives has made it possible to settle this question.

Wills and donations at the beginning of the nineteenth century: were they used to re-establish the male heirs' ancient rights?

To turn to the practice of making donations and wills, there was a great increase in this type of activity after the implementation of the Civil Code. In the Vernon region, with a population of 7–8,000, there were about 3 wills a year entered in the registers of notarised acts (*Enregistrement*) between 1750 and 1789[14]. Between 1807 and 1826 this figure was multiplied by about 17 or 18, with around fifty wills registered each year. The same tendency can be seen with donations, where the frequency increased from around one a year before the Revolution to about 17 a year after the Civil Code was introduced.

In the Pont l'Evêque region, even though the data was taken from a smaller sample, the results lead to the same conclusions. In this case, we did not make a systematic examination of all the notarial acts for the period 1750–1830, but only took a sample from the notarial minutes of Beaumont from two years in the period before the Revolution and two years around 1820. In the 1768 and 1771 minutes of Maître Féral, the notary of Beaumont, we found only 4 wills, as opposed to 34 for the years 1817 and 1822 in the records of Maître Follebarbe, his successor. Testaments were, therefore, nearly ten times as common in the 1820s as they were in the 1770s. As for donations *inter vivos*, there were only two acts in Féral's records as opposed to 8 in Follebarbe's.

In both cases, it is undeniable that this practice grew significantly after the introduction of the Civil Code, which shows that individuals reacted to the new laws by making use of the judicial tools at their disposal.

---

14   This analysis was based on a study of all the acts concerning individuals whose family name began with B, about 10 per cent of the population. See Fabrice Boudjaaba, *Des paysans attachés à la terre?*, *op. cit.*

But which individuals took such action? Was the ability to use the law to preserve a certain method of transmission, and conception of the family, confined to educated and/or wealthy groups, or was it equally shared by all? Given the nature and size of these tallies in the notarial archives, it is clearly difficult to determine the precise profile of those making wills and to claim to have a sociologically representative sample. However, we can show whether the testamentary practices were urban, rural or mixed, and whether they were elitist or from a wider range of social groups.

The sources do not always make it possible to know the exact profession or marital status of the testator[15] and so to make definitive statements about these issues. When profession and status are mentioned in the acts, they may provide evidence as to what milieu the testators belonged to, but without giving precise information about their wealth. It must be remembered that most wills are not equivalent to the succession arrangements of the individual. Except in the case of partition wills (*testaments–partages*), which laid down the succession rather than naming the chosen legatees, the will only tells us about the objects bequeathed, not the whole make-up of the testator's fortune. At Vernon, among the testators in the 12 wills dating from the end of the *ancien régime*, there were two *tonneliers*, a *vigneron, a laboureur,* a former *curé*, a former servant and four women (two widows and two single)[16]. Two things should be noted here: first, the variety of the social groups among the testators, showing that wills were not only for the elites but were also used by the humblest sort; second, the importance of women, who drew up one in three wills. At the beginning of the nineteenth century, the number of wills is larger (160), making it possible to show some of the specific characteristics of this latter group.

In this later period the will-makers of Vernon came from varied backgrounds. There were peasants in the wider sense – farmers (*cultivateurs*) (8), winegrowers (*vignerons*) (14), day-labourers (2), and some landowners (15) – but also artisans (13). Thus, the choice of arranging one's own succession was not just reserved for the elites, which, to me, seems to indicate that even individuals in modest circumstances were familiar with the law. So, even though Normans had for several centuries practised a customary egalitarian division which left little freedom to bequeath, the

---

15   This is particularly the case with wills taken from the summaries in the Enregistrement and not directly from the notarial acts – the notarial acts for the eighteenth century were partially destroyed.

16   For two testators, there is no information on their profession and marital status.

ability to use and manipulate the law was not limited to an educated elite but shared by all social groups. Women, be they single, married or widowed, were also frequent will-makers, accounting for more than a third of the total (58 out of 160). Married women were particularly numerous (39 out of 58) although none had made wills under the old regime. This can be explained by the changes in matrimonial law: the almost total disappearance of the dowry system, which we will discuss below, in favour of community of property between spouses, as well as the full and complete participation of daughters in the inheritance, explains why married women had additional reasons to make a will.

Similar conclusions can be drawn from a study of the records of the Beaumont notary in the Pont l'Evêque region. In the 1820s there was a great variety of occupations, with both peasants (8 out of 32) and artisans (8) exercising their right to make a will. Again, about a third of testators were women (9 out of 32). The fact that women were succeeding to estates, as a result of the Civil Code, is no doubt one of the main reasons they appear here among the will-makers[17].

Overall, drawing up a will, though done by only a minority of those with possessions to bequeath, was a universal practice in that it was not exclusive to any one socio-professional group or sex. In these conditions under an egalitarian regime, even though it discouraged wills, the liberty to make a will was not specific to a precise category of individuals with particular patrimonial interests to defend. Will-making was also not particular to winegrowers or farmers, who were most concerned by problems created by divided estates that threatened the survival and continuation of the farms. A close study of donations *inter vivos* would lead to similar conclusions on these points. Although we cannot claim that these results are in any way representative of the different groups within Norman society, they do suggest that the analysis of testamentary practices can cast light on Norman conceptions of the family and the changes they underwent, whether before the Civil Code or in reaction to it. With this in mind, we now need to look at the content of these wills.

If we set aside the wills of people without descendants, about one third of the wills in the two samples from the nineteenth century, and the small number of wills dealing with secondary aspects of inheritances such

---

17   Fabrice Boudjabaa, "Femmes, patrimoine et marché foncier dans la région de Vernon (1760–1830): le patrilignage normand face au Code civil", in *Histoire et sociétés rurales*, vol. 28, 2007, n. 2, pp. 33–66.

as gifts to faithful servants and bequests to the Church for Masses to be said, the principal item in most of the remaining wills is a donation to the surviving spouse[18].

At Vernon, in the first decades of the nineteenth century, bequests to a spouse made up half of the body of notarial documents studied (18 acts out of 38). One of the most common forms of legacy was to give the surviving spouse full ownership of the movables and the usufruct of the non-movable property. There were, however, many variations, for example: "the usufruct of all movable and immovable property … or one-quarter in ownership and one-quarter in usufruct"[19]; or again, only "half of the immovables in usufruct"[20]. This formula made it possible to ensure the quality of life of the surviving spouse without calling into question the fact that the spouse was not the heir.

Wills favouring the spouse were justified in half of the cases (9 out of 18) by the fact that the couple had no children[21]; this is probably an underestimate since some testators did not specify whether they had children or not. For instance, in Maître Lavoisier's office on 11 November 1819, François Lubin Buisson, day-labourer at Sainte-Colombe, made a gift of half of his possessions in full ownership and half in usufruct to his wife, Marie-Romaine Gorgedoux[22]. The document stated that he was ill at the time. It does not mention the fact, but we know from genealogical evidence drawn from the Vernon demographic database[23] that they had had three children, but that none had survived beyond 1810. He was 43 and his wife was 49. The husband clearly states that he is making the will "in order to provide Marie-Romaine Gorgedoux [his] wife with the means to exist more comfortably after [his] death and to demonstrate the true friendship that [he] has for her". The great majority of bequests to the spouse, in cases where there were no children, were motivated by worries about the

---

18 It should also be noted that the great majority of donations were mutual donations *inter vivos* between spouses.
19 Archives Départementales de l'Eure [ADE], 612 Q 2, testament Beaudot, 25 April 1821.
20 ADE, 4 E 27 179, testament Boucher, 13 May 1824.
21 Four of these wills were, in fact, mutual bequests by the two spouses to the surviving spouse.
22 ADE, 4 E 24 170 étude Lavoisier.
23 Database at the Centre Roland Mousnier, Université Paris-Sorbonne, created by Jean-Pierre Bardet and Jacques Renard. See Fabrice Boudjaaba, *Des paysans attachés à la terre?, op. cit.*, p. 18.

future condition of the surviving spouse. Customary law, which had provided for the dower portion, had been in many ways more advantageous to
the wife than the Civil Code, which, in case of deaths *ab intestat* gave no
right, not even in usufruct, to the possessions of the spouse or to his share
of the community property.

At Beaumont, the proportion of wills designed to protect the surviving spouse was similar. Out of 42 wills, 18, or just under half, aimed to
ensure the future of the surviving spouse. The type of bequest varied and
depended on whether or not there was a child. On 29 May 1817 François
Duplessis, a day-labourer with no children, "gives and bequeaths the ownership and enjoyment of all the property he leaves at his death" to his
wife, Marguerite Lelièvre[24]. Thomas Alleaume, "landlord and farmer" at
Drubec, on 6 August of the same year, "gives and bequeaths to Monique
Leperchey, his wife, who lives with him, half the usufruct of all movable and immovable property belonging to him at the time of his death …
above and beyond the benefit she may derive from the present community
of property between her and him"[25]. He made this bequest on condition
"that she not contract a second or subsequent marriage, and that on the day
of such a marriage the objects bequeathed will cease to belong to her and
may be taken from her by my heirs". It should be noted that at Beaumont,
the wills in favour of the spouse in our sample are almost all in the form
of a mutual bequest: the husband's will is followed on the same day by the
wife's will, which makes a bequest to him in the same terms as his to his
wife.

In the absence of detailed information on the composition of families,
the family relationships and the exact fortune of the testators, it is hard
to grasp the precise meaning of the varying size of bequests. It is clear,
however, that the presence of children tended to reduce their value, even
though the maintenance of the community of property after the death of
the first spouse put off the moment when the heirs received all their due.
It is also likely that the amount of the legacy depended on the size of the
testator's fortune. A modest day-labourer would be more likely to leave all
his property in usufruct, which no doubt would barely suffice to ensure a
decent income for his widow, while a wealthy farmer could more easily
limit the bequest, allowing his heirs to acquire part of the estate on his
death, without leaving his widow in straitened circumstances.

---

24   Archives Départementales du Calvados [ADC], 8ᴱ 28574: will, 29 May 1817.
25   ADC, 8ᴱ 28574, will, 6 August 1817.

Half of the increase in the numbers of wills, but also of *donations entre vifs*, in the post-Revolutionary decades, was thus caused by the spouses' desire to protect each other when they were widowed. The bequest or gift was intended to provide the surviving spouse with the means to set up a new household, alone or with children, in the best possible conditions. This sort of action did not work against the new process of devolution because it only concerned the bequest of usufruct, but it delayed its effect. It did not come about simply because the Civil Code gave Normans greater freedom to bequeath property than under customary law. Rather, these wills constituted a response to the Code's modification of matrimonial law, which profoundly altered the living conditions of widows and widowers. In effect, the Code not only favoured the regime of common property over the dowry regime, so depriving the widow of her dowry (though that was in part compensated for by her share in the common property) but, more importantly, it did away with the dower portion which had allowed widows to benefit from movable property and from part of the non-movable property held by the deceased husband as *propres*.

In general, the drawing up of wills in the two regions never showed signs of any desire to favour one child over another, particularly a son over a daughter; it aimed above all to protect the surviving spouse. In my opinion, this demonstrates the predominance of the marital relationship over any consideration of the family line in matters of inheritance. In this respect, what seems to have worried the Normans about the application of the Civil Code was not that sons were no longer privileged in successions, but that the widow might experience hardship by being deprived of the dower portion bestowed under customary law.

Was the marriage contract a device to exclude daughters?

Marriage contracts also provide a good indication of Norman attitudes to male inheritance privilege and the patrilineal concept of transmission. One of the most distinctive features of Norman customary law was the way it imposed the dowry system on all spouses, even those who did not have the agreement drawn up by a notary. It was said to be a key element in maintaining male lineages since it kept the patrimony of the spouses separate.

It allowed the property of the wife to be returned to her family line in the absence of children but, most importantly, it ensured that all the property acquired by the husband during the marriage remained on his side of the family. Thus, on both sides, it made sure that fixed property and even some of the movables remained in the original family line. From this point of view, the Civil Code caused a small revolution, since it established community of property between spouses as the legal principle.

Like the will, the notarised marriage contract was used by all classes in society, before the Revolution and after. Both peasants and small artisans employed it extensively, although the samples used here are too small to say just how frequently it was used by one or other social group[26]. At the beginning of the nineteenth century, peasants – farmers, winegrowers and day-labourers – made up about half of those signing marriage contracts in the two regions. At Beaumont, this proportion remained much the same after the Revolution as before. But at Vernon, after the Revolution, the share of peasants among those with notarised marriage contracts increased to one out of every two contracts, as opposed to one out of six before.

However, the marriage contract was used in very different ways in the two regions. At Beaumont, a large majority of inhabitants chose the dowry regime. Out of 38 contracts made by Maître Follebarbe between 1817 and 1822, 34 were for dowries, 4 for community of property, and 2 for separation of property. By contrast, between 1826 and 1827, the inhabitants of Vernon (a sample of those with names beginning with the letter B) usually opted for community of property: 26 out of 30 made this decision and only 4 used dowries.

At first glance, the choice of the inhabitants of Beaumont and Pont l'Evêque may seem easier to explain: they took advantage of the possibilities offered by the Civil Code to maintain the old practice. But the path followed by the inhabitants of Vernon seems paradoxical, since they were making contracts for community of property, a system which previously had not required a contract.

However, the behaviour of the Vernon spouses is not in fact paradoxical. If we examine carefully the clauses of the contracts, two main motives emerge. In 9 of the 26 contracts, there was what we may term

---

26   On this point, see Fabrice Boudjaaba, "Le régime dotal normand, un moyen de préserver les intérêts du patrilignage? Une comparaison entre deux régions: Vernon et Pont-l'Évêque (1750–1824)", in *Annales de Démographie Historique*, 1, 2011, pp. 121–139.

an "enlarged community" which, instead of being limited to the property acquired during the marriage, was extended to some of the personal property (*propres*) of each of the spouses. Thus, Marguerite Boudon and Robert Porquerel made a contract before Maître Lavoisier on 22 January 1816[27] which stated "from the property of the future spouses two hundred francs each will be put into the community", thus creating a surplus of 400 francs in the community, taken from their own personal property. In this fashion, these acts created an enlarged estate for the nuclear family.

The second motive was no doubt the more important, since it appeared in all the contracts studied without exception, even in the four that employed the dowry system. This was a mutual donation in favour of the surviving spouse. At the signature of their marriage contract under the common property regime on 11 February 1813[28], the Lapôtre couple, "guided by the sentiments of friendship which they felt for each other and wishing to give proof of them, the said future spouses by these presents do make a mutual and irrevocable donation *inter vivos* to each other and to their survivor, of the usufruct of enjoyment of all the movable and immovable property which on the day of the death of the first to die (…) shall make up his or her succession with no exception or reservation". This donation was to be reduced by half "if there are children". Not all the contracts studied mention the sentiments and friendship that motivated this mutual donation, but all of them contained a donation bearing on the usufruct of the entire succession of the first deceased partner, that is of his or her share of the community and of his or her own property. This clause conformed to article 1094 of the Civil Code[29]. However, although the law provided for the possibility of making a donation partly in usufruct and partly in full ownership, it is significant that all those making contracts chose the other solution, a donation entirely in usufruct. No doubt the couple were seeking a formula in conformity with the new law that was equivalent to the dower portion – one of the central clauses of the

---

27   ADE, 4 E 27 157, étude Lavoisier, marriage Porquerel – Boudon, 22 January 1816.
28   ADE, 4 E 27 157, étude Lavoisier, contract Lapôtre – Bourdon, 11 February 1813.
29   "If there are no children or descendants, the spouse may, either by marriage contract or during the marriage, make over to the other spouse, in ownership, all that he or she would be able to make over to an outsider, and, in addition, the usufruct of all the portion that the law prohibits making over away from the heirs. And in the case where the spouse making the donation leaves children or descendants, he or she may leave to the other spouse either a quarter in ownership and a quarter in usufruct, or half of all the property in usufruct only."

customary dowry system – but with a bigger portion. By mutual gifts of usufruct, they guaranteed the living standard of the surviving spouse, particularly the widow. This preoccupation was certainly not incompatible with those of succession and family line, but the latter became secondary and were not the reason for the contract.

The inhabitants of the Vernon region knew perfectly well how to adapt to the new law to attain certain objectives. They used their legal knowledge, or that of the notary, not to protect patrilineal rights, which would have been perfectly possible within the Code, but to guarantee the best possible living conditions for the widows.

What can be learned from the marriage contracts drawn up at Beaumont by Maître Follebarbe between 1817 and 1822? The clauses are actually very similar since the great majority of dowry system contracts provide, paradoxically, for common ownership of property acquired during the marriage (a *sociéte d'acquêts*) – in fact, exactly 27 of the 34 contracts under the dowry system provided for a commonality of acquisitions. In a way, this drained the dowry system of most of its content, since the only difference between this and a regime of common property was that the furnishings brought into the marriage by the wife returned to her in their entirety, whereas under common property, those brought by the wife and those acquired during the marriage were equally divided between the two spouses. As for non-movable property, the personal shares (*propres*) remained the property of each of the spouses but property acquired during marriage (*acquêts*) was divided.

The content of the dowry was very different if we consider what was put into common property as equivalent to a dowry. In the Beaumont region, it never included anything but mobile property and money. By contrast, at Vernon, fifteen future brides brought land to the common property contracts, showing that the new rules of succession were being applied. Daughters now had land. However, these differences in the type of property brought in do not necessarily mean that the Civil Code was received in a different fashion there, as it may be the result of sociological differences between the two samples. At Vernon, very small properties were extremely common, and this explains why so many women had land. At Beaumont, ownership was more concentrated and the strong presence of farmers (*cultivateurs*) – 15 of the 37 future bridegrooms – no doubt reflects changes in the terms used to designate professions rather than a complete disappearance of landless, or near-landless, day-labourers.

As at Vernon, all the marriage contracts contain a general "mutual and reciprocal" donation *inter vivos* of the ownership of all movable property and of the usufruct of all non-movable goods by the first deceased to the surviving spouse. If there were surviving children, the donation was reduced by half and only bestowed in usufruct.

On the whole, whatever the method chosen, whether it be the dowry system, common property or even separation of property, it is clear that the most important provisions, the recurrent and most detailed ones, were those dealing with the fate of the surviving spouse, particularly the widow. In these circumstances the increased use of the marriage contract in the years following the application of the Civil Code cannot be explained, or only to a very small degree, by the preoccupations of the contracting parties and their families with the family line. The main purpose of the contract was not to ensure the preservation of property in the male line. In only one single exception, in the sample used here, was the dowry destined to be returned to the succession of the bride's parents. The presence of landed property in the Vernon dowries shows, on the contrary, that the new rules for dividing successions were completely accepted and that the exclusion of daughters had been brought to an end.

In fact, the principal aim of the spouses in drawing up a marriage contract at the beginning of the nineteenth century was rather to create an improved dower portion which would allow the widow to have some capital or a usufruct, or even something more, after her husband's death. Under the customary law, the widow had been barred from sharing in goods acquired during marriage (a *société d'aquêts* was forbidden) but had been compensated by rights of usufruct on her husband's personal property (*propres*) and acquisitions (*acquêts*). Under the Civil Code, the dowry system was still possible but the dower portion, which had been an essential part of the matrimonial system in Norman law, had disappeared. This was why donations between spouses developed, to replace the dower portion of the wife and the *don mobile* of the husband, for a half-share of property acquired in marriage (*acquêts*) was often not enough for modest folk, who had little hope of acquiring enough land to guarantee adequate living conditions for the surviving spouse.

Worries about old age and the viability of the widow's or widower's establishment seem to have been the main motive of the contracting parties in the two regions. The transmission of estates in itself was not at the centre of matrimonial agreements.[30] It is significant that in many common-property contracts at Vernon, the participants had no hesitation in extending the community to include part of the personal property of each spouse. What interested the couple was economic equilibrium and future living conditions. The law guaranteed the preservation of immovable property, particularly the personal property on each side, but the marriage contract was above all concerned with the usufruct, which was what counted most in the life of an individual or couple. The shift to the Civil Code did not inspire Normans to seek ways of perpetuating ancient modes of succession even though the flexibility of the Code made this possible; rather, they sought primarily other forms compatible with the new legislation which would permit the equivalent of the dower portion for the women and, to a certain extent, the *don mobil* for the men, and would even permit them to go beyond these old practices.

A flashback to the eighteenth century: early moves towards the nuclear family?

The easy acceptance of the Civil Code, and the upheaval that it created in the patrilineal system that predominated in Norman customary law, leads to questions about earlier transformations of a customary system that is often depicted as changeless. Unless we believe that people's behaviour was motivated only by an overwhelming legalistic mentality, we may wonder if this acceptance of the Code did not stem from earlier changes in the Norman view of the family and its relation to property transmission.

Two questions serve to highlight changes in the Norman family system and to help us understand this very sudden adaptation to principles of family transmission that were so different from those of customary law.

The first is the *don mobil* clause in marriage contracts. It appeared at the end of the sixteenth century and was widespread in Normandy by the eighteenth century. It arose out of the desire to help the husband meet

---

30   There were few legally delicate situations and conflicts over inheritance in the nine-teenth century and those that occurred, in most cases, had begun before the Code was put in place. See David Bastide, "La survivance de la coutume de Normandie dans la juris-prudence au XIXe siècle", in *Annales de Normandie*, vol. 56, 2006, n. 3, pp. 95–114.

household expenses but went far beyond that in practice. The *don mobil* generally consisted of several hundred *livres*. It appears systematically in marriage contracts in Vernon in 1760–1780. All 30 marriage contracts in Beaumont in the years 1768 and 1771 contain this clause. In Jérome Viret's study of marriage contracts in Argences, only 10.5 per cent of the contracts made before 1723 did not have a *don mobil*. That figure dropped further, to only 2 per cent, after 1761[31]. This advantage given to the husband may be seen as a sign of increased attention to the surviving spouse. The *don mobil* and the dowry in general were not only made up of gifts from the parents, but also came from the wife's savings.

The second point to consider is the importance that historians usually assign to legal distinctions between movable and non-movable property. Norman law, which changed very little in the early modern period, made it obligatory to keep landed property in the male line by the exclusion of daughters, and in the male lineage by the *retrait lignager*. This made it difficult to note certain devices, legal or illegal, that went against the spirit of the law. In the nineteenth century, there was a significant trend to include land in dowries and in the property women brought into the marriage. Their absence in the eighteenth century can of course be interpreted as a sign of the desire to preserve the male line at all costs[32]. However, eighteenth-century marriage contracts contain cash dowries of a value often quite comparable to the price of pieces of land such as are found in those contracts of the nineteenth century. The systematic obligation to find a "re-employment" (*remploi*) for this money often meant buying land. In other words, the Civil Code simply made it easier, in a way, to give pieces of land to daughters. If we admit that a dowry of 300 *livres* in cash and a dowry, or contribution to communal property, consisting of a piece of land worth 300 *livres* are more or less the same thing, we can see that from the eighteenth century onwards the patrilineal principle was already being called into question in Normandy. We have even found in our samples from the second half of the eighteenth century two contracts out of 31 at Vernon and one out of 30 in the Beaumont region which explicitly state that the wife brought a piece of land as dowry, in direct contradiction to the Custom. It may also be added that recourse to *retrait lignager*, though

31   Jérôme Viret, *La famille normande, op. cit.,* p. 79.
32   *Ibid.*, p. 135.

covered by a dozen articles in the Custom, was in fact extremely rare[33] and that, in this regard, the prescription of male lineage in Norman law found little concrete expression.

As for the *don mobil*, some of the marriage contracts, despite the Custom, included land. The contract between the cartwright (*charron*) Jean-Charles Buisson and Marie-Marguerite Driancourt[34] was very explicit on this point. The husband brought nothing to the marriage. His future wife, on the other hand, brought 100 *livres* of jewellery and, "not having a trousseau", the sum of 250 *livres* cash. She also had several properties from the succession of Antoine Demay[35] and from the succession of her maternal grandmother, Jeanne Damour: "the said bride-to-be with the authorisation of her parents, gives a third of these properties to her future spouse as a *don mobil*". Similarly, at Beaumont, a piece of land was included in the *don mobil* given to a day-labourer by his wife[36].

On the whole, practice in the second half of the eighteenth century seems to have been much more flexible than the Custom decreed. Landed property was not really kept outside marriage. There are many cases of permeability between the patrimonies of the spouses that contradict the impression of strict patrilineal transmission obtained from a literal reading of the Custom.

Conclusion

It is impossible to study effectively the way in which wills and marriage contracts operated over the long term, that is three or four centuries. But the way in which the Civil Code was received provides a good point from which to observe the changes in the Norman system of family relations and transmission. The Custom favoured a patrilineal system in multiple ways, by distinguishing between fixed and movable property and by its omnipresent

---

33 Viret found more occurrences for the region of Argences between 1762 and 1789. See *Ibid.*, p. 252.

34 ADE, 4E 27 112, étude Trichard, 8 June 1772.

35 The family link between this man and the bride is not stated in the contract. However, although the demographic database does not allow us to establish the exact relationship, it shows that the bride's mother's maiden name was Demay.

36 ADC, 8ᴱ 28505, étude de Beaumont: marriage, 2 December 1771.

dowry system. The Civil Code included daughters and favoured community of property. But the stark contrast between the two did not provoke any resistance from the Normans. Unless we prefer to believe that individuals were motivated by a deep legalistic instinct, the hypothesis suggested by David W. Sabean, Jon Mathieu and Simon Teuscher, that family systems tend to move towards the nuclear form and away from the patrilineal concept, offers an interesting path to follow in the search to understand the acceptance of the new family law in the Civil Code.

Certain changes in the way that wills and marriage contracts were drawn up in Normandy seem to suggest an increased attention being paid to the spouse and a redirection of patrimonial considerations in favour of the nuclear family. These changes, in this writer's opinion, prepared the way for the later introduction of the Civil Code, regardless of the particular forms it took in each region. On this point, the notaries' role as intermediaries was important[37], as they employed various techniques to ease the shift towards a greater emphasis on the conjugal unit. The choice of a regime of common property, as at Vernon, or the dowry system, as at Beaumont, to achieve the same objective (the protection of the surviving spouse) is very significant in this regard.

It should be emphasised that the new concentration of the family system on the nuclear family was a very widespread social phenomenon. It spread outward from the peasant world to affect the whole of Norman society. Land took up a dominant position in marriage contracts during the nineteenth century as soon as the law permitted, even though the Code would also have allowed the opposite, that is the partial maintenance of masculine privilege and a dowry system based solely on movable property. But the peasants were not just following changes in the law. On the contrary, the implementation of the new law seemed to allow for the legal expression of new forms of relationship linking the peasant world, and indeed the whole of Norman society, with the land and with kinship itself; and the signs of this change were already present in the eighteenth century.

Given the chronological limits of our study, it is difficult to determine a date for the beginning of these new attitudes to the main principles of the Custom that had been laid down when it was drawn up in the sixteenth century. Was it a transformation that took place only in the second half of the eighteenth century, or were the seeds of change already present at an earlier date, from the seventeenth century onwards?

---

37   Dionigi Albera, *Au fil des générations, op. cit.*

JÉRÔME LUTHER VIRET

Children leaving Home in Europe in the Modern Age: Towards a Typology taking into account Western European Forms of Authority*

Enlightened by several decades of research, we are well aware of the many solutions sought by families across Europe to distribute work and resources amongst their own, to anticipate the challenges of old age, to establish their children in households, to form alliances and to climb, however modestly, the social ladder. John Hajnal has set out the existence of a western model, characterised by late marriage and by a high proportion of single individuals. He drew a straight line from Leningrad to Trieste, which separated a Europe of early marriage in the east from a Europe of late marriage in the west. He suggested that later marriage was motivated by a desire for a certain standard of living. Despite his caution, he has been held up as a partisan of the theory of "positions". In order to marry and to establish themselves, young people had somehow to acquire a farm or a profession. Marriage certainly involved a property contribution, particularly land in the case of farming communities. If marriage was comparatively late in western Europe, this was because it was necessary to acquire skills and to find the means to set up a home. It was also in order to guarantee a certain standard of living. But who decided what was an acceptable standard of living? Was it the couple themselves, the parents, or even the local authorities? Marriage always involves questions of power, particularly that exerted by parents. Yet this is an area to which historians obsessed by economic questions have paid scant attention. A typology of family systems must incorporate the ways in which power is exercised.

Jacques Dupâquier has interpreted marriage as "a kind of licence to reproduce accorded to a couple by society"[1]. In the case of France, if

---

*   Translation by Alice C. Holt.
1   Jacques Dupâquier, *Histoire de la population française, vol. 2, De la Renaissance à 1789,* Paris, PUF, 1995 [1ere édition, 1988], p. 430.

not of Germanic territories, the hypothesis of institutional control can be rejected[2]. Dupâquier does evoke the role of parents but places particular emphasis on agrarian structures and the return on production. Failing the emergence of a rural industry, the number of rural homesteads could not expand indefinitely. The unwillingness of parents and married children to share a home and the desire for independence led to a rise in the age of marriage. This functioned as a "preventive check" within the land-based structure on the growth of population. This explains to a large extent why the rise in the age of marriage occurred during the sixteenth century and why it affected such vast swathes of western Europe[3]. However, this hardly encourages the study of how couples actually set up home and, in particular, how power was exercised within the family. Few have written in any great detail about how young households were set up. Laurent Herment has shown, at least as far as the Beauce and Gâtinais regions are concerned, that the level of resources brought to the marriage by the couple could be the determining factor. Around 1850, ploughing, manure and seed would require some 250 francs per hectare and, therefore, 6000 francs for 30 hectares. Certainly, children who had inherited from their parents were in a better position, and freer to set up home at a time of their choosing. But that is not to say that the parents, were they still alive, would have blocked the marriage. Unfortunately there has been too little study of all this. Yet it is clear that parents could exert considerable pressure, through their freedom to fix the amount of the dowry or to provide an advance on their child's inheritance. It is this question which will be examined here, as it refers to the rules of inheritance. The aim here is to consider the dynamics of social and family life, on the basis of marriage contracts and the body of common law[4]. Villiers-le-Bel in the Paris area, and Argences

---

2   Georg Fertig, "The Hajnal thesis before Hajnal: the pre-history of the European Marriage Pattern", Historisches Seminar der Universität Münster, mars 2004.

3   Daniel Devolder, *Cycles démographiques et cycles économiques de longue période dans les pays occidentaux, XVᵉ–XXᵉ siècles*, Thèse, Institut d'Etudes politiques de Paris, 1994.

4   In the case of Villiers-le-Bel, the sample consisted of 201 marriage contracts, 148 cases of guardianship appointments, 48 recorded completions of guardianship, 37 records of advance on inheritance. AD 95, 2E4 notarial minutes of Ecouen, 1640–1660. For Argences, use has been made of 92 appointments of guardianship and 255 marriage contracts. AD14, 8E 23630 to 23673. Several annotated works on Parisian and Norman customs have been used, principally Jean Brodeau and Jean Choppin for Paris (1658 and 1614), Basnage and Houard for Normandy (1778 and 1780).

in Normandy, reveal sharply diverging conceptions of the couple and radically different approaches to inheritance transfer[5]. However, the age at first marriage remains fairly similar. How then should we address a typology as crude as that which contrasts early and late marriage, and brings together types of family as different as those found in a Parisian and a Norman province? Have we given a sufficiently comprehensive account by simply stating that the nuclear family triumphs in Paris as it does in Caen in Normandy? The respective positions of the spouses and the conception of the couple and of the family had implications for the age at marriage. But was this really important? Age at marriage, early or late, has significant consequences in terms of fertility. But were families preoccupied above all by this? The control of intergenerational transfers, carefully calculated by parents, was undoubtedly a matter of greater parental concern than the desire to limit the number of children or to improve the lot of the generation to follow. This is what will be shown here, using Norman and Parisian examples. But first, the insights and oversights of the historiography will be briefly touched upon.

The Western European Model

If girls married late in western Europe, this seems to have been because of the nature and composition of the servant population. Mikolaj Szoltsysek has pointed out the existence of significant contrasts between Poland and Belarus, confirming this hypothesis[6]. The presence of complex households had a negative impact on the number of servants. As one moved eastward, family complexity increased and the number of servants fell. Since, in eastern Europe, domestic service was not so important for marriage, it was possible for girls to marry at a younger age. But this can look very

---

5   Jérôme-Luther Viret, *Valeurs et pouvoir. La reproduction familiale et sociale en Ile-de-France. Ecouen et Villiers-le-Bel (1560–1685),* Paris, PUPS, 2004; *Id., La famille normande. Mobilités et frustrations sociales au siècle des Lumières,* Rennes, PUR, 2013.
6   Mikolaj Szoltysek, "Life cycle service and family systems in the rural countryside: a lesson from historical East-central Europe", in *Annales de Démographie Historique,* 1, 2009, pp. 53–94.

different if one does not assume that setting up home was the responsibility of girls. The establishment of children is just as much the responsibility of parents, backed by the inheritance still in their possession, as it is that of the child. Of primary concern, then, is the contribution of the parents. In this type of family structure, parents could marry off their daughters without having to obtain independent settlements for them.

Did parents in the west consider that children ought to find their own means to set up a home? It would seem so, but attitudes varied from one country to the next. In England, in the Low Countries and in Scandinavia, the placing of children in domestic service, while not universal, was at least very widespread, even amongst wealthy peasants[7]. In Sweden, in the eighteenth century, the likelihood of being a servant prior to marriage was very high[8]. In the centre-east of Sweden, 40% of twenty-year-old sons of property owners were servants. However, this proportion rose to 80% amongst those without property. Landless peasants could do nothing for their young folk. The children of those with property shared the same predicament but left home slightly later and in fewer numbers, since they could be found employment on the family land[9]. The size of the holding, therefore, played an essential role. In Sweden, two servants (a man and a woman) were sufficient for a farm of 10 to 15 acres. For larger holdings of 50 to 60 acres, four servants were needed[10]. It was also the case elsewhere that the scale of the area under cultivation, and the existence of livestock requiring a great deal of work throughout the year, caused a boom in the levels of domestic service[11]. However, this was not solely a question of the best use of labour. A child placed outside the home is no longer dependent

7   Ann Kussmaul, *Servants in husbandry in Early Modern England,* Cambridge, Cambridge University Press, 1981; Beatrice Moring, "Migration, Servanthood and assimilation in a new environment", in Antoinette Fauve-Chamoux (ed.), *Domestic Service and the formation of European Identity. Understanding the globalization of domestic work,* Bern-Berlin, Peter Lang, 2004, pp. 43–70.

8   Christer Lundh, "The Social Mobility of Servants in Rural Sweden, 1740–1894", in *Continuity and Change,* 1, 1999, pp. 57–89.

9   Martin Dribe, "Leaving Home as a Family Strategy in Times of Economic and Demographic Stress. The Case of Rural Scania, Sweden, 1829–1866", in Frans Van Poppel, Michel Oris, James Lee (eds.), *The road to independence. Leaving home in western and eastern societies, 16th–20th centuries,* Bern, Peter Lang, 2003, pp. 85–116.

10   Martin Dribe, Christer Lundh, "People on the move. Determinants of Servant Migration in Nineteenth Century Sweden", in *Continuity and change,* 20, 2005, 1, pp. 53–91.

11   Isidro Dubert, "Agricultural Work, Social Structure and Labour Markets of the Rural Domestic Service in Galicia in the mid-Eighteenth century", in Antoinette

on his or her parents. Furthermore, it is not surprising to see them more readily sent away at times of underemployment on the family holding. In other countries, people might have thought differently and preferred underemployment to dishonour. It has been shown that in southern Italy, domestic service was regarded as somewhat humiliating and degrading[12]. The entry into service of widows without parents or means arose from strict and harsh necessity. If they were younger, servants were mainly orphans, abandoned children, or women without relatives and with little prospect of marriage[13]. Equally, in Schwäbisch Hall, in southern Germany, more than half of all servants had lost a parent, and orphaned girls were overrepresented amongst the youngest servants. For girls from good families, entry into domestic service represented a loss of status and class[14]. Powerful sociocultural factors held back the development of domestic service to a certain extent.

The question of domestic service has taken on such importance in the debate on the age of marriage because there is a clear and solidly documented link between the two. Indeed, we know that such employment tended to put off the time of marriage, especially for girls. Valets and other servants enjoyed a reasonably good standard of living, better than many day-labourers. They could work several additional years, beyond what was necessary, to attain a better standard of living. In the Low Countries, in the eighteenth century, Jona Schellekens estimates that at most six years in service were necessary prior to marriage. Why, then, did the children of day labourers, after a period of domestic service, marry so late, on average at 30.8 years for men and 29.4 years for women? The men had neither wives nor children to support. They did not face seasonal unemployment and had a reasonably good standard of living. There was, therefore, most likely another reason to delay marriage. Some saved for longer in the hope of being able to acquire a cottage or small farm. This ambition explains

---

Fauve-Chamoux, (ed.), *Domestic Service and the formation of European Identity*, *op. cit.*, pp. 113–126.

12   Giovanna Da Molin, "Family forms and domestic service in southern Italy from the seventeenth to the nineteenth centuries", in *Journal of Family history*, vol. 15, 1990, n. 4, pp. 503–527.

13   Raffaella Sarti, "Criados, servi, domestiques, gesinde, servants: for a comparative history of domestic service in Europe (XVIth–XIXth)", in *Obradoiro de Historia Moderna*, n. 16, 2007, pp. 9–39.

14   Renate Dürr, "Les servantes de Schwäbisch Hall au XVIIe siècle: destin et appartenance sociale", in *Annales de Démographie Historique*, 1, 2009, pp. 35–52.

why the rise in wages, instead of shortening the length of service, in fact extended it[15]. Conversely, the fall in wages, by reducing the possibility to save, could discourage those hoping to build up resources before marrying and persuade them to wait no longer. Changes to agrarian structures could play a similar role. In 1770, a Norwich newspaper revealed that the number of small farms had fallen sharply. Whereas previously, hard-working men with savings could hope to rent a farm, what good would it do from now on to save? In the eighteenth century, especially after 1750, the hope of achieving autonomy by establishing a small farm fell away. This could have contributed to the fall in the age of marriage[16]. Deprived of land for livestock in the wake of enclosures, the poor also stopped saving, which they had done in the past for the purchasing of animals[17]. In this scenario, it was the absence of prospects, of opportunities for the individual to progress, which explains the drop in the average age of marriage. It should be noted that all these explanations make children solely responsible for their own establishment in life.

Amongst the numerous criteria governing the age of marriage are the number of siblings and the age at which parents died. In the Low Countries, in the nineteenth century, the death of the mother would accelerate the departure of daughters, since the father would remarry. Boys would also leave home earlier after the death of their mother, even if this pattern was less pronounced than for their sisters. In the Belgian Ardennes also, the death of the mother had considerable impact. The attachment to a mother being much stronger, the propensity to remain in the home diminished where the surviving parent was the father[18]. Did the departure of children then depend entirely on the children themselves, in that they were free to remain or to go? The presence of several children of the same sex also increased the tendency of early departure for at least one amongst them. In Sweden, older children with several brothers left home to reduce the

---

15   Jona Schellekens, "Nuptiality during the first industrial revolution in England: explanations", in *The journal of interdisciplinary history*, n. 4, 1997, pp. 637–654.

16   Bridget Hill, "The Marriage Age of Women and the Demographers", in *History Workshop Journal,* 1, 1989, pp. 129–147 (138).

17   David R. Weir, "Rather Never Than Late: Celibacy and Age at Marriage in English Cohort Fertility, 1541–1871", in *Journal of family History*, vol. 9, 1984, n. 4, pp. 340–354.

18   George Alter, Catherine Capron, "*Leavers and Stayers in the Belgian Ardennes",* in Frans Van Poppel, Michel Oris, James Lee (eds.), *The road to independence, op. cit.,* pp. 117–141.

burden on the household[19]. Without this changing the balance of responsibilities, the gender ratio has been highlighted as important. When men left in large numbers, it became more difficult for girls who remained behind to marry[20]. The impact of rural industry on migration patterns was, as is well-known, considerable, and had varying effects depending on gender. In Cardington, more boys left than girls. Lace-making kept girls at home, whereas there were no opportunities for boys to find work[21]. In the Swiss village of Hausen, near Zurich, spinning did not offer sufficient opportunities to keep boys beyond their adolescence. But at Oetwil, boys worked in textiles beyond the age of twenty, since in this area there were better paid jobs in carding or weaving[22]. It is important, therefore, to pay close attention to the organisation and nature of the work being carried out.

Rural industries did not simply have an impact on the age of marriage in terms of the gender ratio and differential migration. They also acted directly on the age of marriage through the issue of savings. Most authors took it for granted that all, or at least most, earnings belonged to the children. This point, taken as given, allowed historians to devote themselves to what was for them the only really serious question: the age at marriage. J.D. Chambers has revealed an unequivocal link between the presence of rural industries and the fall in the age of marriage in the Trent valley around 1740. David Levine has also shown that in the case of Shepshed, textile work brought the age of marriage down[23]. In nineteenth century Hertfordshire, a limited but real tendency on the part of rural industry to bring down the average age of marriage has been observed[24]. However, on the Continent, the effects were not as conclusive. In the Low

---

19   Martin Dribe, "Leaving Home as a Family Strategy", art. cit.

20   James Lehning, *The Peasants of Marlhes: economic development and family organization in XIXth century France,* Chapel Hill, University of North Carolina Press, 1980.

21   Richard Wall, "The Social and Economic Significance of Servant Migration", in Antoinette Fauve-Chamoux, (eds.), *Domestic Service and the formation of European Identity, op. cit.,* pp. 19–43; David Baker, *The inhabitants of Cardington in 1782,* Bedford, Bedfordshire Historical Record Society, 1973.

22   Ulrich Pfister, "Work Roles and Family Structure in Protoindustrial Zurich", in *Journal of Interdisciplinary History,* vol. 20, 1989, n. 1, pp. 83–105.

23   David Levine, "The demographic implications of rural industrialization: A family reconstitution study of Shepshed, Leicestershire, 1600–1851", in *Social History,* 2, 1976, pp. 177–196.

24   Nigel Goose, "Cottage industry, migration and marriage in Nineteenth Century England", in *The Economic History Review,* 61, 2008, 4, pp. 798–819.

Countries, proto-industry did not exert a profound influence on the age of marriage[25]. The same is true of Belm in Germany, Lille or even Marhles, near Saint-Etienne[26]. In Sowerby, the age at marriage of girls fell slightly. If this varied more than it did for boys, it was because economic insecurity was greater for girls and the need to marry was stronger[27]. Single women, excluded from the benefits of the *Poor Laws*, had to find work or marry. A drop in female employment, in general terms, led to earlier marriage[28]. Here and there, the power of parents makes a timid appearance. In Cardington, parents seem to have become dependent on their daughters' work, resulting in the postponement of marriage[29].

It is clear that a great deal of energy has been spent in explaining the average age at marriage of girls, and to a lesser extent that of boys. In accordance with a particular conception of the family, which emphasises the responsibilities of children, the age of marriage pitches the individual against the labour market. Late marriage can be explained in economic terms by the simple desire of children to make a better start. All this leaves aside the question of parental responsibility. One question, however, remains on the table. Is it possible, on the basis of the average age

25   François M. M. Hendrickx, "Family, farm and factory: labor and the family in the transition from protoindustry to factory industry in nineteenth century Twente, the Netherlands", in *The History of the Family*, vol. 8, 2003, n. 1, pp. 45–69; Pat Hudson, Steve King, "Two textiles townships 1660–1820, a comparative demographic analysis", in *Economic History Review*, vol. 53, 2000, n. 4, pp. 706–741.

26   Jurgen Schlumbohm, "Micro-history and the Macro-Models on the European Demographic system in Pre-industrial Times: life-course patterns in the Parish of Belm (Northwest Germany), Seventeenth to the Nineteenth centuries", in *The history of the Family*, 1, 1996, 1, pp. 81–95; Paul Spagnoli, "Industrialization, Proletarianization and Marriage: a Reconsideration", in *The Journal of Family History*, vol. 8, 1983, n. 3, pp. 230–247; James Lehning, "The timing and prevalence of women's marriage in the French department of the Loire, 1851–189", in *The Journal of Family History*, vol. 13, 1988, n. 1, pp. 307–327.

27   Pat Hudson, Steve King, "Two textiles townships", art. cit.

28   Roger Schofield, "English marriage patterns revisited", in *The Journal of Family history*, 1, 1985, pp. 2–20; Keith D. M. Snell, *Annals of the labouring poor. Social change and agrarian England, 1660–1900,* Cambridge, Cambridge University Press, 1985; John. R Gillis, *For better, for worse. British marriages, 1600 to the present,* Oxford, Oxford University Press, 1985.

29   Richard Wall, "Real property, marriage and children: the evidence from four pre-industrial communities", in Richard M. Smith (ed.), *Land, Kinship and Life-cycle,* Cambridge Studies in Population, Economy and Society in Past Time, Cambridge (Eng.) and New York, Cambridge University Press, 1984, pp. 443–479.

at marriage, which is relatively steady in the west, to resist elaborating a typology of forms of family organisation? Is the indifference of parents regarding their offspring a generally held attitude or merely a particular way of regulating the financial relationship between generations?

The exclusion of girls and marital freedom

Most writers have seen saving money as a necessary stage on the road to marriage, yet generally their work devotes only a few lines to the issue of parental responsibility. Hilde Bras and Jan Kok show that, for example, in Zeeland, children's earnings belonged to the parents as long as the child continued to live with them. However, the situation changed after the child left home[30]. It seems that the daughters of agricultural labourers, who became domestic servants, returned part of their earnings to their parents. Martin Dribe has also confirmed that part of the income of children placed in service was paid back to the home[31]. As the daughter's distance from home and age increased, parental control was weakened. However, Hilde Bras is mainly concerned with age. Children gave their earnings to the parents until they were 16 to 18, after which they kept a growing proportion, and eventually a majority, for themselves[32]. It is regrettable that there has not been more interest in this question. We know that girls who left home to work on a farm or even in town frequently switched employers, and also had a freer choice of husband than girls who stayed at home with their parents. In France, in regions dominated by the nuclear family, at least outside of the elite, parents would loosen their control, even on daughters who remained where they were. The identity of the husband was

---

30 Hilde Bras, Jan Kok, "'Naturally, Every Child Was Supposed to Work'. Determinants of the Leaving Home Process in the Netherlands, 1850–1940", in Frans Van Poppel, Michel Oris, James Lee (Eds.), *The road to independence, op. cit.,* pp. 403–450.

31 Martin Dribe, "Leaving Home as a Family Strategy", art. cit.

32 Hilde Bras, "Domestic service, migration and the social status of women, The case of a Dutch sea province, Zeeland, 1820–1935", in *Historical Social research,* 3, 1998, pp. 3–19; Hilde Bras, Jan Kok, "'Naturally, Every Child Was Supposed to Work'", art. cit.; Hilde Bras, "Maids to the city: migration patterns of female domestic servants from the province of Zeeland, the Netherlands (1850–1950)", in *The History of the Family,* vol. 8, 2003, n. 2, pp. 217–246 (226–227).

less of an issue where girls and parents did not cohabit. The child, it would seem, was left free to choose a spouse. But the widespread principle of homogamy in marriage presupposed that the child would bring a marital contribution of some significance. Yet parents would still contribute to the marriage. As a result, the choice of spouse was not as entirely free as one might think, unless the child waited and saved up meticulously to attain the required amount. Late marriage was as much the price of freedom as it was the price of material comfort. This issue was made more complicated if the child wished to give a part of his or her earnings to the parents. Distance, in this respect, was not an insurmountable obstacle, because even if children did move further away, it was not necessary to return more than once a year to deliver the funds, since salaries were paid on an annual basis.

An analysis of marital customs and contracts in the countryside around Paris and in Normandy illustrates the importance of saving. These two provinces were particularly subject to the laws of custom. People living in such strict provinces of France were constrained or strongly limited in what they could do, and the same was true for parents who wished to exercise discretionary power. There was a preference to remain loyal to the habits of the community. The details of property arrangements between spouses were, however, set out in the marriage contract. Contracts generally respected prevailing customs, with very little room for manoeuvre. Practices in Normandy and around Paris changed only slightly between the sixteenth and the end of the eighteenth centuries. Whereas Norman custom forbade any community of property between spouses, in the Parisian region it was considered virtually obligatory. A wife living in the Parisian area was an associate in the marriage, whereas in Normandy wives effectively worked for their husbands. Even if the situation of wives in Norman towns was slightly better than it was in the countryside, it was still advantageous for women to marry in Paris. For daughters too, it was preferable to be born close to Paris. Whereas girls and boys inherited equally in Paris, girls in Normandy were excluded from inheriting in favour of their brothers. This was an effect of masculine bias. The condition of daughters and wives, and particularly that of widows, of comparable social standing was, therefore, better in Paris than in Normandy.

Almost all marriage contracts drawn up in Villiers-le-Bel listed the value of movable property brought by the daughter – only 12 out of 201 contracts do not make such reference. All cite an advance on the inheritance, in other words an advance on any future legacy. The exact amount is almost always mentioned. This was in fact indispensable for Parisian inheritance arrangements. On the death of each parent, the child had to record what he or she had received on marriage, so that there could be the fairest possible division between all the children. On the very rare occasions when the amount of the advance was not indicated, it was because the parents had been unable to commit themselves to a precise amount. As Didier Michel explained in 1651, he would give his daughter "as much as was in his power to give".[33] The mother of Hélène Daujon also committed herself to give her daughter as an advance on the inheritance "as much movable property as she could without inconvenience to herself".[34] Finally, Jeanne Rocancourt explained to her daughter that she would do "the best that she could".[35] Apart from these rare exceptions, the amount of the advance on the inheritance was always known. But the most important point is that money came in part from the child's earnings, whether at home or elsewhere, without it being necessary for it to be recorded, since in law all the child's earnings belonged to the parents. It is important not to interpret the failure to mention a daughter's earnings as a sign of disdain for her work. On the contrary, people in the Parisian area were extremely aware of the value of any services and work carried out. Orphans would obtain from their guardians as exact an evaluation as was possible of their "services". This mattered because the value of work carried out by minors increased their rights to inheritance. The accounts of guardians observed this scrupulously.[36] In Normandy, it was the custom, by contrast, to impose a strict dowry regime and to rule out any community of property between spouses. What the woman brought to the marriage was, therefore, carefully recorded. This contribution did not constitute an advance on the inheritance, because it was utterly separate and there was no subsequent levelling out. If the sum of the woman's contribution was carefully set out in the marriage contract, it was not to facilitate her inheritance, but to obtain the return of her dowry if she was to be widowed.

The marriage of children, and particularly that of daughters, in Normandy, was an important moment. For many girls in Normandy, and all those

---

33   AD 95, notarial minutes of Ecouen, 7 February 1651.

34   AD 95, notarial minutes of Ecouen, 30 June 1640.

35   AD 95, notarial minutes of Ecouen, 30 January 1651.

36   See, for example, AD 95, notarial minutes of Ecouen, marriage contracts of 24 October 1658, 3 June 1659, 14 February 1659 and 21 November 1660.

with brothers, it was even the defining step of their lives. Endowment by the parents was a one off payment. A girl with a dowry in Normandy could never return to claim additional money or property as a legitimate heir. It is true that, in some cases, parents did leave an inheritance to their daughters, which allowed them to inherit alongside sons. This happened in very precise circumstances and among certain social groups. It was groups of the most modest social standing that did this, and not those with established wealth. The increase in these "entitlements to succession" in the eighteenth century was more the product of economic hardship than rising equality. None of this changes the basic pattern. In people's minds, girls would be totally excluded from further inheritance by virtue of the dowry provided by the parents. The sum total of the contribution brought by the daughter and retained by her from the age of majority – 20 in Normandy against 25 in Paris – could be added to by a contribution from her parents. It is possible to calculate the average size of the parental contribution. It was 110 pounds where there was a specified entitlement (46 contracts) and 150 pounds where there was no such entitlement (73 contracts). Girls entitled to an inheritance along-side their brothers would receive lower amounts, but it must be remembered that this applied to the poorest in society. It was because they received so little that they would go on to inherit, and not the inverse. In the second half of the eighteenth century, and thus rather late, men subtly corrected the dis-advantage imposed by custom. If they could not help their daughters as much as they might wish at their marriage, they promised a little more to come. The wealthier among them did not feel compelled to treat girls and boys equally. For them, the marriage of daughters remained a question of cutting them out as cheaply as possible. The contribution of men at the marriage of their daughters, where there was no future entitlement, fell within a range of 40.3% to 42.8% of the total provision[37]. The daughters' savings represented, therefore, over half of the total provision, and often two thirds or more. It should be added that one in four girls married without any parental contri-bution. This is a figure comparable to records for Dijon in 1780–1781[38]. In these cases, the sum total of the provision came from the girls' earnings.

In order fully to understand the difference between Paris and Nor-mandy, it is important to bear in mind that the age of majority was 20

---

37   Jérôme-Luther Viret, *La famille normande, op. cit.*
38   Michel Petitjean et Françoise Fortunet de Loisy, *Les contrats de mariage à Dijon. Contribution à l'étude des comportements juridiques*, Dijon, Faculté de droit de Dijon, 1980, p. 67.

in Normandy and 25 in Paris. The rarity of female emancipation before the age of 20 in Normandy indicates that girls waited to reach this age to leave the parental home. Shortly after the adoption of the law of 17 Nivôse in the year II, establishing throughout France equality between all children regardless of sex, petitions began to arrive at the Convention. They referred to Normandy and explained that an equal share of movable property with married sisters would be an injustice, since boys "bestowed work and even income on the paternal home". The decree of 22 Ventôse set out that "in the division of inheritance, it could only upset the social order to take into account the number of years children remained in the family home or the greater or lesser amount of work which each of them had contributed"[39]. It is clear from these discussions that daughters tended to leave, whereas their brothers remained with the parents[40]. Unmarried girls over 20 who had left home to work elsewhere kept their earnings, whereas those of boys were added to the family coffers. Boys whose earnings went straight to their families could hardly consider it an injustice since they, to the exclusion of their sisters, were the sole heirs. Thus, girls would leave the parental home around the age of 20 and save up for marriage for a number of years. In Argence, this was until an average age of 24.7[41].

Conclusion

The departure of children, and more particularly of girls, from home, did not have the same significance in Paris and in Normandy. In Normandy, girls only had the right to a lump sum payment, with the amount fixed arbitrarily by the father. It was only relatively late that men seem to have developed some scruples. Fathers, for the most part, clung to the provisions of Norman custom, which imposed no obligation on them. This must have encouraged girls to leave home quickly and to build up their own dowries. Parents felt they had few obligations. Things were different in Paris. The father would pay an advance on the inheritance, which the work of girls

---

39 Decree of 22 Ventôse Year II, interpreting the law of 17 Nivôse Year II, article 1.
40 Jérôme-Luther Viret, *La famille normande, op. cit.,* p. 130.
41 Calculation made by means of a reconstitution of families and indications of age in the marriage contracts of 135 women.

would help to augment. Fathers deemed it a point of honour to give the same advance to all their children. As a result, the unequal contributions of children were not taken into account. Several legal disputes reveal that parents believed they had a claim on their children's work. This was the expected return on care given to children in childhood. A precise evaluation of services rendered occurred only in the case of orphans. Fathers did not measure out their affection. Above all, they did not distinguish between boys and girls. If advances on the inheritance were not always equal between the children, it was because difficulties arose, or more commonly because the funds available dwindled as more children were born. The last child to marry often received less than the others.

This comparison, by contemporary standards, is somewhat unfavourable with regard to Normandy. But the fact that girls played a more direct role in their own establishment in Normandy than in the Parisian countryside could have carried certain advantages. Perhaps this gave them a little more freedom. There is no evidence in Normandy in the eighteenth century of the equivalent of the marital "pools" seen in Villiers-le-Bel in the middle of the seventeenth century, whereby a number of linked families systematically gave each other their children in marriage over the course of a few years. Unusual marriages, such as the marriage of several brothers with several sisters, seem also to have been more common in the Parisian area than in Normandy. Perhaps the Parisian region was simply behind the times. Customs changed in the eighteenth century, allowing greater freedom for girls, in Normandy as elsewhere[42]. Girls in the south, where statute law applied, were more dependent on their parents and married earlier than in the north. The average age at marriage in the countryside of southern France was 24.8 years between 1740 and 1789, while it was 26.6 years in the northern half of the kingdom[43]. This amounts to a difference of almost two years. The latter also often benefited from better dowries than the younger women, who were the victims of the structure prevailing in areas of unequal property inheritance.

A large number of factors affected age at marriage. Local demographic and economic conditions, but also the place and status of the couple in society, as well as the way in which the work of children was regarded,

---

42   Anne Fillon, *Les trois bagues aux doigts. Amours villageoises au XVIIIe siècle*, Paris,
      R. Laffont, 1989.
43   Louis Henry, Jacques Houdaille, "Célibat et âge au mariage aux XVIIIe et XIXe siècles.
      II. Age au premier mariage", in *Population*, vol. 34, 1979, n. 2, pp. 403–442 (421).

all determined the ease and age of marriage. The situation was different again where families formed communities. A legal expert and seasoned observer of matrimonial practice in Nivernais explained that "people in the village married their children off very young, motivated by a desire to increase numbers in family homes as early as possible". In the Panné-Garreau family of Préporché (Nièvre), a large proportion of the boys, and an even higher proportion of the girls, married before their eighteenth birthday[44]. As in eastern Europe, the married child who would remain in the home had no need to build up a nest egg. The necessity to form large communities of workers, and to attract a male labour force, weighed in favour of early marriage for girls. It was not so much the ease with which girls could marry that was at stake, as has often been argued, but rather the desire to attract more young men as quickly as possible. It was for the same reason that in La Courtine, in the Limousin region, in the eighteenth century, the average age at marriage for girls was 19.6 years. As many as 20% of these girls were married before the age of 14, and 62% before the age of 19[45]!

In the past families were, above all, communities of people living and working together. Marriage was seen differently depending on whether income was generated by land farmed in common or by wage labour. It was also experienced differently depending on whether or not women were partners in the marriage, and on whether or not men were unduly privileged. Marriage was not simply a "licence to reproduce", as it involved transfers of wealth which parents, on occasion, would seek to reduce, in order to benefit their own wellbeing and old age. Where parents felt a responsibility at the marriage of their children, the intensity of this feeling could be very different depending on the local culture. In Normandy, it was accepted that a child, particularly a daughter, could keep the entirety of her income from the age of 20. Sons, if they left home, could also retain their savings. There was a strong incentive to leave. It was different closer to Paris, where the expectations of parents with regard to their children remained strong in terms of work; but so equally did those of children with

---

44   Jacqueline Bernard, André Paris, Christian Bouchoux, *Une communauté familiale avant la Révolution: les Panné-Garreau de Préporché (Nièvre)*, Chateau-Chinon, Académie du Morvan, 2006, p. 36.

45   Jean-Claude Peyronnet, "Vie conjugale et vie familiale en Limousin du XVIIe siècle à l'époque contemporaine", in *Bulletin de la Société d'archéologie et histoire du Limousin*, t. CXXVI, 1998, pp. 148–150.

regard to their parents when it came to receiving the advance on an inheritance. In France and western Europe, family, marriage and the contribution of children to the domestic economy were seen differently. Marriage
was not simply a "licence to reproduce". It was also the most frequently
used route to emancipation. Moreover, the age of marriage depended on
numerous factors, both internal and external to the family. The general
tendency to marry later in western Europe must not obscure the differences between two neighbouring provinces of France. In this respect, it is
the job of historians interested in questions of power to put that issue at the
core of any typologies of the family. In Europe, there were many different
approaches to the exercise of power, founded on the collective customs
of a particular group or an entire province. Caught between France and
England, Normandy was, on the one hand, attached to French tradition,
hostile to arbitrary power on the part of the family when it came to sons,
and beholden to the English tradition of "laissez faire" when it came to
daughters. Inequality, permissible between daughters, was unacceptable
between sons. The even-handed and egalitarian character of the Parisian
family, on the other hand, and its rejection above all of any individual arbitrary control, made such distinctions between male and female children
impossible.

Michaël Gasperoni

Reconsidering Matrimonial Practices and Endogamy in the Early Modern Period. The Case of Central Italy (San Marino, Romagna and Marche)

In recent decades, several studies have focused on the real increase, or even explosion, of marriages between close relatives between the mid-eighteenth century and World War One[1]. According to Gérard Delille, this dramatic

---

This paper is part of a broader study carried out as part of a doctoral thesis, which is based on a study of matrimonial practices through the exhaustive reconstruction of two central Italian populations, one Christian and the other Jewish, over a long period of time (1450–1900). The study has systematically cross-referenced many different sources and has used computer tools, particularly the software Puck (Program for the use and computation of kinship data), making use of the perspectives provided by demographic, economic and social history, as well as the network analysis. See Michaël Gasperoni, *De la parenté à l'époque moderne: systèmes, réseaux, pratiques. Juifs et chrétiens en Italie centrale*, Paris, École des hautes études en sciences sociales, 2013. The software Puck was developed by K. Hamberger as part of the project TIP ("Traitement Informatique des phénomènes de Parenté en histoire et en ethnologie"), financed by the National Research Agency of France, coordinated by C. Grange and M. Houseman. The results of the group's work were published in a special issue of the journal *Annales de démographie historique*, 2, 2008. For an introduction to Puck, cf. Klaus Hamberger, Michael Houseman & Cyril Grange, «La parenté radiographiée», *L'Homme*, vol. 191, 2009, n. 3, pp. 107–137.

1   See in particular Gouesse, "L'endogamie familiale dans l'Europe catholique au XVIIIᵉ siècle. Première approche", in *Mélanges de l'Ecole française de Rome. Moyen-Age, Temps modernes*, 1, 1977, pp. 95–116; *Id.*, "Mariages de proches parents (XVIᵉ–XXᵉ siècle)", *Le modèle familial européen: normes, déviances, contrôle du pouvoir*, École française de Rome, 1986; Gérard Delille, *Famille et propriété dans le Royaume de Naples (XVᵉ–XIXᵉ siècle)*, Rome, École française de Rome, 1985; *Id.*, "Réflexions sur le système européen de la parenté et de l'alliance", in *Annales. H.S.S.*, 2, 2001, pp. 369–380; *Id.*, "Représentation, généralisation, comparaison. Sur le système de parenté européen", in *Annales. H.S.S.*, 11, 2007, pp. 137–157; David Warren Sabean, *Kinship in Neckarhausen, 1700–1870*, Cambridge, Cambridge University Press, 1998; David Warren Sabean, Simon Teuscher, Jon Mathieu (eds.), *Kinship in Europe: approaches to long-term development (1300–1900)*, New York – Oxford, Berghahn Books, 2007.

increase in endogamous marriages coincides with, and is intimately linked to, the parallel boom in totally exogamous marriages, which began to prevail from the second half of the nineteenth century. David W. Sabean, on the other hand, insists in the intensification of kinship ties between close relatives, proposing more recently, with other authors, the importance of integrating phenomena of kinship in a long term but nonlinear perspective, taking into account two major transitions: first, from the end of the Middle Ages to the Early Modern Era and, secondly, from the mid-eighteenth century onwards[2]. On the other hand Laurent Barry, in a theoretical essay on kinship, insists in an anthropological perspective on the continuity of the European system of kinship up to the present day[3].

Whilst, in the wake of microhistory, the efforts of theorisation and generalisation have opened the field to numerous regional studies, putting the more general phenomena of kinship into the shade, Dionigi Albera has charted a third path and discussed the articulation between general and regional models, that is to say between macro and micro analysis. In this way, he has recalled the need to interrogate the local or regional processes through the *longue durée* perspective in order to incorporate broader phenomena and more general dynamics on a larger scale[4].

Following this methodological and heuristic approach, I propose to combine, in a multi-scale perspective, a quantitative approach to the study of populations with the methods of network analysis and social history, focusing on the kinship system over the long term in a part of Central Italy, in the region of the Republic of San Marino and Rimini. A systematic and extensive study of matrimonial practices generated a database that has been analysed with informatic tools. The use of the computer is intended not only to verify the supposed enforcement of the endogamy starting from the second half of the eighteenth century, but also to explore several aspects of the economic and social life of the past, using the history of the family and kinship as the main key to

---

2   David W. Sabean, Simon Teuscher, "Kinship in Europe. A New Approach to Long Term Development", in David Warren Sabean, Simon Teuscher, Jon Mathieu (eds.), *Kinship in Europe, op. cit.*, pp. 1–32.

3   Laurent Barry, *La parenté*, Gallimard, 2008, pp. 481–635.

4   Dionigi Albera, *Au fil des générations. Terre, pouvoir et parenté dans l'Europe alpine (XIVᵉ–XXᵉ siècles)*, Grenoble, PUG, 2011.

interpretation[5]. The exhaustive study of the demographic documentation and the systematic reconstruction of a population on an intermediate scale (between local and regional) may contribute to the interrogation in depth of more general kinship phenomena.

Reconstructing and analysing an entire population

Fig. 1: The field and sources

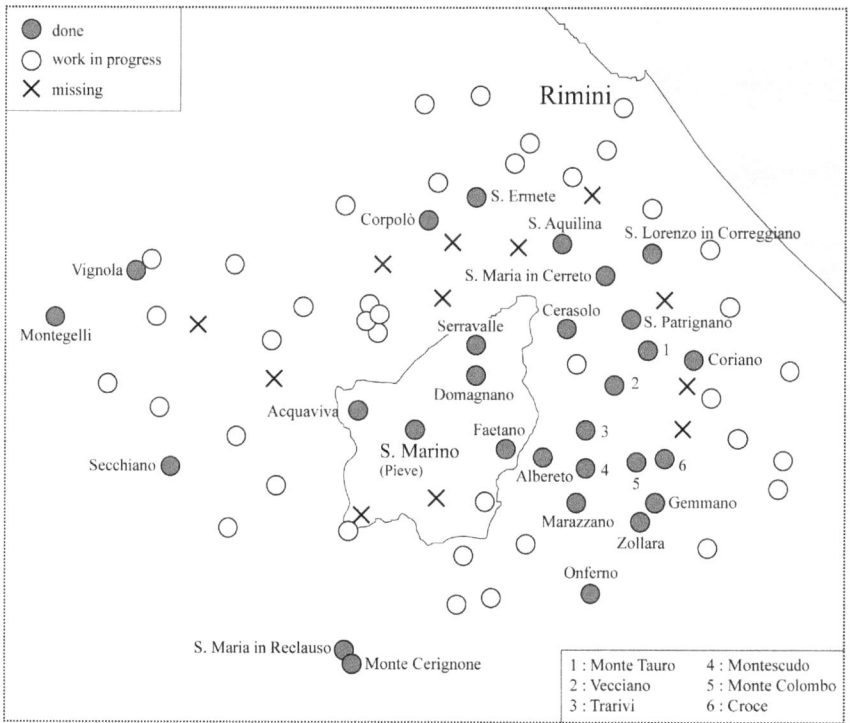

5   For the encounter between network analysis and the history of family and kinship, see Claire Lemercier, "Analyse de réseaux et histoire de la famille : une rencontre encore à venir?", in *Annales de démographie historique*, 1, 2005, pp. 7–31.

The starting point of this work is the reconstruction of an entire population – that of the Republic of San Marino, an old state that is still independent, between Marche and Romagna in Central Italy, populated by about 3,000 people at the beginning of the eighteenth century and 7,080 by 1864[6]. We will not dwell on the methodological problems related to this type of approach, even though they are essential for understanding not only its results, but also the more general results of historiography dealing with kinship. For example, in the region considered here, it should be said that the onomastic system was not yet established: in fact, many families still did not have a surname in 1650, and some even lacked one at the beginning of the nineteenth century[7].

The research is based on the intensive and exhaustive use of all available documentation: the most important documents are the parochial records of the Republic and surrounding districts; also all notarial protocols preserved from 1450 to 1850. Finally, I studied land records, family and private archives, and fiscal and judicial sources. Indeed, a complete reconstruction was necessary, since all the individuals and families in the genealogical corpus are connected. In fact, at least until 1640, the noble families contracted matrimonial alliances with families of lower rank, artisans or peasants. The genealogical corpus is composed of 10,164 marriages and 33,224 individuals (18,913 men, 14,309 women, and 2 individuals of unknown sex), with a genealogical depth of 22 generations and an average genealogical depth of 3.96[8]. The chronological distribution of the individuals in the dataset reflects the typology of the sources used for the census: while, starting in the sixteenth century, the parish records allow us to know better the whole of the population, more "qualitative" sources from earlier periods, such as notarial archives (wills, endowments, etc.), accentuate the gender imbalances. These imbalances must lie at the centre of any methodological reflection before starting to analyse the matrimonial structures within the family networks.

---

6   On the population of San Marino, cf. Carlo Verducci, *Popolazione ed emergenze economico-sanitarie a San Marino tra Medioevo e Ottocento*, San Marino, Centro Sammarinese di Studi Storici, 1995.

7   Roberto Bizzocchi, "Marchigiani senza cognome. Un'inchiesta nell'Italia napoleonica", in *Quaderni storici*, vol. 134, 2010, pp. 533–584.

8   Average genealogical depth is calculated by dividing, for every generation starting from one individual, the number of ascendants known by the number of ascendants expected, aggregating the obtained values. Cf. Marie-Hélène Cazes, Pierre Cazes, «Comment mesurer la profondeur généalogique d'une ascendance?», in *Population*, vol. 51, 1996, n. 1, pp. 117–140.

Biases: scientific evaluation of genealogical databases

In most cases, we have more information on men than women, and this discrepancy grows the further back we go. If we are unaware of the many matrimonial relationships that pass through women, some parts of the network, and therefore of the social reality, will escape us. This genealogical incompleteness causes significant methodological problems, especially in the context of network analysis[9].

Historical datasets, however, have a notable advantage compared to those created by anthropologists: their genealogical depth can reach up to tens of generations and can cross multiple centuries. Historians can therefore grasp matrimonial structures over the long term, can study their evolution, measure them over both shorter and longer periods of time, and perceive accelerations and decelerations. Historical datasets allow us to measure the consanguineous loops and the more distant re-linkings, or the consanguinity in a geographically endogamous population.

Analysis of the sources

The advantage of a serial analysis of kinship networks is that we are able to compare the trends shown by the sources and the genealogies systematically reconstructed. This allows us, for example, to identify possible consanguineous marriages below the fourth canonical degree (which did not require a dispensation). Vice versa, we may be faced with a dispensation even if the union was not surveyed at the computer level, because the genealogy of the couple in the dataset is incomplete, and therefore their marriage does not appear as consanguineous. The systematic cross-referencing of all the available sources allows an accurate recreation of the population and a precise measurement of the proportion of forbidden marriages in relation to the total number of marriages.

---

9   On this point, see Laurent Barry, Michael Gasperoni, «L'oubli des origines. Amnésie et information généalogiques en histoire et en ethnologie", in *Annales de démographie historique*, 2, 2008, pp. 53–104.

The main parish of the Republic of San Marino: Pieve (1588–1823)

The parish of Pieve includes both the urban districts (with families of artisans, merchants and the local ruling class) and the surrounding countryside. Consanguineous marriages in the seventeenth century principally involve the aristocracy. The unions of closer degree allow the elites to form themselves into a new body, detached and distinct from the rest of the society[10]. Peasant families evolve in a different context: "repetitions of alliances" and re-linkings, with almost no marriages needing the dispensation from consanguinity. In the eighteenth century, however, the trend is reversed: the urban elite, then incorporated into a "true" nobility, adopts an attitude of total exogamy, characterised by a general trend of allying themselves with families from the pontifical aristocracy of the surrounding cities. On the other hand, a certain increase in consanguineous marriages can be noted in the peasant class and the "bourgeoisie" at the start of the eighteenth century, like an echo of the previous reinforcing phase of the aristocracy.

There is not so much an "explosion" of consanguineous marriages as a steady increase, and an openness towards alliances between the aforementioned social groups. Marriages between very close relatives become possible, but they are not the norm within the group of consanguineous marriages. The end of the eighteenth century is likewise marked by a considerable increase in familial and above all socially exogamous marriages.

The declarations of dispensation in the marriage records and in marriage banns

– 1588–1670: the record of marriages

The scrutiny of the only marriage record that has been preserved between 1588 and 1670 allows us to identify only eleven declarations of dispensation for consanguinity, representing 1.63% of the total number of marriages (674) that were recorded. There are multiple methodological

---

10　Cf. Donatella Fioretti, *Dalla democrazia alla aristocrazia elettiva: il ceto dirigente a San Marino nei secoli XVII e XVIII*, San Marino, Centro Sammarinese di Studi Storici, 1994; M. Gasperoni, *De la parenté à l'époque moderne, op. cit.*

precautions to be taken in the face of this type of documentation: for example, the aim of these records is, first of all, to record marriages and not dispensations[11]. Thus, consanguineous marriages could sometimes escape registration because the bonds of parentage that unite the bride and groom are unknown or undeclared. However, these cases are not frequent, in the sense that the actors deploy a sometimes surprising genealogical memory[12]. It is therefore possible that a slightly more significant number of marriages required dispensations.

We have subdivided the period covered by the marriage record into four phases in order to have a complete view of potential changes or ruptures. The moment that corresponds to the closing of ranks (matrimonially) by the elites, around the middle of the seventeenth century, is also that of the growth in consanguineous marriages (Tab. 1). These marriages between close relatives probably fostered a common identity within an elite that was progressively defining itself as a true "nobility". Endogamy seems to be a behaviour aimed at creating a homogeneous social group, closed and inaccessible to the other members of society. Inter-class marriages become impossible when the dowries of high-class women increase considerably, thus blocking access to the matrimonial market of the upper classes[13].

---

11   We used notarial and diocesan archives where possible, particularly those of Pennabilli. Unfortunately the documentation related to dispensations is not yet organised and is spread across different sources. Cf. ADP, *Parishes of San Marino*, b. 16–19.

12   On this point I do not agree with the critiques of Jon Mathieu, "Kin marriages: Trends and Interpretations form the Swiss Example" in David. W. Sabean, Simon Teuscher, Jon Mathieu (eds.), *Kinship in Europe, op. cit.*, pp. 220–221 and François-Joseph Ruggiu, "Histoire de la parenté ou anthropologie historique de la parenté? Autour de Kinship in Europe", in *Annales de démographie historique*, 1, 2010, p. 228, directed towards Gérard Delille, contesting the fact that genealogical memory of the actors exceeds three generations. In reality, and as Merzario has demonstrated (see *Il paese stretto. Strategie matrimoniali nella diocesi di Como, Secoli XVI–XVIII*, Torino, Einaudi, 1981, pp. 7; 35–38), the memory of the "elders" of the villages (relatives, neighbours and in particular women, see p. 115) who were often the first witnesses in the investigations about parentage, could certainly ensure a longer memory, if parents or grandparents of Ego were not available. The reoccurring appearance of "licences" for the fourth and fifth degree in our matrimonial records seems to confirm the importance of the oral tradition. However, the question remains complex, as we are reminded by Vincent Gourdon, in his work on the history of grandparenthood in France (*Histoire des grands-parents*, Paris, Perrin, 2012, pp. 357–409).

13   M. Gasperoni, *De la parenté à l'époque moderne, op. cit.*, pp. 368–373.

Tab. 1: Dispensations of consanguinity (1588–1670).

Years	Number of dispensations	Marriages (total)	% of the whole
1588–1609	1	182	0,55
1610–1629	0	184	0
1630–1649	7	169	4,14
1650–1670	3	138	2,17

– *1588–1826: the set of marriages surveyed*

Lacking parish records after 1670, we used banns of marriage (1659–1826)[14]. 1,142 additional marriages were surveyed for this particular period, making a total of 1,816. Globally we counted 38 dispensations and licences, a number that must again be taken alongside the methodological precautions mentioned above.

Four categories of family were taken into consideration in order to classify these consanguineous marriages (Tab. 2): the nobility, which resided within the walls of the Terra; the "bourgeoisie", linked to crafts or trade, dwelling in the urban districts and sometimes in the nearby country-side; the "wealthy peasantry", corresponding to families who have always been landowners, had a constant representation in the Council of the Republic, and a frequent presence of churchmen in its ranks; and finally the "lower" strata of San Marino's society, namely the small peasant class, with reduced, crumbling or even non-existent property.

Tab. 2: Dispensations for consanguinity according to social class.

	Nobility	Bourgeois	Wealthy Peasantry	Small Peasantry	Number of dispensations	Marriages (total)	%
1588–1599	1	0	0	0	1	107	0,93
XVII c.	5	3	2	0	10	578	1,73
XVIII c.	2	5	7	3	17	816	2,08
1800–1826	0	2	5	3	10	315	3,17
Total	8	10	14	6	38	1816	2,09

---

14 From 1670 until the end of the century only eleven marriage banns are preserved. However, the series is complete from the year 1700.

Over the entire period, the rate of consanguineous marriages that required a dispensation is not particularly high (2.09%) except for the first third of the eighteenth century, during which 11 dispensations were granted[15], representing 6.3% of all the marriages[16]. Over thirty years (1708–1738), as many dispensations were conceded as during the entire century before. Yet the aristocracy is no longer the most endogamous group. While at the time of its establishment, the aristocracy was reinforcing the links of kinship internally, its later attitude is characterised by the extension of the field of its alliances beyond "national" borders and by the integration of new foreign families.

Though fourth-degree dispensations are still the most numerous, it becomes more common at the end of the eighteenth century to marry closer relatives and, in particular, second-degree cousins. Marriages between very close relatives remain, however, marginal and are also the least favoured by the Church, which always considered kinship as necessarily exogamous. It is no coincidence that the majority of requests for dispensations concern the impediment in the 4th degree (Tab. 3), a transitory moment in terms of what is known and perceived as kinship, and the very moment when families desire to renew it[17].

---

15   Only one for the aristocracy, four for the bourgeoisie and six for families of the wealthier peasantry.

16   It could well be that the increase in the dispensations for consanguinity from the eighteenth century onwards has an explanation in the church authorities' improved ability to check for consanguineous marriages, thanks to the establishment of parish records a little more than a century before, which allowed a reconstruction of four or five generations. Before that, only oral memory, especially of the elders of the villages, made that possible.

17   See an example in Laurent Barry, Michael Gasperoni, "L'oubli des origines", art. cit., pp. 55–56. R. Merzario's research shows the great prevalence of 4th degree dispensations in the diocese of Como, both in the case of consanguinity (76.23% of the total dispensations) and in that of affinity (63.21% of the dispensations). Cf. Raul Merzario, *Il paese stretto, op. cit.*, pp. 54–55.

Tab. 3: Types of dispensations granted (1588–1826).

4th and 5th degree	2
4th degree	19
3rd and 4th degree	8
3rd degree	4
2nd and 3rd degree	1
2nd degree	2
Unknown	2
Total	38

It is necessary to consider marriages between close relatives not only in the context of their timing, but also in the context of the whole family network they are part of, starting from complete reconstructions of the families. In his works on "Arab marriage", Laurent Barry highlighted how important it was to analyse the matrimonial behaviours of the actors by reintegrating them into the matrimonial network of their ancestors[18]. Observing the genealogies and the consanguinity dispensations, one can note how marriages between close relatives often included some families that constantly bent the rules, although most other families respected them by using repetitions of alliances and re-linkings to maintain and reinforce bonds with particular groups of families.

Some sedentary families of the wealthy peasantry, 56 families in total, frequently requested dispensations. Most of these (three quarters) made such requests only once, but some benefited from two (9 families), three (2 families) or four (2 families) dispensations during the period considered. Furthermore, almost a third of the dispensations granted (ten out of thirty-eight) concerned individuals whose parents were immigrants, as if in some way a consanguineous marriage in the following generation was a way to integrate themselves fully within the host population, by reinforcing the bonds of kinship with it. Moreover, consanguineous marriage is not always synonymous with geographic endogamy. A combination of geographic exogamy and familial endogamy is observed in San Marino and other parishes, as we will see later. This also demonstrates the efficacy of the Church's control, which is well aware of the fact that a marriage with a spouse from outside the parish could be a marriage between

---

18   Laurent Barry, "Les modes de composition de l'alliance : le 'mariage arabe'" , in
      L'Homme, 3, 1998, pp. 17–50.

close relatives. In the actor's perception, however, it is still very probable that a close relative residing far away is less forbidden – or perceived as such – than a slightly more distant relative residing nearby, almost as if geographic distance relativised, in some way, genealogical proximity[19]. In fact, one of the rare marriages between very close relatives surveyed in the mid-1800s, between first-degree cousins (FBD), concerns a noble couple in which the groom, at the time of the marriage, resided tens of kilometres away from the bride[20].

Rural parishes in the Republic of San Marino

In other parishes in the Republic of San Marino, the same trends can be observed as in the main parish. The proportion of matrimonial dispensations increases but remains low, even at the end of the period considered when geographic endogamy is growing[21]. Constant immigration, particularly of men, allows for a constant renewal of the familial lines, while exogamous marriages with members of other parishes allow the widening of kinship circles.

Again, there are several matrimonial dispensations granted to couples where one of the spouses is originally from another parish. Furthermore, one does not notice an "explosion" of dispensations, or of marriages between very close relatives (Tab. 4 and Tab. 5). Most of the dispensations concern marriages on the border of the prohibition, and they are very rarely below the third degree (only one out of 21 dispensations).

---

19   T. Jolas, Y. Verdier and F. Zonabend observe that in Minot, in Châtillonnais, "a cousin that lives in a distant village and that is rarely met becomes a spouse somehow less forbidden than a more genealogically distant cousin that lives in the same village", see Tina Jolas, Yvonne Verdier, Françoise Zonabend, "'Parler famille'", in *L'Homme*, 3, 1970, pp. 14–15.

20   ASRSM, *Census*, 1865, Pieve Parish, City Section, n. 590.

21   In the main parish of San Marino, Pieve (1588–1670), 71.3% marriages involve spouses coming from the parish itself and 80.4% involve spouses from San Marino, figures comparable to the other parishes of the Republic (72.75 and 81.2 in Serravalle (1705–1850); 61.72 and 87.72 in Domagnano (1672–1850); 68.93 and 86.87 in Acquaviva (1746–1850) and 70.53 and 81.61 in Faetano between 1794 and 1850), cf. M. Gasperoni, *De la parenté à l'époque moderne, op. cit.*, pp. 353–363.

Tab. 4: Matrimonial dispensations, consanguinity (1670–1850).

	1670–99	1700–49	1750–99	1800–50	Dispen-sations (total)	Marriages	% of the whole
Acquaviva (1746–1850)	–	0 (6)	1 (133)	2 (162)	3	301	0,99%
Domagnano (1672–1850)	1 (49)	3 (149)	1 (126)	4 (124)	9	448	2%
Faetano (1794–1850)	–	–	0 (11)	4 (174)	4	185	2,16%
Serravalle (1705–1850)	–	1 (154)	0 (195)	4 (266)	5	615	0,81%
Total	1 (49)	4 (309)	2 (465)	14 (726)	21	1549	1,35%
% of the whole	2,04	1,29	0,43	1,93			

Tab. 5: Typologies of consanguinity dispensations (1670–1850).

	2°	2°-3°	3°	3°-4°	4°	4°-5°
Acquaviva	0	0	1	1	1	0
Domagnano	0	0	2	2	5	0
Faetano	0	1	0	1	2	0
Serravalle	0	0	3	2	0	0
Total	0	1	6	6	8	0

Is San Marino a singular local case? Surveys in the surrounding parishes (Rimini-Pesaro)

I expanded the inquiry to 24 other parishes in the area around San Marino[22]. Though the state of preservation of the archives greatly varies, we note a similar trend to that observed in San Marino: the increase in matrimonial dispensations is significant but not homogeneous, both at the

---

22   I am still working on ten other surrounding parishes. The genealogical database "San Marino" used here has grown in the meantime, and a new version will be available on the website of the project *Kinsources*, financed by the ANR (French National Research Agency).

quantitative and at the qualitative (that is, between very close relatives) level (Tab. 6 & Tab. 7). Furthermore, we must remember that the rise in dispensations must always be placed in the context of the total number of marriages contracted, which increases in many parishes. For instance in Monte Colombo there is a strong increase in the number of dispensations between the eighteenth and nineteenth centuries: from five dispensations between 1750 and 1799 to eleven dispensations between 1800 and 1850. However, over the same time periods the number of marriages increases from 199 to 305, and therefore the rate of dispensations only increases from 2.51% to 3.61%[23]. Some parishes, such as Albereto, Vecciano and Trarivi, show an opposite trend, with a decrease in the number of dispensations. It is noteworthy that in some parishes, we encounter few or no dispensations. Moreover, the increase in matrimonial dispensations in some parishes is not characterised by a shift towards lower degrees. In many parishes, a number of dispensations concern geographically exogamic marriages. In the small parish of Vignola (near Sogliano on the Rubicone), for example, 4 out of 5 dispensations concern partners coming from different parishes. These involve also high degrees (three in the 4°, one in the 4/5° and one in the 3/4° degree), which suggests that the actors can activate, by means of oral tradition and parish documents, a genealogical memory beyond the parish of residence. Finally, the high number of endogamous marriages which alternate with exogamous marriages over the generations, reminds us of the necessity of putting the sequence of dispensations within the framework of the history of each family.

---

23   The increase of dispensations is unequal depending on the parish, but the increase in the number of marriages is general.

Michaël Gasperoni

Tab. 6: Consanguinity dispensations and marriages (1550–1850), provinces of Rimini and Pesaro.

	1550–1599	1600–1649	1650–1699	1700–1749	1750–1799	1800–1850	Total Dispensations	Total Marriages	% of the total
Albereto (1598–1839)	0 (8)	10 (157)	3 (100)	3 (130)	1 (114)	0 (85)	17	594	2,86
Cerasolo (1751–1850)	–	–	–	–	0 (93)	2 (145)	2	238	0,84
Coriano (1778–1838)	–	–	–	–	0 (170)	3 (284)	3	454	0,66
Corpolò (1573–1850)	1 (138)	1 (29)	2 (83)	1 (139)	1 (160)	0 (202)	6	751	0,80
Croce (1791–1850)	–	–	–	–	0 (46)	5 (292)	5	338	1,48
Gemmano (1736–1850)	–	–	–	0 (39)	1 (151)	0 (209)	1	399	
Gemmano (Marazzano, 1769–1850)	–	–	–	–	0 (58)	1 (95)	1	153	0,65
Gemmano (Onferno, 1713–1850)	–	–	–	0 (56)	–	5 (103)	5	159	3,14
Gemmano (Zollara, 1649–1850)	–	0 (11)	1 (45)	2 (74)	0 (71)	0 (106)	3	307	0,98
Monte Cerignone (1715–1850)	–	–	–	2 (59)	1 (60)	2 (62)	5	181	2,76
Monte Colombo (1635–1850)	–	1 (64)	–	2 (77)	4 (199)	11 (306)	18	646	2,79
Monte Tauro (1576–1688)	0 (40)	2 (70)	0 (56)	–	–		2	166	1,2

	1550–1599	1600–1649	1650–1699	1700–1749	1750–1799	1800–1850	Total Dispensa-tions	Total Mar-riages	% of the total
Montegelli (1680–1850)	–	–	2 (46)	3 (74)	1 (69)	1 (109)	7	298	2,35
Montescudo (1681–1850)	–	–	2 (54)	2 (180)	4 (204)	10 (305)	18	743	2,42
S. Aquilina (1731–1850)	–	–	–	0 (43)	0 (83)	0 (94)	0	220	0
S. Ermete (1689–1850)	–	–	1 (34)	7 (209)	3 (201)	4 (187)	15	631	2,38
S. Lorenzo in Correggiano (1685–1850)	–	–	0 (50)	1 (155)	1 (145)	3 (273)	5	623	0,8
S. Maria in Cerreto (1637–1850)	–	0 (48)	0 (135)	0 (166)	0 (133)	0 (217)	0	699	0
S. Maria in Reclauso (1679–1850)	–	–	0 (8)	0 (47)	0 (54)	0 (61)	0	170	0
S. Patrignano (1743–1850)	–	–	–	0 (10)	1 (111)	1 (118)	2	239	0,84
Secchiano (1680–1850)	–	–	1 (30)	1 (48)	1 (82)	3 (125)	6	285	2,10
Trarivi (1671–1850)	–	–	5 (89)	5 (136)	3 (163)	3 (226)	16	614	2,6
Vecciano (1677–1837)	–	–	3 (40)	1 (105)	0 (88)	0 (72)	4	305	1,31
Vignola (1670–1850)	–	–	2 (36)	0 (58)	1 (79)	2 (72)	5	245	2,04
Total	1 (186)	14 (379)	22 (806)	30 (1,805)	23 (2,534)	56 (3,748)	146	9,458	1,54
%	0,54	3,69	2,73	1,66	0,91	1,49			

Michaël Gasperoni

Tab. 7: Typologies of consanguinity dispensations.

	2°	2°–3°	2°–4°	3°	3°–4°	4°	4°–5°	Unknown	Total
Albereto	0	0	1	1	5	10	0	0	17
Cerasolo	0	0	0	0	1	1	0	0	2
Coriano	0	0	0	0	3	0	0	0	3
Corpolò	0	0	0	0	0	6	0	0	6
Croce	0	1	0	0	1	3	0	0	5
Gemmano	0	0	0	0	0	1	0	0	1
Gemmano (Marazzano)	0	0	0	0	0	1	0	0	1
Gemmano (Onferno)	0	0	0	1	1	3	0	0	5
Gemmano (Zollara)	0	0	0	0	0	2	1	0	3
Monte Cerignone	0	0	0	2	0	3	0	0	5
Monte Colombo	0	1	0	5	4	8	0	0	18
Monte Tauro	0	0	0	0	0	2	0	0	2
Montegelli	0	0	0	0	1	5	1	0	7
Montescudo	0	1	0	2	2	10	3	0	18
S. Aquilina	0	0	0	0	0	0	0	0	0
S. Ermete	0	1	0	3	4	7	0	0	15
S. Lorenzo in Correggiano	0	0	0	1	0	3	0	1	5
S. Maria in Cerreto	0	0	0	0	0	0	0	0	0
S. Maria in Reclauso	0	0	0	0	0	0	0	0	0
S. Patrignano	0	0	0	1	0	1	0	0	2
Secchiano	0	0	0	1	1	3	1	0	6
Trarivi	0	0	0	0	1	15	0	0	16
Vecciano	0	0	0	0	0	4	0	0	4
Vignola	0	0	0	0	1	3	1	0	5
Total	0	4	1	17	25	91	7	1	146

Reconsidering dispensations in their context

The example of the parish of Monte Colombo, where the number of dispensations is among the highest, demonstrates how the dispensations must be reconsidered in the light both of the local socio-economic context and of an in-depth study of the trajectories of the families.

Of the twenty dispensations surveyed, half of them (nine of consanguinity and one of affinity) involve spouses coming from different parishes or where one of the parents – often the father – is a migrant and only recently established in the parish. This trend is found in all the parishes considered in this study. On the one hand, therefore, dispensations concern families characterised by a notable and constant geographic mobility. On the other, as we saw for San Marino, some families characterised by a long residential stability also tend to request dispensations, sometimes in the same generation. Still in Monte Colombo, some families, often related and members of the sedentary group of wealthy peasants, do alternate marriages between close relatives and exogamous marriages outside the parish for one or two generations. There are also cases of consanguineous marriages that concern sedentary agnatic groups related through women originally from other parishes.

Let us quickly examine the case of three closely related families, between the second half of the eighteenth century and the second half of the nineteenth century. The alternation of exogamic marriages outside the parish with marriages between close relatives (five 3rd degree dispensations and one 4th degree), over successive generations, is accompanied by relinking, which reinforces the overall structure also in the context of exogamous marriages. The case of the two brothers Giovanetti, who marry two sisters originally from another parish (Saludeccio, approximately 15 km away), is typical of this. These three families are the source of five dispensations[24] out of fifteen granted for the entire parish from 1750 to 1850 (Fig. 1).

---

24   One was not accounted for, because the marriage was contracted in 1859.

Fig. 1: Genealogy of the families Giovanetti, Graziosi and Ugolini from Monte Colombo.

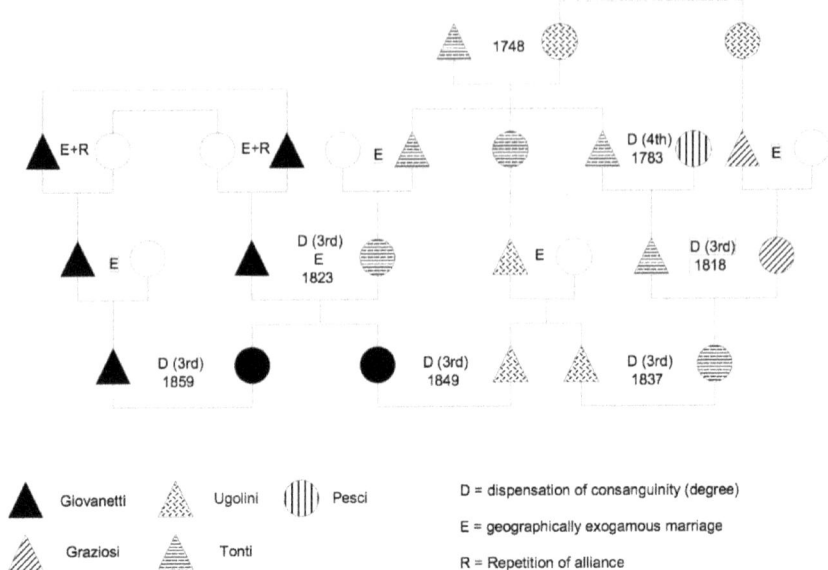

Matrimonial census of the genealogical dataset using Puck

Although the parish records are very accurate and specify whether a marriage needed a dispensation of any kind (consanguinity, affinity or spiritual kinship), the computer census using the Puck software allows us to verify if some consanguineous marriages could have been with-held from the manual count or the declarations in parochial or diocesan archives. Therefore this allows us to count the large number and variety of consanguineous marriages more accurately, and also allows us to understand the matrimonial circuits within the network over the entire period under consideration.

Consanguineous marriages

The results from the computer census confirm the trend observed in the sources: marriages below the fourth canonical degree represent a very small proportion of the total number of marriages, only 0.78%. As has emerged from this study of the sources, it is at the border of the impediments that the families often decided to renew the ties of kinship between them, to reactivate bonds as they were about to disappear, or simply because as soon as the impediment was overcome, the marriage became possible[25].

As soon as the impediments were overcome, the proportion of consanguineous marriages increased in every successive degree (Tab. 8). It rises from 330 consanguineous marriages at the fourth canonical degree (3.24% of total marriages within the dataset) to 771 marriages at the fifth degree (7.58%), then to 1,352 at the sixth degree (13.3%). From the eighth degree, we note a stabilisation of consanguineous marriages, the level of which remains rather high (more than 20% of all marriages). The values are obviously higher in the more distant degrees (≥5th degree) if we consider only the results from the eighteenth and nineteenth centuries, for which there is a greater genealogical completeness. This demonstrates how an important geographic endogamy generates, over the long term, a coefficient of high biological consanguinity among the members of a community, a dense and very complex network of kinship, even if they avoid marriages between close relatives.

Tab. 8: Consanguineous marriages of degree surveyed using the software Puck.

	Number of consanguineous marriages	% of total marriages	Diff.
≤ 2nd degree	3	0,03	
≤ 3rd degree	80	0,78	+ 0,75
≤ 4th degree	330	3,24	+2,46
≤ 5th degree	771	7,58	+4,34
≤ 6th degree	1352	13,30	+5,72
≤ 7th degree	1827	17,97	+4,67
≤ 8th degree	2185	21,49	+3,52
≤ 9th degree	2374	23,35	+1,86
≤ 10th degree	2454	24,14	+0,79

---

25   G. Delille, *Famille et propriété dans le Royaume de Naples, op. cit.*, pp. 281–283.

If we observe the different typologies of consanguineous marriages, we are surprised by the great variety of matrimonial configurations (namely 29,582 circuits[26] for 2,454 marriages at the tenth degree, whereas we find only 125 different circuits for 330 marriages at the fourth degree). No typology is particularly prevalent. In all the marriages at the tenth degree, only one circuit appears more than ten times, and this is an agnatic typology of marriage, which puts parallel patrilateral relatives at the fifth degree in relation, that is, just after the impediments imposed by the Church (FFFFBSSSD); two others, cognatic, are present ten times in the network (FFZSD and MFFBSSD). 27,032 circuits appear only once. This clearly indicates that there are not any particular "preferences" (Tab. 9).

Tab. 9: Recurrence of matrimonial circuits.

Number of times a circuit appears	Number of cases
12	1
11	0
10	2
9	1
8	3
7	4
6	4
5	21
4	71
3	295
2	2147
1	27032

Marriages with the same surname

In a limited territory like San Marino, surnames provide an effective means to immediately recognise or assume consanguinity and kinship. A

---

26   A matrimonial circuit is a chain of kinship that is "closed" with a marriage. On matrimonial circuits, cf. Klaus Hamberger et Isabelle Daillant, « L'analyse de réseaux de parenté: concepts et outils », in *Annales de démographie historique*, 2, 2008, pp. 42–43.

name is both an indicator and a carrier of identity and familial memory. Consanguinity becomes immediately visible, but the same cannot be said when the consanguineous relationship passes through women, since then there is the alternation of surname in each generation. This requires both a quite significant genealogical memory and an effective check by the religious authorities which, over the centuries, had the "logistical" means to conduct such checks, systematically keeping the records of marriages, banns of marriage, etc.

As Gérard Delille pointed out, same-name marriages are rare in the modern age, after the appearance and the establishment of surnames and their transmission along the patrilineal line in the course of the late Middle Ages, which allows us easily to identify groups of descendants[27]. In fact, none of the thirty-eight matrimonial dispensations found in the parish of Pieve involve individuals who bear the same patronym and who are parallel patrilateral relatives. Basically, alliances between individuals with the same surname are *a priori* almost always outside the canonical prohibitions[28].

In the rural parishes, however, some marriages were contracted between spouses with the same surname with matrimonial dispensations: between relatives at the 3rd degree in Domagnano in 1751, at the 3rd and 4th degrees in Serravalle in 1821 and at the 2nd and 3rd degrees in Faetano in 1810[29]. These marriages between agnatic relatives below the 4th degree

---

27 G. Delille, "Parenté et alliance en Europe occidentale. Un essai d'interprétation générale", in *L'Homme*, 1, 2010, pp. 75–135. See also the critical article by Élie Haddad, "Deux modèles récents de la parenté à l'épreuve de la noblesse française d'Ancien Régime", in *L'Atelier du Centre de recherches historiques. Revue électronique du CRH*, 9, 2012.

28 This is, for example, the case with the marriage between Bernardino and Fiordigrana Belluzzi, whose family tree, as we reconstructed it, demonstrates that they are relatives at the sixth degree. The same is true of the marriage between Alessandro and Vincenza Belluzzi (7th degree), between Aurelio and Caterina Martelli (6th degree) and Giovanni and Maria Antonia Di Biagio (5th degree), see APSM, *matrimoni*, 2.VI.1602; 18.II.1631; 16.XI.1664 and *pubblicazioni*, 1819. We note that in some parishes, as for example in Monte Colombo, which we will address later, where there were many branches of the Ugolini family, there are many cases of marriages between persons bearing the same name, with hardly any dispensations.

29 APDo, *matrimoni*, 8.II.1751; APSe, *matrimoni*, 1.VIII.1821; APFa, *matrimoni*, 1.IX.1810.

therefore appear late and are almost nonexistent before the second half of the eighteenth century.

The census carried out with the aid of Puck confirmed the low number of unions between parallel patrilateral relatives at the 4th degree or below the limit allowed by the Church; it also allowed us to discover some others which are not in the sources. There are very few marriages between agnates, and they represent only 0.2% of all matrimonial relationships in the genealogical corpus[30]. Only two marriages between first cousins (FBD) were counted. Occurring in the 1830s, they concern a couple of cousins from a noble family and one from a family of small peasants. In the first case, the groom did not reside in the same parish as the bride (he had grown up about ten kilometres from San Marino) and his geographic distance probably made the alliance less "close".

Instead, seven marriages between the offspring of first cousins (FFBSD) were counted: two were contracted in the second half of the nineteenth century and involved peasant families; two others were contracted at the beginning of the eighteenth century, one involving an influential Borgo family, the other two involving members of the peasant elite. Four marriages were between parallel relatives at the 4th degree (FFFBSSD). Two of these involved the noble family Belluzzi, and one of these two marriages is particularly interesting because it falls within a "combination" of alliances in which three consanguineous marriages between agnates are involved: FFFBSSD, MFFBSSD and FFFFBSSSD.

Beyond the 4th degree, sixteen marriages between parallel patrilateral relatives were counted, seven of which were at the 5th degree and only two of which were at the 6th degree (Tab. 10). Marriages between close relatives, whether they be agnatic, uterine (with only twelve cases between the 3rd and 8th degrees) or cognatic, are infrequent, though they increase slightly from the end of the eighteenth century.

---

30   Or 21 unions from the 2nd to the 4th-5th degrees, out of a total of 10,164 marriages.

Tab. 10: Marriages between parallel patrilateral relatives (matrimonial census with Puck).

Type of marriage	Degree of kinship (canonical comput)	Number of cases
FBD	2nd	2
FBSD	2nd and 3rd	1
FFBSD	3rd	7
FFBSSD	3rd and 4th	3
FFFBSSD	4e	4
FFFFBSSD	4th and 5th	1
FFFBSSSD	4th and 5th	3
FFFFBSSSD	5th	7
FFFFBSSSSD	5th and 6th	1
FFFFFBSSSSD	6th	1
FFFFFFFBSSSSSSD	8th	1
FFFFFFFBSSSSSSSD	8th and 9th	1
FFFFFFFFBSSSSSSSD	9th	1
Total		34

The limited number of unions between people of the same surname – who were without a doubt more visible and therefore liable to attract attention from the Church – must, however, be considered alongside the total number of consanguineous marriages. It is possible to agree with L. Barry, that these agnatic marriages, which are among the most numerous within the set of consanguineous marriages (though rare within all marriages), were perhaps not considered closer – in terms of identity and of kinship – than uterine unions. A famous doctor from Milan in the nineteenth century, P. Mantegazza, established a decreasing hierarchy of matrimonial hazards that could strike relatives who married each other, particularly cousins[31]. First of all, he highlighted that the marriages of two children of sisters (MZD) would be the most risky, followed by that between the son of a brother and the daughter of a sister (FZD) or vice versa (MBD); finally, the marriage of two children of brothers (FBD) would be the least risky for their descendants. In the hierarchy of danger and of consanguineous proximity established by Mantegazza, the prevalence of uterine connections was clearly an important factor.

---

31   R. Merzario, *Il paese stretto, op. cit.*, pp. 253–254.

Marriages between affines

If there is one concept that we can say has profoundly marked the European system of kinship, it is certainly that of *una caro*. Based on the notion of *contagio carnalis*, which led to the extension of the impediments of affinity, the *una caro* logic turns all who are related by law into relatives affected by the incest prohibition[32].

Matrimonial dispensations due to affinity are quite rare in the records, although historiography has highlighted a significant increase from the second half of the eighteenth century, parallel to that of dispensations due to consanguinity. We found only one such dispensation in the records in Pieve (4th degree, 1737); another, later and closer, in Serravalle (1st and 2nd degrees, 1820); one in Acquaviva (4th degree, 1759); and none in Domagnano or Faetano (Tab. 11). Similar trends were observed in the parishes around San Marino: matrimonial dispensations for affinity are fairly rare[33]. Another type of dispensation rarely appears in the sources: dispensations because of spiritual kinship, which often assume an age difference between the spouses and/or the status of widow for one of them[34].

Tab. 11: Dispensations for Affinity.

Parish	Number of dispensations	Number of marriages	Period
Pieve	1	1575	1588–1826
Serravalle	1	615	1705–1850
Domagnano	0	448	1672–1850

32 On the *una caro*, see Laurent Barry, *La parenté, op. cit.*, pp. 572–635 and Anita Guerreau-Jalabert, "Flesh and Blood in Medieval Language about Kinship" and Simon Teuscher, "Flesh and Blood in the Treatises on the Arbor Consanguinitatis (Thirteenth to Sixteenth Centuries)", in Christopher H. Johnson et al. (eds.), *Blood & kinship: matter for metaphor from ancient Rome to the present*, New York – Oxford, Berghahn Books, 2013, pp. 61–82 and 83–104.

33 Among the total number of marriages between affines, there is only one in the second degree, 2 in the 2/3°, 4 in the 3rd, 6 in the 3/4°, 9 in the 4th, 2 in the 4/5° degree, and 5 where the exact degree is unknown.

34 We found only three cases, the first of which comes from the parish of Monte Colombo (*matrimoni*, 27.08.1841). Here, the bride had been the godmother of a son from the husband's first marriage (cf. APMC, *battesimi*, 27.02.1825). The second case is from the parish of Monte Cerignone (29.10.1850), the third from Corpolò (02.07.1855). There is also a case from Secchiano, a dispensation both for the second degree of affinity and for spiritual kinship.

Parish	Number of dispensations	Number of marriages	Period
Faetano	0	185	1794–1850
Acquaviva	1	301	1746–1850
Albereto	3	594	1598–1850
Cerasolo	0	238	1751–1850
Coriano	0	454	1778–1850
Corpolò	3	751	1573–1850
Croce	2	338	1791–1850
Gemmano	1	399	1736–1850
Gemmano (Marazzano)	1	153	1769–1850
Gemmano (Onferno)	1	159	1713–1850
Gemmano (Zollara)	1	307	1649–1850
Monte Cerignone	2	181	1715–1850
Monte Colombo	2	646	1635–1850
Monte Tauro	0	166	1576–1850
Montescudo	2	743	1681–1850
S. Aquilina	0	220	1731–1850
S. Ermete	2	631	1689–1850
S. Lorenzo in Correggiano	0	623	1685–1850
S. Maria in Cerreto	0	699	1637–1850
S. Maria in Reclauso	1	170	1679–1850
S. Patrignano	1	239	1743–1850
Trarivi	2	614	1671–1850
Vecciano	4	305	1677–1850
Total	31	11754	1573–1850

The statistical analysis of the matrimonial corpus undertaken with the Puck software confirms that the matrimonial prohibitions that concern in-laws were particularly observed, even at the end of the period considered (1750–1880). Only two marriages of the sororate (WZ) or levirate (BW) typology were counted out of a total of 10,164 matrimonial relationships. These are late (1867 and 1870) and involve peasant families, one wealthy and the other of labourer status. Only one marriage was counted at the 1ˢᵗ and 2ⁿᵈ degrees, between a man and the daughter of the sister of his deceased wife (WMZ) in 1820. Only one marriage was found between a man and the widow of his parallel patrilateral cousin (FBSW, 1730); and only one between a man and the widow of the matrilateral cross-cousin of his father (FMBSW, 1773). Beyond that, and until the 4ᵗʰ degree, there are only 29 marriages between in-laws, and they are spread evenly, without any typology appearing to be more prevalent.

Re-linkings

Analysing re-linkings with Puck, we observe a similar situation, except that the proportion of re-linkings within the total number of marriages is much higher. Therefore it may be that this phenomenon already played an essential role in the European system of kinship, as some anthropologists have pointed out[35]. Re-linkings allow families to negotiate close and constant matrimonial alliances with one or more families over the long term, in order to create a dense kinship without having to violate the prohibitions imposed by the Church. A sign of the importance of this phenomenon is certainly the inability of our computer to count re-linkings after the 5ᵗʰ canonical degree, which means that the implied circuits are in the hundreds of thousands (Tab. 12).

Tab. 12: Re-linkings from the 1ˢᵗ to the 5ᵗʰ canonical degree.

Degree	Number of marriages	% of total marriages	Number of circuits	Types of circuits
≤ 1	559	5,5	293	8
≤ 2	1303	12,82	823	95
≤ 3	2954	29,06	3757	1271
≤ 4	4330	42,6	21757	13039
≤ 5	5643	55,52	145609	110145

The interpretation of this data is not simple. It raises the question of whether it is only an automatic consequence of the complex interweaving of the links created by marriages or a consequence of the density of the network that results from the repetition of alliances between groups

---

35   Tina Jolas, Yvonne Verdier, Françoise Zonabend, "Parler famille", *op. cit.*

over the long term. François Héran wonders if it could be, in the end, less "a deliberate and meaningful practice than a global measurement of the density of the networks, which is itself a function of local endogamy on a general level"[36]. Finally, not all of these marriages should be placed on the same level: considering the different typologies of re-linkings (Tab. 13), some categories clearly stand out and should not be underestimated. In particular, the "repetitions of alliances", like double marriages (BWZ) or exchanges of sisters (ZHZ), stand out clearly in the set of re-linkings, more than marriages with the sister of the husband of either the parallel patrilineal cousin (FBDHZ) or the crossed matrilateral cousin (MBDHZ).

It is necessary to compare these results with matrimonial censuses from other geographical areas. One of the first findings of the TIP project was that double marriages – that is, between two brothers and two sisters – occurred more often than exchanges of sisters. This imbalance could be explained by either an economic (the transfer of property from one family to another) or a demographic hypothesis[37]. We will therefore only emphasise the extreme variety of re-linkings, as we did for consanguineous marriages.

Tab. 13: Typologies of the ten most common re-linkings.

Typology	Occurrences
BWZ	153
ZHZ	127
FBDHZ	28
MBDHZ	24
BWFZD	24
FZSWZ	21
FZHBD	18
MBWBD	18
FZHFBSD	18
ZHBD	17

---

36 François Héran, *Figures de la parenté: une histoire critique de la raison structurale*, Paris, PUF, 2009, pp. 252–253.

37 For a formal approach to network analysis, see Camille Roth et al., "Random alliance networks", in *Social Networks*, vol. 35, 2013, n. 3, pp. 394–405.

Conclusion

The analysis, which has cross-referenced between the sources and the genealogical dataset, shows the continuity of matrimonial practices throughout the period considered. The quite low number of consanguineous marriages below the 4th degree contrasts with a particularly high rate of consanguinity in the following degrees, a consequence of an important geographic endogamy which, over time, causes nearly all the individuals of a territory to be related, first by alliance, then by blood.

Given the number of dispensations and the total number of marriages (even if sometimes one or the other is not precisely known), it becomes clear that, from the second half of the eighteenth century, the number of consanguineous marriages is not large, although it increases. We can only agree with François-Joseph Ruggiu, who emphasises that this increase in consanguineous marriages remains low "for a phenomenon presented as structuring for European populations and that, furthermore, cannot be retraced to all social classes"[38].

The study of dispensations must always be placed within the local context because, as we have seen, these consanguineous marriages are part of a particular socio-economic dynamic that often reaches beyond a single locality: significant geographical mobility requires a study on a regional scale over the long term. Surveys conducted in the Republic of San Marino and in the surrounding areas, but also in urban contexts such as Rimini and Pesaro[39], instead show a stability and a continuity of the practices: while it becomes possible to marry a close relative, these marriages remain rare. What seems remarkable, instead, is not so much the rise of consanguineous or affine marriages between close relatives, as the decrease in traditional matrimonial practices, which emphasised solidarity (for example through the repetitions of alliances or re-linkings), in favour of a more individual choice, even if the latter was not entirely disconnected from the collective project, since kinship always remains an essential social point of reference[40].

---

38   François Joseph Ruggiu, "Histoire de la parenté ou anthropologie historique de la parenté? Autour de Kinship in Europe", art. cit., p. 235.

39   ADRn and ADPs, *Matrimoni*, 1570–1850.

40   This phenomenon should therefore be analysed in the light of recent works show-ing the reinforcement of the intra-familial ties of spiritual kinship and ties between spouses and witnesses during the same period. See Vincent Gourdon, "Les témoins

Alongside this phenomenon, we see the emergence of a greater geographic and social mobility in the investigated area from the second half of the eighteenth century. Though social homogamy remains an ideal norm, marriages between members of different classes do appear: after a period of narrow homogamy from the first half of the seventeenth century, some noble families again contract unions with families of craftsmen or peasants.

It is important to consider kinship, demography, and socio-economic and cultural factors as interwoven; it is also important to consider them over a long period of time, using different methods of analysis, in order to understand their multi-dimensional significance. Whilst the actors (some in particular) are sometimes able to bypass the rules of incest prohibition, these rules are in general respected, as the results of this systematic study in this geographical area show. It would be necessary to carry out similar studies in other European contexts in order to verify the extent of the increase in marriages between close relatives: studies conducted on a larger scale and, in particular, focusing on urban contexts, which still lack extensive research.

Archival sources

Republic of San Marino
ASRSM: Archivio di Stato

Archivi parrocchiali:
APSM: Pieve
APA: Acquaviva
APDo: Domagnano
APSe: Serravalle
APFa: Faetano

---

de mariage civil dans les villes européennes du XIXᵉ siècle : quel intérêt pour l'analyse des réseaux familiaux et sociaux?", in *Histoire, économie & société*, 2, 2008, pp. 61–87; Guido Alfani, Vincent Gourdon (eds.), *Spiritual kinship in Europe: 1500–1900*, New York, Palgrave Macmillan, 2012; Guido Alfani, Vincent Gourdon, Isabelle Robin, *Le parrainage en Europe et en Amérique. Pratiques de longue durée (XVI–XXIᵉ siècle)*, Bruxelles (et all.), Peter Lang, 2015.

Province of Rimini
ADRn: Archivio diocesano

Archivi parrocchiali:
APCe: Cerasolo
APCor: Coriano
APCorp: Corpolò
APGe: Gemmano (Gemmano, Marazzano, Onferno, Zollara)
APM: Montescudo (Montescudo, Albereto, Trarivi)
APMC/APCr: Monte Colombo & Croce
APMT: Monte Tauro
APSLC: San Lorenzo in Correggiano
APSP et APVe: Ospedaletto (San Patrignano & Vecciano)
APSMC: Santa Maria in Cerreto
APSe: Sant'Ermete
APSo: Sogliano (Montegelli & Vignola)

Province of Pesaro-Urbino
ADPs: Archivio diocesano di Pesaro
ADP: Archivio diocesano di Pennabilli
Archivi parrocchiali:
APMCe: Monte Cerignone & Santa Maria in Reclauso
APSec: Secchiano

Vincent Gourdon

Godparenthood in Western Europe from the Sixteenth to the Twentieth Century. Plurality of Models and Dynamics of Convergence

In 2006, Guido Alfani and I created *Patrinus*, the "European network for the social and cultural history of baptism and godparenthood", which has since welcomed around a hundred researchers from across the world. Many themes have been treated during the network's various scientific meetings[1], one of the most popular of which was the analysis of the social and economic functions of godparenthood, and the description and understanding of models for choosing godfathers and godmothers in terms of number per child and of gender, but also in terms of the quality of the relationship: godparents chosen from within the kinship group – known as "intensive" – and those from outside – or "extensive" – relationships, along with distinctions between the different statuses of those who were called upon; whether they were social equals, inferiors, or superiors; secular or religious, etc.

In this regard, Guido Alfani's research on how the Council of Trent brought changes to the way spiritual parents were chosen in Northern Italy between the sixteenth and the early seventeenth centuries has been decisive, not only because he questions the historicity of mobilisation models, but also because this work was the first to provide a typology of godparenthood models[2]. Many *Patrinus* network members have built upon the themes outlined in this work to look at different parts of Europe and time periods other than those studied by Guido Alfani.

1   Guido Alfani, Philippe Castagnetti, Vincent Gourdon (dir.), *Baptiser. Pratique sacramentelle, pratique sociale (XVIᵉ–XXᵉ siècles)*, Saint-Étienne, Publications de l'Université de Saint-Étienne, 2009; Guido Alfani, Vincent Gourdon (eds.), *Spiritual Kinship in Europe, 1500–1900*, London, Palgrave Macmillan, 2012; Guido Alfani, Vincent Gourdon, Isabelle Robin (dir.), *Le parrainage en Europe et en Amérique. Pratiques de longue durée (XVIᵉ–XXIᵉ siècle)*, Bruxelles, Peter Lang, 2015.
2   Guido Alfani, *Fathers and Godfathers. Spiritual Kinship in Early-Modern Italy*, Aldershot, Ashgate, 2009 (Italian version, 2006).

I will draw on existing studies and on the main results presented by researchers involved in the *Patrinus* network to paint a broad picture of the great secular movements of Western European godparenthood models in both Catholic and Protestant countries[3]. I will look for points of convergence between societies and will emphasise the continued existence of substantial nuances in national or regional trajectories and the existence of very variable temporalities[4].

Plurality of godparenthood in Western Europe at the end of the Middle Ages and the beginning of the Early Modern era

Prior to the religious reforms of the sixteenth and seventeenth centuries, the practice of godparenthood was largely unaffected by ecclesiastical regulations and their insistence that baptisms be attended by a small number of spiritual parents who had been chosen according to their religious preparedness for the task. Although some theologians, like Gratian, writing around 1140[5], or Pope Boniface VIII in the thirteenth century[6], supported the idea of a single godfather, it is clear that an extreme plurality on the number and/or the sex of spiritual parents of each baptized child prevailed in late Medieval Europe, and that multi-godparenthood was quite frequent. This pattern can be seen in the parish registers of various Northern Italian communities (Table 1) up to the closure of the Council of Trent in 1563[7]. There are no comparable registers for France in the late Medieval period, but we find a number of different rules in synod statutes of the time: from four spiritual parents in Cambrai to two in Marseilles and Lyons, and just

---

3   In this chapter, greater place is given to France and Italy because more works have been conducted on these two countries.
4   I do not intend to discuss the effectiveness of social and economic support through godparenthood here. For an analysis and concrete examples, see Guido Alfani, Vincent Gourdon, "Il ruolo economico del padrinato: un fenomeno osservabile?", in *Cheiron*, 45–46, 2006, pp. 129–177; Guido Alfani, Vincent Gourdon (eds.), *Spiritual Kinship in Europe, 1500–1900, op. cit.*
5   Didier Lett, *Famille et parenté dans l'Occident médiéval Vᵉ–XVᵉ siècle*, Paris, Hachette, 2000, p. 72.
6   Guido Alfani, *Fathers and Godfathers, op. cit.*, p. 23.
7   *Ibid.*, pp. 31–32.

one in Dax and Cahors[8], with three in Île-de-France[9] and Nantes[10], composed of two godfathers and a godmother for the baptism of a boy, and two godmothers and a godfather for a girl. This ternary model, inspired by the Holy Trinity, appears to have been equally dominant in contemporary Scandinavia and England, although precise data are not available. Research conducted by Antonio Irigoyen in the Spanish region of Murcia, on the other hand, found that around 1450 the model was for four or five spiritual parents per child, and here too there was a slight predilection for godparents of the same sex as the baptised baby[11]. This fragmentation of local models shows that the "godfather-godmother" model was far from dominant in Europe at this time. Godfathers and godmothers were not seen as potential substitutes for the parental couple, and were far from being considered as guardians or adoptive parents[12].

Table 1: Average number of godparents in Northern Italy (before 1562).

	Bellano	Ivrea	Turin	Azeglio	Voghera	Finale	Gambellara	Mirandola
N° baptisms	574	1,399	108	583	4085	976	567	8,449
First year of records	1533	1473	1551	1543	1534	1481	1541	1484
Average number of godfathers	2.86	2.55	2.44	2.34	2.18	1.57	1.40	1.15
Average number of godmothers	2.35	1.27	0.43	1.60	0.00	1.50	1.38	1.19

Source: Guido Alfani, *Fathers and Godfathers. Spiritual Kinship in Early-Modern Italy*, Aldershot, Ashgate, 2009, pp. 31–32.

---

8   *Ibid.*, pp. 24–25.
9   Camille Berteau, Vincent Gourdon, Isabelle Robin-Romero, "Réseaux sociaux et parrainage: les conséquences de l'application du Concile de Trente dans une paroisse française, Aubervilliers (1552–1631)", in *Obradoiro de Historia Moderna*, 19, 2010, pp. 279–306.
10   Etienne Couriol, "Godparenthood and social relationships in France under the *Ancien Régime*: Lyons as a case study", in Guido Alfani, Vincent Gourdon (eds.), *Spiritual Kinship in Europe 1500–1900*, *op. cit.*, pp. 124–151.
11   Antonio Irigoyen, "Ecclesiastical Godparenthood in Early Modern Murcia", in Guido Alfani, Vincent Gourdon (eds.), *Spiritual Kinship in Europe 1500–1900*, *op. cit.*, pp. 74–95.
12   Anita Guerreau-Jalabert, "*Spiritus* et *Caritas*. Le baptême dans la société médiévale", in Françoise Héritier-Augé, Elisabeth Copet-Rougier (dir.), *La parenté spirituelle*, Paris, Éditions des Archives contemporaines, 1995, pp. 133–203; Ead., "Qu'est-ce que l'*adoptio* dans la société chrétienne médiévale?", in *Médiévales*, 35, 1998, pp. 33–49.

As shown by studies produced by members of the *Patrinus* network, the strategies used by families of those being baptised to choose a godparent were equally varied, especially once the practice of multi-godparenthood allowed for the accumulation of multiple selection logics[13]. Smaller communities showed a predominance of horizontal choices directed towards neighbours, colleagues, economic partners (merchants, craftsmen), and political allies. Nonetheless, social superiors were also called upon in the context of clientelism and patronage, and even, in some rare cases, the godparents were social inferiors, poverty-stricken or beggars[14]. The latter could serve to demonstrate one's "charitable" nature and could therefore be seen as part of a spiritual approach[15], but for other families it was mainly a way to avoid arranging the often elaborate festivities and the customary gifts that were normally associated with godparenthood[16]. In some cases, poverty stricken godparents were thought to have a talismanic effect, diverting bad luck away from the child and providing protection from the dangers of infant mortality. According to local traditions midwifes were often chosen as godmothers, since it was they who performed the symbolic function of "courier" from death to life[17]. It was also common for parents to call upon clergymen to act as godfathers. Nonetheless, the preference for ecclesiastical godparents varied widely from one place to another. In the case of some Northern Italian communities, Guido Alfani has found that up to one godfather in seven was an ecclesiastic before the Council of Trent. This was true, for example, in early sixteenth century Bellano, but elsewhere there were fewer than one in a hundred (eg. Gambellara, Voghera)[18]. In the rural parish of Aubervilliers near Paris, too,

---

13   Guido Alfani, *Fathers and Godfathers, op. cit.*

14   Agnès Fine, *Parrains, marraines. La parenté spirituelle en Europe*, Paris, Fayard, 1994; Julian Pitt Rivers, "Le parrain de Montesquieu", in Françoise Héritier-Augé, Elisabeth Copet-Rougier (dir.), *La parenté spirituelle*, Paris, EAC, 1995, pp. 1–16.

15   On the Florentine case, see Christiane Klapisch-Zuber, "Parrains et filleuls: étude comparative", in *La maison et le nom. Stratégies et rituels dans l'Italie de la Renaissance*, Paris, EHESS, 1990, pp. 109–122.

16   On the importance and cost of baptismal gifts and banquets, see Guido Alfani, Vincent Gourdon, "Il ruolo economico del padrinato", art. cit.

17   On Venice, see Jean-François Chauvard, "'Ancora che siano invitati molti compari al Battesimo'. Parrainage et discipline tridentine à Venise (XVIᵉ siècle)", in Guido Alfani, Philippe Castagnetti, Vincent Gourdon (dir.), *Baptiser. Pratique sacramentelle, pratique sociale (XVIᵉ–XXᵉ siècles), op. cit.*, pp. 341–368.

18   Guido Alfani, "La famille spirituelle des prêtres en Italie septentrionale avant et après le Concile de Trente: caractéristiques et transformations d'un instrument

only one percent of godfathers were priests before the parish adopted the Tridentine creeds around 1620[19]. One may wonder why a family would wish to have a priest as godparent. This can in part be explained by the parish priest's central position in the local community and his ability to provide access to a wider social network. Obtaining a priest's agreement to become godfather was certainly seen as a mark of prestige for the family concerned. In any case, apart from the priest being ideally suited to over-seeing his godchild's religious instruction (though this was probably not the parents' primary motive), there were many other factors that made this choice "socially useful"[20]. Firstly, a godfather priest did not create future matrimonial impediments in relation to spiritual kinship, and secondly, his central position within the parish *compèrage* network[21] meant that he was an essential source of local information while, on the other hand, dis-cretion and confidentiality were guaranteed to his godchildren and their families. Finally, having a solid relationship with a priest represented an advantage for those faithful who wished to advance their own religious devotion. For his part, the godfather priest was able, through *compérage,* to become a member of a social network within his community; a benefit which, of course, he could not gain access to through marriage.

If the use of different types of mobilization depended on the total number of godparents and godmothers per child, it can also be seen to vary according to local customs, sometimes differing even at the parish community level. Another decisive factor was the social one: the poorest families tended to turn more frequently to hierarchical superiors, whereas families from higher classes made more horizontal choices. However, the essential point is, rather, the low incidence of choices made within the kinship network. Kinship is generally measured through an approximate indicator: the godfather or godmother and the father and/or mother of the

---

d'intégration sociale", in *Annales de Démographie Historique*, 1, 2004, pp. 137–161 (139).

19 Camille Berteau, Vincent Gourdon, Isabelle Robin-Romero, "Réseaux sociaux et parrainage", art. cit.

20 Louis Haas, *The Renaissance Man and his Children: Childbirth and early Childhood in Florence, 1300–1600*, New York, Macmillan, 1998; Guido Alfani, "La famille spir-ituelle des prêtres en Italie septentrionale avant et après le Concile de Trente", art. cit.

21 *Compère* and *commère* are French forms of the Latin terms *compater* and *comater*, from the notion of *compaternitas*. The godparents are linked in *compérage* with the natural parents of the baptised child. *Compérage* is therefore a "horizontal" tie link-ing the blood parents with their spiritual counterparts.

baptised child are considered kin if they share the same surname. This indicator tends to underestimate the impact of kinship, since not all kin would have the same name as the child's parents, like a maternal grand-mother, or an in-law, for example. However, since a maximum of 10% of godfathers and godmothers fall into the above category, historians work-ing in the field of godparenthood in Italy up to the sixteenth century are universally of the opinion that intensive choices in kinship were very rare in Italy during this period[22]. The situation is less clear for England[23] where the proportion was around 20%, with similar figures for France[24].

Religious reforms: divergences and convergences

Religious reforms introduced in the sixteenth century caused a major divide in the practice of godparenthood. Protestantism came to reject the notion of "spiritual kinship" which, for Luther and Calvin, had no scrip-tural basis and should therefore be discontinued, particularly in terms of matrimonial impediments. Despite this, the idea of godparenthood itself maintained its popularity. For Luther it was a good and laudable custom, and a creator of social ties between different individuals and families within the religious community. There were those who supported the idea of preserving the role of a guide to assist in the religious instruc-tion of the newly baptised, or at least to welcome them into the com-munity. The reformers' attitude towards godparenthood was also forced to take account of people's attachment to this ritualised social tie. In Geneva Calvin initially tried to abolish godfathers and godmothers, but

---

22 Christiane Klapisch-Zuber, "Parrains et filleuls: étude comparative", art. cit.; Guido Alfani, *Fathers and Godfathers, op. cit.*

23 Christiane Klapisch-Zuber, "Parrains et filleuls: Une approche comparée de la France, l'Angleterre et l'Italie médiévales", in *Medieval Prosopography*, 6, 1985, pp. 51–77; Michael Bennett, "Spiritual Kinship and the Baptismal Name in Traditional Society", in Dave Postles, Joel T. Rosenthal (eds.), *Studies on the Personal Name*, Kalamazoo, Western Michigan University, 2006, pp. 115–146.

24 For Aubervilliers, Camille Berteau, Vincent Gourdon, Isabelle Robin-Romero, "Réseaux sociaux et parrainage", art. cit.; *Id.*, "Familles et parrainages: l'exem-ple d'Aubervilliers entre XVIe et XVIIe siècles", in *XVIIe siècle*, 249, 2010, 4, pp. 597–621.

was forced to abandon the idea when faced with popular resistance[25]. A century later the English Puritans would also come up against opposition when they tried to eradicate godparenthood under Cromwell[26].

The suppression of spiritual kinship led to the substitution of spiritual parents with "baptismal witnesses"[27], although the terms "godfather" and "godmother" often returned quite quickly[28]. This process had the effect of weakening the theological and liturgical value of the baptismal tie while at the same time, paradoxically, the abolition of true spiritual kinship ended up fostering the preservation, or even the growth, of multi-godparenthood in the Protestant world. In the Church of Sweden as many as two or three godfathers and godmothers were allowed in the mid-sixteenth century, with the limit becoming much more flexible in the seventeenth century: in 1686, the Code of the Church of Sweden simply indicated that "few" were necessary. This resulted in a great deal of variation, especially between different social groups, with Swedish noble families sometimes calling upon up to 8 or 9 individuals per baptism. Differences also arose from one area to another, as was the case in the territories controlled by the Kingdom of Sweden at the beginning of the eighteenth century; we find between 2 and 4 godparents in the diocese of Viborg, there were generally 4 in the parish of Vihti in the South of Finland, and as many as 6 in Jalasjärvi in South Ostrobothnia. In the Finnish parish of Valkeala, the average number of godparents solicited per child rose from about 3.5 in 1706–1710 to 4 by 1736–1738[29].

---

25 Karen E. Spierling, *Infant Baptism in Reformation Geneva*, Aldershot, Ashgate, 2005.

26 Will Coster, *Baptism and Spiritual Kinship in Early Modern England*, Aldershot, Ashgate, 2002, p. 91.

27 For instance, in Lutheran Sweden the term "*vittnen*" (witness) appeared (Tom Ericsson, "Who wants to be a godparent? Baptisms in a Lutheran Church in Paris, 1755–1804", in Guido Alfani, Vincent Gourdon (eds.), *Spiritual Kinship in Europe, 1500–1900, op. cit.*, pp. 227–243 (230)).

28 Certain French Protestant baptismal registers at the end of the sixteenth century designated godparents as the persons who "presented" or "named" the child. These alternative formulations disappeared in the seventeenth century (Margreet Dieleman, "Protestant and Godparenthood in the Western Provinces of France, 1560–1685", communication at the European Social Science History Conference, Valencia, March 2016).

29 Kari-Matti Piilahti, "Kin, neighbours or prominent persons? Godparenthood in a Finnish rural community in the first half of the eighteenth century", in Guido

This rise occurred despite restrictions imposed by reformed parishes or Lutheran church leaders: in the eighteenth century the French reformed church of Frankfurt set the limit at 2 godfathers and 2 godmothers[30]; in 1539 it was 4 godparents in Denmark, rising to 5 in 1607[31]; in Iceland it was 3 godparents from 1746, while in the same period the limit was set at 5 godparents in Sweden and in Norway[32]. Nevertheless, as Absjorn Thomsen has suggested with regard to eighteenth century Denmark, it appears that the actual number of socially-recognised godparents was higher than is suggested by the entries made in parish registers[33].

Fig. 1: Proportion of ternary godparenthood per year in Aubervilliers 1552–1631 (ambiguous cases excluded).

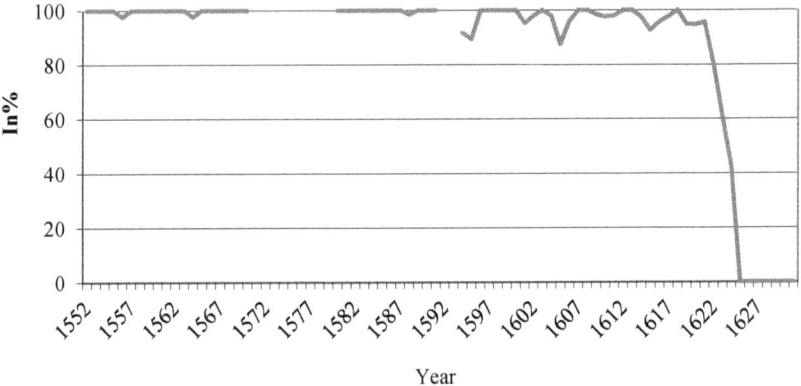

Source: Catholic registers of the parish of Aubervilliers.

Alfani, Vincent Gourdon (eds.), *Spiritual Kinship in Europe 1500–1900, op. cit.*, pp. 207–226 (213).

30   Tom Ericsson, "Who wants to be a godparent?", art. cit., p. 234; Janine Drian-court-Girod, *Ainsi priaient les luthériens. La vie religieuse, la pratique et la foi des luthériens de Paris aux XVIIᵉ et XVIIIᵉ siècles*, Paris, Cerf, 1992, p. 121.

31   Asbjørn Romvig Thomsen, "Le parrainage dans la société rurale danoise entre 1750 et 1830", in Guido Alfani, Vincent Gourdon, Isabelle Robin (dir.), *Le parrainage en Europe et en Amérique. Pratiques de longue durée (XVIᵉ–XXIᵉ siècle), op. cit.*, pp. 227–257.

32   Gísli Ágúst Gunnlaugsson, Loftur Guttormsson, "Cementing Alliances? Witnesses to Marriage and Baptism in Early Nineteenth-Century Iceland", in *The History of Family*, vol. 5, 2000, n. 3, pp. 259–272.

33   Asbjørn Romvig, Thomsen, "Le parrainage dans la société rurale danoise", art. cit.

The Catholic world, meanwhile, followed the opposite trend. The Council of Trent (1545–1563) was, in effect, marked by a reaction against the social uses of medieval godparenthood and in particular multi-godparenthood. The latter posed particular concerns in that it multiplied the risks of spiritual incest. The Catholic Church chose to preserve the notion of spiritual kinship that had been abandoned by Protestantism, while at the same time reducing its significance by, on the one hand, restricting the number of relationships between baptismal actors who would have been carriers of spiritual kinship[34], and on the other hand by limiting the number of godparents to only one per baptised child, or two at most as long as they were of different sexes.

This logic of restrictive convergence was applied immediately in Northern Italy, between the 1560s and 1580s[35], and after the Council of 1583 in the diocese of Murcia in Spain[36]. It came into force a little later in France due to the Wars of Religion and because the French monarchy did not recognise the decrees produced by the Council of Trent. The abandonment of the ternary model, then, took place between the very end of the sixteenth century (or around 1600 in Mans) and the 1630s (about 1622 in Aubervilliers, Figure 1; between 1610 and 1632 in Orleans; 1635 in Saint-Denis), according to the policy of individual bishops and to the negotiations carried out between the local clergy and their parishoners[37].

---

34 The notion of *fraternitas spiritualis* between the children of godparents and the baptised was thus rejected (Agnès Fine, *Parrains, marraines, op. cit.*, pp. 22–24).

35 Guido Alfani, *Fathers and Godfathers, op. cit.*

36 Antonio Irigoyen, "Ecclesiastical Godparenthood in Early Modern Murcia", art. cit., p. 88.

37 Camille Berteau, Vincent Gourdon, Isabelle Robin-Romero, "Réseaux sociaux et parrainage", art. cit, p. 283; Martine Barilly-Leguy, 2006, *'Livre de mes Anciens grands pères'. Le livre de raison d'une famille mancelle du Grand Siècle (1567–1675)*, Rennes, Presses universitaires de Rennes, 2006, pp. 109–110.

Fig. 2: Reduction in the number of godfathers and godmothers after the Council of Trent. The case of Ivrea (Italy).

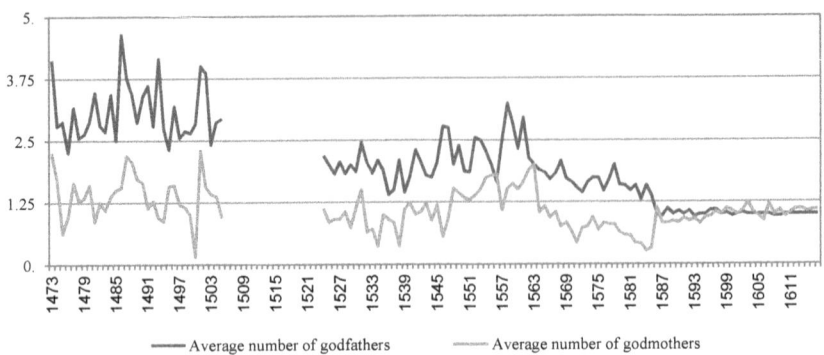

—— Average number of godfathers   —— Average number of godmothers

Source: Guido Alfani, *Fathers and Godfathers, op. cit.,* p. 94.

From then on in France, as in most of the Northern Italian communities studied by Guido Alfani (Figure 2)[38], the dominant model became that of the "godfather-godmother" couple. In other Catholic regions where the decrees of the Council of Trent were more strictly applied, the dominant model was that of the single spiritual parent – without exclusivity -, like in Veneto up to the nineteenth century, where the preference was usually for one godmother[39], or in Rome in the eighteenth and early nineteenth centuries[40]. Sometimes the accepted model was subject to variations, like in Murcia where the "godfather-godmother" couple dominated during the seventeenth century, but gave way to the single spiritual parent model in the early eighteenth century before returning to its former position at the end of the same century[41]. This last development reveals what appears to have been a long-term trend, that is the victory of the "godfather-godmother" couple model. The same development took place in Rome in the mid-nineteenth century; and happened only very recently in Veneto, according to Cristina Munno's study of Ormelle and Follina, which shows

38   Guido Alfani, *Fathers and Godfathers, op. cit.,* ch. 5.
39   Cristina Munno, "Prestige, intégration, parentèle. Les réseaux de parrainage dans une communauté de Vénétie (1834–1854)", in *Annales de Démographie Historique,* 1, 2005, pp. 95–130.
40   Personal research in the registers of Archivio Storico del Vicariato di Roma.
41   Antonio Irigoyen, "Ecclesiastical Godparenthood in Early Modern Murcia", art. cit.

it took place in the twentieth century, as late as the 1950s-60s[42]. Today in France and in Italy, nearly all children who are baptised into the Catholic faith have both a godfather and a godmother, but internal differences continue to exist, since the choice of a single spiritual parent is still the preferred one in many parts of Italy[43].

While the networking uses of godparenthood may have remained unchanged in the Protestant world (and thus the multiplicity of strategies linked to such choices[44]), the at times drastic reduction in the number of godfathers and godmothers had recognisable social effects during the Early Modern period in the Catholic world. As highlighted by Guido Alfani, this evolution restricted parents' range of choices and led godparent-selection strategies to become concentrated on those candidates who were considered most essential[45]. In Northern Italy at the end of the sixteenth century, Alfani observed a decline in horizontal choices and an increase in socially superior godparents: master craftsmen or traders, independent professions, and, above all, "seigneurs". The seventeenth century, then, was a golden age for vertical, clientelistic godparenthood. The study of the French parish of Aubervilliers confirms this observation, showing that the proportion of godfathers with an honourific title ("*avant-nom*") doubled in the years following the desertion of ternary godparenthood (Table 2).

Another factor worth taking note of is that the decrease in ecclesiastical godparenthood observed in Northern Italy did not take place in Aubervilliers or in Murcia in Spain: in the Murcian parish of St Bartolomew the proportion of clerical godparents rose from 8% in 1611–1630 to 13% in 1671–1675, and to 9% in 1751–1780, with annual peaks of 15%, 20% and 30% in the 1750s. The custom did not disappear until after the 1770s, when the single godparent model gave way to that of the "godfather-godmother" couple, which suggests that the elimination of ecclesiastical godparenthood was not directly related to a matter of godparents' quorum. Other

---

42 Cristina Munno, "De Marco Caco au 'cœur d'Allah'. Le baptême et les parrainages en Vénétie entre 1830 et 2010", in Guido Alfani, Vincent Gourdon, Isabelle Robin (dir.), *Le parrainage en Europe et en Amérique. Pratiques, op. cit.*, pp. 429–458.

43 Guido Alfani, Vincent Gourdon, Agnese Vitali, "Social Customs and Demographic Change: The Case of Godparenthood in Catholic Europe", in *Journal for the Scientific Study of Religion*, vol. 51, 2012, n. 3, pp. 482–504.

44 On this point see, for example, the case of a Finnish rural parish in the eighteenth century in Kari-Matti Piilahti, "Kin, neighbours or prominent persons?", art. cit., pp. 220–223.

45 Guido Alfani, *Fathers and Godfathers, op. cit.*

selection criteria, such as the choices made by slaves or converted Muslims, or by migrants looking to better integrate into an Episcopal city, explain the long-standing appeal of ecclesiastical godparenthood in the seventeenth and eighteenth centuries[46].

Table 2: *Percentage of laymen godfathers with honorific titles in Aubervilliers 1552–1631.*

	1552–1614	1615–1624	1625–1631	1552–1631
No. godfathers	3395	733	426	4554
Laymen with honorary title	68	20	22	110
In %	2.00	2.73	5.16	2.42

Sources: Catholic registers from the parish of Aubervilliers; Camille Berteau, Vincent Gourdon, Isabelle Robin-Romero, "Godparenthood: driving local solidarity in Northern France in the Early Modern Era. The example of Aubervilliers families in the sixteenth-eighteenth centuries", in *The History of the Family*, 17, 4, 2012, pp. 452–467 (460).

A new trend, the "familialization" of godparenthood

In France, from the 1970s, mainstream academics have insisted on the domination of intensive godparenthood (that is to say, the custom of choosing kin as godparents) since the beginning of the Early Modern period[47]. The explanation for this domination lies particularly in the link between godparenthood and child-naming, where the child would be named after the godfather or godmother, so that families would have tended to choose kin godparents so as to guarantee the transmission of family first names[48]. Social history studies on godparenthood in France tend to contradict this

---

46   Antonio Irigoyen, "Ecclesiastical Godparenthood in Early Modern Murcia", art. cit.
47   André Burguière, "Prénoms et parenté", in Jacques Dupâquier, Alain Bideau, Marie-Elizabeth Ducreux (textes recueillis par), *Le prénom, mode et histoire. Les entretiens de Malher 1980*, Paris, EHESS, 1984, pp. 29–35; Agnès Fine, "Parrainage et relations familiales dans la société française contemporaine", in Tiphaine Barthélémy, Marie-Claude Pingaud (dir.), *La généalogie entre science et passion*, Paris, C.T.H.S., 1997, pp. 273–294.
48   André Burguière, , "Prénoms et parenté", art. cit.; Françoise Zonabend, "La parenté baptismale à Minot", in Tina Jolas *et alii*, *Une campagne voisine*, Paris, MSH, 1990, pp. 215–240.

vision, which had been inherited from Levi-Straussian historical anthropology. Founded on a large corpus of baptism documents and not on isolated examples of noble or merchant families, these studies show that godparenthood was slightly weighted in favour of familial godfathers throughout the sixteenth and seventeenth centuries. On the evidence of shared surnames between godfathers or godmothers and the baptised child's father and mother, there appears to have been a dramatic increase during the eighteenth century in intensive choices right across France, in villages as well as cities, in Paris and in the provinces (Table 3).

Table 3: Proportion of spiritual parents with the same surname as their godchild's father or mother. French samples in sixteenth-eighteenth centuries.

Aubervilliers	1552–1631	19.7
	1705–1710	24.2
	1745–1749	24.7
	1785–1790	31.6
Lyons (Saint-Nizier)	1655	12.0
	1740	27.8
Bouafles	1740–1791 (all baptism)	46
	1720–1792 ("three generations" selection)	55
Preuilly-sur-Claise (Catholic sample)	October 1629-February 1632	20.0
Preuilly-sur-Claise (Protestant families)	1590–1683	27
Dijon (Notre-Dame parish)	1655–1657	12
	1735–1737	37
	1775–1777	46
Dijon (Saint-Philibert parish)	1663–1665	8
	1748–1750	22.5
Dijon (Saint-Pierre parish)	1650–1654	24.5
	1671–1679	19
	1701–1705	23
	1728–1730	26.5
	1753–1757	27.5
Bordeaux (Sainte-Croix parish)	1730 (January-June)	17.6
	1780 (January-June)	30.3

Sources: Camille Berteau, Vincent Gourdon, Isabelle Robin-Romero, "Le parrainage à Aubervilliers XVIᵉ–XIXᵉ siècles", in Guido Alfani, Vincent Gourdon, Isabelle Robin (dir.), *Le parrainage en Europe et en Amérique, op. cit.*, pp. 39–68 (51); Etienne Couriol, "La place de la parenté dans les baptêmes d'une paroisse lyonnaise d'Ancien Régime", in *Ibid.*, pp. 293–313 (296–297); Jean-Pierre Bardet, "Angelots, famille, patrie: parrains et marraines à Bouafles (Eure) au XVIIIᵉ siècle", in Guido Alfani, Philippe Castagnetti, Vincent Gourdon (dir.), *Baptiser. Pratique sacramentelle, pratique sociale, op. cit.*, pp. 167–184; Vincent Cousseau, 1995, "Sociabilité, parenté baptismale et protestantisme. L'exemple de Preuilly 1590–1683", in *Bulletin de la Société d'Histoire du Protestantisme français*, 141, 1995, pp. 221–246; Philippe Salvadori, "Communauté catholique et société: fabriques et parrainages dans trois paroisses de Dijon (vers 1650 – vers 1750)", in *Annales de Bourgogne*, 71, 1999, 1–2, pp. 139–156; Stéphane Minvielle, "Baptême et parrainage à Bordeaux sous l'Ancien Régime", in Guido Alfani, Vincent Gourdon, Isabelle Robin (dir.), *Le parrainage en Europe et en Amérique, op. cit.*, pp. 259–291 (291).

This process continued into the nineteenth century, although at a slower pace than in the preceding century. It concerned Catholic areas (Provence, Aubervilliers, La Rochelle, Tables 4, 5, 6[49];) just as much as it did Protestant ones (for Paris, see Table 7).

Table 4: Surname homonymy between spiritual parents and parents. Aubervilliers in sixteenth-nineteenth centuries (in %).

	1552–1631	1705–1710	1745–1749	1785–1790	1841–1844	1881*
% of godparents who share a parent's surname	19.7	24.2	24.7	31.6	39.1	31.2
Total number of godparents	9055	904	616	939	706	862

Sources: Catholic registers from the parish of Aubervilliers (Camille Berteau, Vincent Gourdon, Isabelle Robin-Romero, "Le parrainage à Aubervilliers XVIᵉ–XIXᵉ siècles", art. cit.).

NB: The criterion used in this table designates the cases in which a godfather or a godmother has the same surname as the baptised child's father or mother.

*Between 1840 and 1881, Aubervilliers ceased to be a rural parish and became a growing industrial suburb of Paris with many migrants.

---

49   For Paris, Vincent Gourdon, "What's in a name? Choosing kin godparents in nineteenth-century Paris", in Guido Alfani, Vincent Gourdon (eds.), *Spiritual Kinship in Europe 1500–1900, op. cit.*, pp. 155–182.

Table 5: Proportion of baptised child's kin among godfathers and godmothers in Western Basse-Provence, 1770–1880 (in %).

	1770–1780	1820–1830	1870–1880
Godfather and godson	30	36	41
Godfather and goddaughter	30	36	41
Godmother and godson	28	28	33
Godmother and goddaughter	26	33	33

Source: Bernard Cousin, "Le prénom des ancêtres", in Jean-Noël Pelen (dir.), *La quête des ancêtres*, Musée dauphinois, collection *Le Monde alpin et rhodanien*, 2009, pp. 103–114 (108–109). Bernard Cousin's figures take namesakes into account, as well as references to kinship made in certificates.

Table 6: Surname homonymy between spiritual parents and baptized children's parents in two La Rochelle parishes in the nineteenth century.

		1805	1841	1881
Saint-Louis parish	No. baptisms	59	36	41
	% of shared surnames	32.2	38.9	43.9
Saint-Sauveur parish	No. baptisms	61	68	56
	% of shared surnames	33.6	39.0	42.0
Total	No. baptisms	120	104	97
	% of shared surnames	32.9	38.9	42.9

Source: Diocesan archive of La Rochelle.

NB: The criterion used in this table designates the cases in which a godfather or a godmother has the same surname as the baptised child's father or mother.

Table 7: Godfathers' and godmothers' relationship to their godchild in Parisian reformed churches in the nineteenth century.

	1821	1841	1861
No. baptisms	168	287	425
No. godfathers/godmothers	339	573	863
Shared surnames (%)	35.1	37.7	38.8
Shared surnames and/or relation (%)	37.5	43.1	47.9

Source: Registers from the reformed church of Paris (Library for the History of French Protestantism, Paris)

NB: Shared surname and/or relation = godfather (or godmother) has the same surname as the child's father or mother, and/or a kinship tie with the child is mentioned in the baptismal certificate.

These findings do not challenge the idea of a certain precociousness in the familialisation of godparenthood in France with respect to the rest of Europe, but they do certainly put its supposed exceptionality into perspective. The rise of kin godparenthood can be observed elsewhere in Western Europe from the eighteenth century, and was taking place across the entire area from the nineteenth century. David Sabean noted this phenomenon in eighteenth century Westphalia[50], just as Piilathi did in Finland around 1750[51]. In Follina, in the Veneto region, the trend began in the second half of the nineteenth century, but the kin godparents did not represent an overall majority until the 1950s[52]. We are still very far from possessing coherent and precise data for the whole of Western Europe, especially since each author tends to have their own method for measuring kinship. Nonetheless, the general direction is clear. An ongoing investigation conducted in Italy and France among students born mostly in the 1980s and 1990s has shown that in these two countries the proportion of godfathers and godmothers whom respondents identified as family members currently represent more than three-quarters of the total (Table 8). Vertical-type choices (for example, employer godfathers), or at least those of which we know, considering that some such choices may be hidden within the "friends" category, have become rare. However, in Italy an interesting divergence between the North and the South does exist, with the inhabitants of the latter, ostensibly more "traditional" part of the country, opting more often to choose non-kin godparents[53].

---

50   David W. Sabean, *Kinship in Neckarhausen, 1700–1870*, Cambridge, Cambridge University Press, 1998.

51   Kari-Matti, Piilahti "Kin, neighbours or prominent persons?", art. cit., p. 222.

52   Cristina Munno, "De Marco Caco au 'cœur d'Allah'", art. cit.. For Sweden in the nineteenth century, see N. A. Bringéus, "Svenska dopseder", in *Fataburen*, 1971, pp. 63–84.

53   Guido Alfani, Vincent Gourdon, Agnese Vitali, "Social Customs and Demographic Change", art. cit.

Table 8: Choice of godparents, Italy and France.

Choice of Godfather	Italy		France		Choice of Godmother	Italy		France	
	N	%	N	%		N	%	N	%
Relative	427	86	171	88	Relative	415	85	143	71
Non-relative	69	14	23	12	Non-relative	75	15	58	29
N	496	100	194	100	*N*	490	100	201	100
Relative:					**Relative:**				
Uncle	266	53.6	115	59.0	Aunt	246	50.2	97	48.3
Grandfather	84	16.9	8	4.1	Grandmother	86	17.6	7	3.5
Cousin	54	10.9	41	21.0	Cousin	57	11.6	26	12.9
Other relative	20	4.0	7	3.6	Other relative	22	4.5	10	5.0
Non-relative:					**Non-relative:**				
Parents' friend	66	13.3	22	11.8	Parents' friend	72	14.7	56	27.9
Parents' colleague	3	0.6	1	0.5	Parents' colleague	3	0.6	2	1.0
Parents' neighbor	3	0.6	0	0.0	Parents' neighbor	4	0.8	3	1.5
Parents' employer	0	0	0	0	Parents' employer	0	0	0	0
N	496	100	194	100	*N*	490	100	201	100

Notes: Numbers refer to a sample of Catholic baptisms of people born in the period 1981–91 in those cases where the relevant information on godparents is available. Cases of multiple godfathers or godmothers are excluded. "Other relative" can be a great-uncle, elder brother, or stepfather (or a great-aunt, elder sister, or stepmother).

For the moment, this process remains open to interpretation, and many partially overlapping hypotheses have been presented.

One of the first elements to be taken into account is the social dimension of such a phenomenon. The tendency to choose family members as godparents first appeared among social "elites", and in higher social classes there was a greater proportion of kin throughout all the Early Modern period[54]. However, in the nineteenth century family-focused choices became almost universal among the bourgeoisie. This situation can be observed by looking at the case of Parisian Protestants (Table 9). The working classes, on the other hand, tended more often to make

---

54   Vincent Cousseau, "Sociabilité, parenté baptismale et protestantisme. L'exemple de Preuilly 1590–1683", art. cit.; Philippe Salvadori, "Communauté catholique et société", art. cit.; Camille Berteau, Vincent Gourdon, Isabelle Robin-Romero, "Familles et parrainages: l'exemple d'Aubervilliers", art. cit.

extensive choices, showing that, in the nineteenth century they were more sensitive to the protection and social integration offered by extensive god-parenthood (by building connections with neighbours and with patrons). Socialist and radical leaders cited the need to provide a child with material support as their motivation for introducing the practice of civil godpar-enthood around 1890 in Paris, where working class society was charac-terised by a particularly anti-clerical sentiment which inspired families to refuse Catholic baptism[55]. These working class families were much less interested in promoting kinship through godparenthood than bourgeoise or aristocratic families, who saw each of their members as a carrier of social resources.

Table 9: Godfathers and godmothers chosen from kin, according to the profession of the child's father, Parisian Protestants in the nineteenth century.

		1807	1821	1841	1861
Elite*	N.	21	37	45	53
	Average n. of kin per baptized child	1.57	1.11	1.42	1.51
Unnamed father (usually meaning the child is illegitimate)	N.	5	8	8	36
	Average n. of kin per baptized child	0.80	0	0	0.28
Tailor	N.	6	4	16	13
	Average n. of kin per baptized child	0.33	0.25	0.69	0.31
Merchant, Fruit seller	N.	9	5	8	13
	Average n. of kin per baptized child	1.00	1.00	1.13	1.15

Source: Registers from the Reformed Church of Paris (Library for the History of French Protestant-ism, Paris)

*Bankers, doctors, merchants, diplomats, landlords, Protestant ministers, etc.

In bourgeois and aristocratic circles, furthermore, identity was firmly tied up with the family unit and the constant reinforcement of kinship ties, an aspect which fits with the need to continually defend the centrality of family ties within society. This logic is very clear in literary works from the period, where not choosing a relative as a child's godparent is described as a moral transgression, an error, a challenge to the "Family". Some works

---

55   Gourdon Vincent, "What's in a name? Choosing kin godparents in nineteenth-century Paris", art. cit.

even speak of a "right of blood" in connection with the role of godparent. Social etiquette in the nineteenth century and the early twentieth century dictated that godparents be chosen according to a strict hierarchy: grandparents for the eldest children, uncles and aunts for their younger siblings followed by cousins and, if necessary, close family friends[56]. A point worthy of note is that this predilection for kinship completely contradicted the theological tradition of spiritual kinship based on a strong conceptual distinction between "carnal kinship" and "spiritual kinship"[57]which encouraged extensive choices in the interest of keeping the peace (*caritas*). In Catholic countries this contradiction could be interpreted as representing a weakening of Church authority.

This obsession on the part of the upper classes with familial godparenthood and their insistence on the need to continually reforge family ties, especially between branches of the same wider family, accompanied other processes that have been highlighted elsewhere: an increase in endogamous alliances between different branches of the family[58], a growing tendency to choose family members as witnesses at weddings[59], and a general expansion throughout the nineteenth century of ritual traditions that enhanced family involvement and promoted its unity both in life and in death.

In addition, the familialisation of godparenthood had a strong reciprocal connection to another phenomenon which involved the horizontalization of choices. Some studies, and in particular Cristina Munno's work on the rural community of Follina in the Veneto region, have found that there was an increase in the choice of godparents from within the same

---

56   *Ibidem.*
57   Anita Guerreau-Jalabert, "*Spiritus* et *Caritas*. Le baptême dans la société médiévale", art. cit.
58   David W. Sabean, Simon Teuscher, Jon Mathieu (eds.), *Kinship in Europe: Approaches to Long-Term Development (1300–1900)*, New York, Berghahn Books, 2007.
59   Vincent Gourdon, "Les témoins de mariage civil dans les villes européennes du XIXe siècle: quel intérêt pour l'analyse des réseaux familiaux et sociaux?", in *Histoire, Économie, et Société*, 2, 2008, pp. 61–87; Koen Matthijs, "Demographic and sociological indicators of privatisation of marriage in the nineteenth century in Flanders", in *Revue Européenne de Démographie*, 19, 2003, n. 4, pp. 375–412.

social group[60]. In short, people were becoming more and more "classist" in their choices[61].

It should also be noted that in nineteenth century guides to etiquette (this is true, at least, of those produced in France) it is seen as acceptable to reject requests to become godparents if they came from non-relations. In order to safeguard the higher interests of the family, it was morally permissible to refuse a request from outside if, for example, it came from a poor family.

Middle and upper class families were withdrawing from local community integration. Stéphane Minvielle has observed how, from the end of the eighteenth century, children from elite Bordeaux families no longer have beggar godparents[62]. Luc Boisnard, in studying the nobility of Tours, suggests that after the Revolution and under the Restoration this custom was carried on by just a few rural noble families in small parishes, and then only those families who were most attached to the idea of restoring the Ancien Régime[63]. The urban aristocracy, in contrast, and even the imperial nobility of Tours shunned this practice, and even found it quite strange.

At the opposite end of the scale, the gradual democratisation of society made the logic of protection less and less acceptable in that it implied a recognition of inequality between individuals and families: fewer and

---

60   Cristina Munno, "Rinchiudersi in famiglia? Dinamiche di una transizione nascosta: legami parentali e scelta del padrino di battesimo (un caso veneto – Follina 1834–1888)", in Alessandro Rosina, Pier Paolo Viazzo (a cura di), *Oltre le mura domestiche. Famiglia e legami intergenerazionali dall'Unità d'Italia ad oggi*, Udine, Forum, 2008, pp. 119–141.

61   Horizontalization also resulted in a great increase in godparenthood choices within the local community (see Sandro Guzzi-Hebb, "Spiritual kinship, political mobilization and social cooperation: a Swiss Alpine valley in the eighteenth and nineteenth centuries", in Guido Alfani, Vincent Gourdon (eds.), *Spiritual Kinship in Europe 1500–1900, op. cit.*, pp. 183–203 (196)). The verticalization of choices also encouraged parents to focus on a small number of influential figures, sometimes indirectly (by calling upon their wives or children to act as godparents), cf. Camille Berteau, Vincent Gourdon, Isabelle Robin, "Familles et parrainages: l'exemple d'Aubervilliers", art. cit.; Cristina Munno, "Prestige, intégration, parentèle", art. cit.

62   Stéphane Minvielle, "La place du parrain et de la marraine dans la vie de leur filleul(e). L'exemple des élites bordelaises du XVIIIᵉ siècle", in Guido Alfani, Philippe Castagnetti, Vincent Gourdon (dir.), *Baptiser. Pratique sacramentelle, pratique sociale (XVIᵉ–XXᵉ siècles), op. cit.*, pp. 243–260.

63   Luc Boisnard, *La noblesse en Touraine de Louis XVI à Mac-Mahon*, PhD thesis, University of Paris-4, 1989.

fewer working class families were willing to subject themselves to such a humiliation. The decline in vertical choices in turn led to the familialization of godparenthood.

At this point we should make mention of one remaining underlying factor: it seems that the emphasis had increasingly moved towards the tie of godparenthood (the relationship between godparents and godchild), and away from *compérage* (the relationship between godparents and the godchild's parents), which had been the main focus of the relationship created at baptism during the Early Modern era. Literature treating codes of etiquette was inundated with debates on "the child's interests" in godparenthood choices (selecting someone not too old who could be useful in the mid to long term) at the end of the nineteenth and beginning of the twentieth century[64].

This process fits into a long-term trend that was underway in France since the eighteenth century and was causing godparenthood to become more associated with the notion of guardianship. For example during the French Revolution when Jacobin leaders planned to replace Christian baptisms with civil ceremonies, they tried to preserve the socializing function of godfathers and godmothers, who were sometimes called "birth witnesses", and entrusted them with the guardianship of orphaned children[65]. Contemporary French studies on civil godparenthood show how this blurring of the lines between godparents and guardians often motivated the choices made by families[66]. It should be noted that the confusion stemmed from the language used by parents (the godfather was required to "take care of or protect the child in case of trouble"), and not from that of the institutions, since this role of guardian has never been legally recognized despite various proposals to do so in France over the last 20 years. It is likely that this alignment between godparenthood and the guardianship of orphans played a role in the current success of the "godfather/godmother" couple model. It also undoubtedly explains, in part, the preference on the part of an increasing number of parents to choose godfathers and godmothers from their own generation.

---

64   Vincent Gourdon, "What's in a name? Choosing kin godparents in nineteenth-century Paris", art. cit.

65   *Id.*, *Les révolutions du baptême en France de 1789 à nos jours*, Paris, Habilitation thesis, University of Paris-Sorbonne, 2014.

66   Agnès Fine, *Parrains, marraines. La parenté spirituelle en Europe*, op. cit., pp. 46–52.

Conclusion

The developments which have been briefly presented here are, alas, largely based on French and Italian data. Thanks to the *Patrinus* network, we are beginning to broaden the spectrum of regional and national patterns over the long term[67], but we still lack contemporary data for a number of European countries, particularly those with a Protestant culture. Here, we can only regret the weak interest of sociologists in the family or the religious for this issue.

Whatever the case may be, the familialization of godparenthood appears to have developed in Western Europe[68] over the last two to three centuries, thus contradicting schematic views of the effect that "modernity" has had on the level of mobilization of kinship in society. However, such an analysis is in need of refinement. All of the available data show the existence of very different chronologies, which vary according to social environment, region, country, and possibly according to different Christian confessions, too. Local traditions remain more or less strong, as in the case of single godparenthood in certain areas of Catholic Italy.

One issue that needs to be further pursued, for example, is the question of which family members were the most sought after for the role of godparent. In nineteenth century France, bourgeoisie etiquette codes, as well as sources from folklore collected by Arnold Van Gennep in his *Manuel de Folklore contemporain*[69], gave precedence to grandparents, at least for the baptism of the first-born child. Similar findings come from a study of the parish of Notre-Dame-de-Bonne-Nouvelle in Paris during the same period (Table 10), where more than a third of godfathers and godmothers whose relationship to the baptised child is given in the baptismal certificate were grandparents, great-uncles or great-aunts. This figure is significant for a society in which fewer people survived to become grandparents, and their numerous appearances in baptismal records indicates the importance of vertical lineage: godparenthood served to honour the oldest members of the family, and to pay a debt to the elderly. This rationale was abandoned

---

67   Guido Alfani, Vincent Gourdon, Isabelle Robin (dir.), *Le parrainage en Europe et en Amérique, op. cit.*

68   This is less clear in the Orthodox world as shown in some works from the Patrinus network, for example on contemporary Romania.

69   Arnold Van Gennep, *Le Folklore français*, vol. 1, Paris, Robert Laffont, 1998.

during the twentieth century, in France just after the First World War, as shown by various studies on the Bigouden region[70], Burgundy[71] or the Pays-de-Sault in the Pyrenees[72]. In the Franco-Italian study looking at contemporary godparenthood, grandparents now represent less than 4% of all godparents in France. Parents now show a preference for one of their own siblings, or sometimes for a spouse of their siblings as godparent. The child's uncles and aunts are also the most popular choices in Italy (Table 8), although the proportion here does not seem as significant, since a fall in fertility in this country over the last forty years has created a shortage of brothers and sisters in younger generations[73]. When there are no siblings to choose from, Italian families opt for grandfathers and grandmothers by default, resulting in a larger proportion of grandparents as godparents than in contemporary France and mid-nineteenth-century Italy. It appears, then, that each situation must be understood by taking account of its specific complexity, and by combining social, cultural, economic and demographic factors. There are certain to be numerous nuances in the overall pattern and the summary that has been presented here must also be read as a call for further studies.

Table 10: Distribution of explicit kinship ties between godfathers/godmothers and godchildren in the baptisms of Notre-Dame-de-Bonne-Nouvelle in 1820–89 (in %).

Godfathers		Godmothers	
Explicit kinship ties	445	Explicit kinship ties	447
Grandfather (in %)	31.5	Grandmother (in %)	31.5
Great-uncle (in %)	2.7	Great-aunt (in %)	2.7
Uncle (in %)	47.2	Aunt (in %)	45.9
Cousin (in %)	6.1	Cousin (in %)	7.4
Brother (in %)	12.3	Sister (in %)	12.3
Father-in-law (in %)	0.2	Niece (in %)	0.2

Source: Céline Georges, *La pratique du baptême dans une paroisse parisienne au XIXe siècle, Notre-Dame-de-Bonne-Nouvelle*, Paris, History master, University of Paris-4, 2002, pp. 141–142.

---

70   Martine Segalen, *Quinze générations de bas-bretons*, Paris, PUF, 1985.
71   Françoise Zonabend, "La parenté baptismale à Minot", art. cit.
72   Agnès Fine, *Parrains, marraines, op. cit.*
73   Guido Alfani, Vincent Gourdon, Agnese Vitali, "Social Customs and Demographic Change", art. cit.

Abstracts

Dionigi Albera, From the Alps to Europe: Combining Long-Term Approaches to Family and Kinship History

The article discusses some remarks generated during recent years by the author's book *Au fil des generations* (2011) dedicated to domestic organisation in the Alpine area from the late Middle Ages to the twentieth century. After better defining what he meant by the expression "third phase" in the history of family and kinship in Europe, the author recalls some aspects of the design of the comparative approach developed in that monograph. Then he discusses the articulation of his regional typology with other scales of analysis, smaller or larger. In particular, he is concerned with the question of the relationship with microhistory, suggesting that this perspective is fundamental, but that it demands to be articulated with a wider historical narrative. Moreover, he argues that the models of Alpine historical processes that he proposes in *Au fil des générations* may be compatible with, and complementary to, the broad hypotheses presented by David Sabean and Simon Teuscher in *Kinship in Europe* (2007).

Fabrice Boudjaaba, Changes in the Norman Inheritance System: A Legal Revolution or an Anthropological Evolution of Kinship in the Eighteenth and Nineteenth Centuries?

Normandy serves as an interesting laboratory in which to examine the second phase of long-term changes in the kinship system in the form that Sabean *et al.* have proposed. Unlike mountain areas or among the aristocracy, the main type of living arrangement in Normandy was the nuclear family. It was, however, a region where customary family law in the early modern period had a strong patrilineal component for the whole population. This article will consider two questions. How did the Normans accept the Civil Code of 1804, which brought in perfect equality of inheritance between sons and daughters? And how did the peasants and small artisans respond to this change, which was, above all, political and legal? If they accepted it, were they imitating the other social classes, or were they anticipating that the law would change? In other words, was the nineteenth-century trend towards a family founded on the married couple the result of the institutional change signaled by the introduction of the Civil Code, or did the change originate in earlier developments in the Norman family dating from before the legal transformations of the Revolutionary era?

Michaël Gasperoni, Reconsidering Matrimonial Practices and Endogamy in the Early Modern Period. The Case of Central Italy (San Marino, Romagna and Marche)

This paper aims at reconsidering the increase in family endogamy towards the end of the early modern period that has repeatedly been stressed in historiography. What underpins our considerations is the systematic study of a vast archive documentation regarding around thirty central Italian parishes (San Marino and within the provinces of Rimini/Pesaro) that we used to entirely reconstruct their populations. Questioning the rise of endogamy between the 17th and 18th century, we cross and confront the sources by an informatical analysis of our genealogical dataset (circa 30,000 individuals) changing levels of analysis and insisting upon the necessity to set interpretations in the respective local context in order to fully understand the given data. Our results show that, when taking the whole of marriages into consideration, there is no considerable relational augmentation of marriages between close relatives in this part of Italy. Neither is there one in terms of consanguinity, nor in terms of affinity. Finally, we demonstrate how those close unions must be analyzed taking the demographic, economic and social particularities into account.

Vincent Gourdon, Godparenthood in Western Europe from the Sixteenth to the Twentieth century. Plurality of Models and Dynamics of Convergence

Continuing the previously existing works and the main results of researchers engaged in the *Patrinus* network, this chapter aims to draw in broad strokes the great secular movements of godparenthood models in Western Europe in the Catholic world and the Protestant world alike. The sixteenth-century religious reforms introduced a major divide in terms of godparenthood. Protestant reformers cancelled the notion of spiritual kinship, but, paradoxically, this abolition had the effect of maintaining or even favoring the possibility of multi-godparenthood in the Protestant world. On the contrary, the Council of Trent limited strictly to one or two the number of godparents by child in the Catholic areas. However, this chapter demonstrates some global convergences, for instance a process of "familialization" of godparenthood since the eighteenth-century, but also emphasizes the maintenance of great nuances in national or regional trajectories and the existence of very variable temporalities.

Sandro Guzzi-Heeb, The Uses of Kin. Kinship, Social Networks and Identities in the Swiss Alps (Eighteenth-Nineteenth Centuries)
The analysis of kinship and devolution structures has been a crucial pillar in the fields of anthropology and historical anthropology. The study of social networks, on the other hand, was conceived of as providing an opportunity to reveal social dynamics which are partly independent of structures like kinship or class. How compatible are the two approaches? The question remains largely open. The detailed study of marriages in the Swiss village of Bovernier in the 19th century suggests that alliance structures are deeply influenced by existing personal and familial networks, particularly when those involved belong to the same political group and to a similar sexually permissive or repressive network. Especially cousin marriages often take place between partners belonging to a similar ideological and sexual milieu. The logic of social, political or sexual networks and identities can, therefore, partly determine structures like alliance patterns, as well as the way in which women and men choose the relatives with whom they wish to cooperate, their active kinship, through roles such as spiritual kin, political allies or sexual partners.

Elie Haddad, Times and Spaces of Noble Kinship (France, Sixteenth-Eighteenth Centuries)
Looking through the prism of the evolution of transmission in the French early-modern nobility, this article questions the social differentiation of domestic organisations. The aim is to establish whether nobility experienced a specific type of domestic organisation, to investigate how it might have been different from what happened in the other social groups, and to ascertain if there was a further internal diversity according to the location or position in the social scale of noble families. Doing so, it intends to explain changes in the noble domestic organisation in relation to the more general social and political evolutions of the kingdom. Thus, it is possible to consider how such changes took place in terms of the general models of European kinship.

Margareth Lanzinger, Patterns of Domestic Organisation: The Transfer of Goods and of Relatives
This contribution aims to bring together two research topics that are crucial to any discussion of domestic organisation: the transfer of goods and

the transfer of relatives. Firstly, the article inquires as to the significance of marital property regimes. Not only various inheritance practices, but also community and separation of marital property had vastly differing consequences in terms of access to resources as well as familial structures and power relations. Secondly, the article focuses on crisis situations caused by the death of the wife, thereby examining the importance of relatives in the context of male widowhood. Particular attention has been paid to marriage projects with the deceased wife's sister, who was simultaneously the aunt of the half-orphans and had often already adopted the role of housekeeper. This specific constellation can, in cases where small children of a widower needed to be cared for, be viewed as an intersection at which affinal and converged.

Luigi Lorenzetti, Regional Spaces and Domestic Organisation. Homogeneity, Transversality and Trans-Cultural Diffusion in the Agnatic Alpine World (Sixteenth-Nineteenth Centuries)
This paper analyses the variety of domestic organization forms in regions where the alpine agnatic model developed and took root in the course of the modern age. Applying a comparative approach, the article seeks to capture the heuristic value of this variety, by linking it to the level of internal "coherence" of the domestic agnatic organization. Subsequently, our analysis dwells on the transversal elements underpinning some political and cultural points of contact of the agnatic area and of the areas traceable to the *Bourgois* model. The features shared by these two models seem to have nothing to do with diffusionistic mechanisms. What they suggest, on the other hand, is that the connections between political structures, juridical models and forms of domestic organization do not answer causal processes but more subtle dynamics, which today are difficult to pinpoint without resorting to a micro-analytical approach.

Jon Mathieu, Transitions in the Domestic Organisation of the Alpine Area, from the Late Middle Ages to Modernity
This chapter offers a historical reading of Dionigi Albera's book *Au fil des générations. Terre, pouvoir et parenté dans l'Europe alpine, XIVᵉ-XXᵉ siècles* (2011) that proposes a threefold "contextual typology" of the domestic organisation in the alpine area from the late Middle Ages onwards. The first section of the chapter provides some personal information of its making after the first manuscript version of 1995. The second section singles out the transition processes described, or hinted at, in the book in

order to obtain an overview. The forms of intergenerational transmission are used as a proxy for the types of domestic organisation. The systematisation could be useful for future studies that would deepen our knowledge about the speed and modalities of the transitions. The third section, finally, deals with the relationship of Albera's typology to the two phased model of kinship history proposed by David Sabean and Simon Teuscher. It argues that they are roughly compatible. Much depends on the rigidity respective flexibility given to the definitions of the regional and chronological types.

Simon Teuscher, Problems of Scale and Mediation in Studies of Kinship in the Past

The chapter departs form Dionigi Albera's book and discusses problems of scale and mediation in kinship studies. First, it asks about the research agendas that stand behind a focus on either the local, regional, or continental levels. A discussion of scales has to take into account that the field of kinship studies since its beginnings in early anthropology has been conceptualized as one of global comparison – with the West as significant blind spot. Second, the chapter pleads for more attention to how structures of kinship are mediated. Kinship structures look very different in the same place according to whether they are expressed through property devolution, name giving, or scientific diagrams. This is particularly relevant to the study of Europe, where kinship never has been a matter of practice only. Here, kinship has been heavily theorized in theology, law, and medicine – which gave rise to interactions and contradictions between different articulations of kinship.

Jérôme Luther Viret, Children Leaving Home in Europe in the Modern Age: Towards a Typology Taking into account Western European Forms of Authority

The departure of children, and more particularly of girls, from home, did not have the same significance in Paris and in Normandy. In Normandy, girls only had the right to a lump sum payment, with the amount fixed arbitrarily by the father. This must have encouraged girls to leave home quickly and to build up their own dowries. In Paris, the girls received an advance of inheritance. They came later to the succession next to their brothers. Fathers did not distinguish between boys and girls. These financial modalities, at the same time as other factors, acted on the age of marriage. A large number of factors affected age at marriage. Local demographic and economic conditions, but also the place and status of the couple and the way in which the work of children was regarded, facilitated or delayed the marriage. Marriage was seen differently depending on whether income was generated by land farmed in common or by wage labour. It was also experienced differently depending on whether or not women were partners in the marriage, and on whether or not men were unduly privileged.

Authors

Dionigi Albera is director of research in the Centre national de recherches scientifique CNRS and directs the Institut d'Ethnologie Méditerranéenne, Européenne et Comparative IDEMEC at the Maison méditerranéenne des sciences de l'homme MMSH (Université Aix-Marseille). Albera has published widely about the Alpine area and about Mediterranean regions. His latest monograph is *Au fil des générations. Terre, pouvoir et parenté dans l'Europe alpine*, Grenoble 2011.

Fabrice Boudjaaba, Phd in history, is researcher at French National Center of Scientific Research (CNRS) in Centre de Recherches Historiques (EHESS). He is co-editor of *Annales de Démographie Historique*. His interests lie with the social and family reproduction in preindustrial societies.

Michaël Gasperoni holds a PhD in modern history, and he is currently member of the École française de Rome. After his thesis dedicated to the history of Jewish and Christian kinship in central Italy, he has focused his research on the social and economic history of the Jewish Ghettos in Italy.

Vincent Gourdon (CNRS, France) is chief editor of the journal *Annales de Démographie Historique*. A historian of the family, he is an expert on the history of baptism and godparenthood in Early Modern and Modern Europe; on this topic, he has published *Le parrainage en Europe et en Amérique. Pratiques de longue durée (XVIᵉ–XXIᵉ siècles),* Bern 2015, with Guido Alfani and Isabelle Robin.

Sandro Guzzi-Heeb is maître d'enseignement et de recherche at the University of Lausanne. He is the author of *Passions alpines. Sexualité et pouvoir dans les montagnes suisses* (1700–1900), Rennes 2014 and of *Donne, uomini, parentela. Casati alpini nell'Europa pre-industriale* (1650–1850), Torino 2007. He published numerous articles on the history of kinship and sexuality in various national and international journals.

Elie Haddad is researcher at the CNRS, member of the Centre de Recherches Historiques (Paris) and is working on the social history of the French early-modern nobility. His investigations deal especially with the relation-ships between kinship, seigneurial domination and the socio-political power of nobility. He is the author of *Fondation et ruine d'une "maison". Histoire sociale des comtes de Belin (1582–1706)* (Limoges, 2009).

Margareth Lanzinger teaches history and gender theory at the Univer-sity of Vienna. Her research interests are within the area of micro-history, historical anthropology and gender history, especially on the topics: kin-ship, marriage, property and the power of disposal, legal and administra-tive practice, relations between norms and practice, the construction of heroes as well as historiographic topics.

Luigi Lorenzetti is professor at the Università della Svizzera italiana where he is also coordinator of the Laboratorio di Storia delle Alpi and chief editor of the journal *Histoire des Alpes – Storia delle Alpi – Geschichte der Alpen.* His research concerns the history of the family, as well as the economic and social history of the Alps.

Jon Mathieu is professor of history at the University of Lucerne, Switzer-land. He has published especially about mountain regions in the modern period. His latest books are: *The Third Dimension. A Comparative History of Mountains in the Modern Era*, Cambridge 2011; *Die Alpen. Raum – Kultur – Geschichte*, Stuttgart 2015.

Simon Teuscher is professor of medieval history at University of Zurich. His research interests include kinship and other personal relationships, rural society, and administrative culture of the late Middle Ages in Western and Northern Europe. Along with David Sabean and Jon Mathieu he has edited the volume, *Kinship in Europe. Approaches to Long-Term Development (1300–1900)*, New York 2007.

Jérôme Luther Viret, Professor of Modern History, teaches at University of Metz-Lorraine since 2016. He has published since 2014 several works on the family and social reproduction, which approach the theme of the family, in Paris region or in Normandy. He is also the author of a synthesis examining the question in France since the Middle Ages (*Le sol et le sang*, CNRS, 2014).

Population, Family, and Society
Population, Famille et Société

Edited by / Édité par
Michel Oris

Cette collection a pour ambition d'accueillir et de promouvoir le dialogue entre les démographes et les spécialistes de la famille, dialogue qui renouvelle profondément tant l'histoire sociale que la sociologie contemporaine. Animée par un réseau international qui s'appuie sur le *Laboratoire de Démographie et d'Etudes Familiales* de l'Université de Genève, la collection est largement ouverte et veut refléter les dynamiques de recherche les plus récentes. Elle privilégie les perspectives comparatives, internationales, ainsi que les approches interdisciplinaires, celles qui mêlent les apports de l'histoire, de l'économie, de la statistique, de la sociologie, de la géographie, de la démographie, de l'anthropologie culturelle, etc. L'innovation méthodologique, dans les domaines du qualitatif aussi bien que du quantitatif, qui permet de refonder les problématiques et d'articuler de nouvelles questions, est particulièrement saluée. La collection accueille aussi bien des contributions individuelles que collectives. Dans le premier groupe se rangent les monographies ou travaux de synthèse issus du milieu scientifique suisse et international, en ce compris les meilleures thèses de doctorat. Le second groupe réunit des recueils d'articles organisés autour d'un thème qui émerge dans le débat scientifique, et qui requiert le croisement de regards venus de multiples horizons disciplinaires et/ou géographiques.

La collection accueille des ouvrages en langue française, anglaise et allemande.

Vol. 1   Frans van Poppel, Michel Oris & James Lee (eds). *The Road to Independence. Leaving Home in Western and Eastern Societies, 16th–20th centuries.* 2004.
ISBN 3-906770-61-3 / US-ISBN 0-8204-5949-6

Vol. 2   Guy Brunet, Michel Oris & Alain Bideau (éds). *Les minorités. Une démographie culturelle et politique, XVIIIe-XXe siècles / Minorities. A Cultural and Political Demography, 18th–20th centuries.* 2004. ISBN 3-03910-220-6 / US-ISBN 0-8204-6874-6

Vol. 3   Erwin Zimmermann & Robin Tillmann (éds/Hrsg.). *Vivre en Suisse 1999-2000. Une année dans la vie des ménages et familles en Suisse / Leben in der Schweiz 1999–2000. Ein Jahr im Leben der Schweizer Familien und Haushalte.* 2004. ISBN 3-03910-370-9

Vol. 4   Jean-Marie Le Goff, Claudine Sauvain-Dugerdil, Clémentine Rossier & Josette Coenen-Huther. *Maternité et parcours de vie. L'enfant a-t-il toujours une place dans les projets des femmes en Suisse?* 2005. ISBN 3-03910-666-X

Vol. 5   Claudine Sauvain-Dugerdil, Henri Leridon & Nicholas Mascie-Taylor (eds). *Human Clocks. The Bio-Cultural Meanings of Age.*
2006. ISBN 3-03910-785-2 / US-ISBN 0-8204-7570-X

Vol. 6   Michel Oris, Guy Brunet, Eric Widmer & Alain Bideau (éds). *Les fratries. Une démographie sociale de la germanité.*
2007. ISBN 978-3-03911-255-5

Vol. 7   Angélique Janssens (ed.). *Gendering the Fertility Decline in the Western World.*
2007. ISBN 978-3-03911-311-8

Vol. 8   Laurence Leitenberg. *La population juive des villes d'Europe. Croissance et répartition, 1750-1930.*
2008. ISBN 978-3-03911-478-8

Vol. 9   Eric D. Widmer & Riitta Jallinoja (eds). *Beyond the Nuclear Family: Families in a Configurational Perspective.*
2008. ISBN 978-3-03911-704-8

Vol. 10   Antoinette Fauve-Chamoux and Emiko Ochiai (eds).
The Stem Family in Eurasian Perspective. Revisiting House Societies, 17th–20th centuries.
2009. ISBN 978-3-03911-739-0

Vol. 11   Michel Oris, Guy Brunet, Virginie De Luca Barrusse & Danielle Gauvreau (éds.).
Une démographie au féminin – A Female Demography. Risques et opportunités dans le parcours de vie – Risks and Chances in the Life Course.
2009. ISBN 978-3-03911-738-3

Vol. 12   Reto Schumacher
Structures et comportements en transition. La reproduction démographique à Genève au 19ᵉ siècle.
2010. ISBN 978-3-0343-0302-6

Vol. 13   Laurent Heyberger
L'histoire anthropométrique.
2011. ISBN 978-3-0343-0586-0

Vol. 14   Irenka Krone-Germann
Part-Time Employment in Switzerland. Relevance, Impact and Challenges.
2011. ISBN 978-3-0343-0614-0

Vol. 15   Guy Brunet
Vie et mort dans la Dombes des étangs aux XVIIIᵉ et XIXᵉ siècles.
2011. ISBN 978-3-0343-0669-0

Vol. 16   Marjorie Bourdelais
La Nouvelle-Orléans: croissance démographique, intégrations urbaine et sociale (1803-1860).
2012. ISBN 978-3-0343-1200-4